GIRLS WHO WORE BLACK

GIRLS
WHO WORE
BLACK

Women
Writing the
Beat Generation

Edited by

Ronna C. Johnson

and Nancy M. Grace

RUTGERS UNIVERSITY PRESS

NEW BRUNSWICK, NEW JERSEY, AND LONDON

Library of Congress Cataloging-in-Publication Data

Girls who wore black: Women writing the Beat generation / [edited by] Ronna C. Johnson and Nancy M. Grace.

    p. cm.

    Includes bibliographical references and index.

    ISBN 0-8135-3064-4 (cloth : alk. paper) — ISBN 0-8135-3065-2 (pbk. : alk. paper)

    1. American literature—Women authors—History and criticism.   2. Beat generation.

3. Women and literature—United States—History—20th century.   4. American literature—

20th century—History and criticism.   I. Johnson, Ronna.   II. Grace, Nancy M., 1952–

PS228.B6 .W66 2002

810.9′11—dc21

                                         2001048399

British Cataloging-in-Publication information is available from the British Library.

For permissions of copyrighted works see Acknowledgments and Permissions.

Manufactured in the United States of America

To Girard and Tom

Contents

Foreword

Did women play an important part in the literature of the Beat Generation? About a decade ago, educated women readers began asking this question, and they usually answered with a resounding NO. At the beginning of the 1990s, women first posed this question as a challenge to the claim that the writing of men like Jack Kerouac, Allen Ginsberg, and William S. Burroughs had effected major changes in the consciousness of their readers in the 1950s and 1960s.

True, works like *On the Road*, "Howl," and *Naked Lunch* challenged a prevailing climate of racism and homophobia in the United States. But discerning readers couldn't help noticing that these works failed to depict women in anything but traditional gender roles. Authors are free to write about whatever they want, of course, so over the decade, the question slowly evolved into a more sharply focused, if more disquieting, inquiry, one that wouldn't go away: had the Beat men encouraged the writing of the women who were involved with them in this literary movement?

The second wave of feminism, which began in the late 1960s, occurred after the publication of Kerouac's, Ginsberg's, and Burroughs's most influential books. Although in her pioneering *Sexual Politics* (1970) Kate Millet had challenged Norman Mailer's misogynistic portrayal of women (Mailer was then often associated with the Beats), it took twenty years of feminist literary criticism before attention began to be paid to the complex role played by Beat women as writers themselves. When Beat writing first appeared, it was attacked acrimoniously by critics in both the popular press and conventional intellectual journals, who were appalled by the social and stylistic challenges of Beat poets and novelists. The more recent attacks by feminist critics claiming that the Beat males didn't support Beat women have been similarly heated. It is now widely acknowledged that many of the Beat males were no more sensitive to the needs of the intellectual women in their midst than many other males of their generation were to the needs of women they worked and lived with.

As a woman reader, I have always found women writers to be an important part of the Beat Generation. In fact, the author of the book that influenced me more than any work I ever read by Kerouac, Ginsberg, or Burroughs was a woman. The book was *Dinners and Nightmares*, a collection of short sketches describing the life of a young woman writer in New York City published in 1961 by Diane di Prima. It impressed me so strongly that although I was embarked upon a traditional education in graduate school, my admiration for di Prima's book helped me make the important decision to involve myself in the study of writing by Beat authors as a literary scholar in 1966, shortly after I had completed my doctorate in American literature at Columbia University.

When I was an undergraduate English major at the University of California, Berkeley, from 1953 to 1957, the professors who taught me to become a close reader were males. If the protagonist of a work of fiction was a male, as in novels by Henry James or James Joyce, I read the plot as symbolizing the experiences of a soul or of a human being. According to this theory, the same gender-free readings were available to male readers encountering heroines in novels by Jane Austen or George Eliot. In colleges throughout the United States during the mid-twentieth century, gender roles might have been studied in psychology classrooms, but in my experience they were completely ignored by English professors when they professed textual criticism.

I can't recall the circumstances of the first time I read *Dinners and Nightmares*, although I probably first picked it up from a stack of newly published books while I browsed in the Eighth Street Bookshop in Greenwich Village, after I began to teach at a college in New Hampshire. But I do remember really reading it closely two years later, in the autumn of 1963, after I returned to New York to live in a tenement apartment on West 109th Street as a student in the Columbia University doctoral program. Then it made such a deep impression on me that I wanted to give copies of the little paperback book to all my friends for Christmas.

If Kerouac's *The Dharma Bums* offered me a nostalgic view of my past as a Berkeley undergraduate in the rosy way I wanted to remember it, then di Prima's *Dinners and Nightmares* projected a beatific vision of my life as I would have loved to live it in New York City at the time. Instead of being straitjacketed by doctoral reading lists and degree requirements, spending long, solitary hours taking notes in my enthusiastic pursuit of knowledge about nineteenth-century American literature, I could imagine myself, while immersed in di Prima's pages, free of the past, independently trusting the present, happily dining on oysters and Oreos with my lovers and friends in my raffishly furnished bohemian pad downtown in the Village. I was poor, and so was di Prima, but in her book she had the courage to live for art, rather than for money. As she joked in one of her "Three Laments" in the book:

> alas
> I believe
> I might have become
> a great writer
> but
> the chairs
> in the library
> were too hard.
>   (119)

Unlike me, di Prima didn't bury herself in the library stacks, allowing herself to be immersed in the past just as an insect becomes silently embalmed in transparently luminous amber. She had style. She appeared to live on her own terms completely in the present, trusting her own experience, exploring the range and exuberance of her own colloquial language as she created her autobiographical prose sketches and poetry. I loved her and envied her for it.

I now understand that part of my delight in my encounter with *Dinners and Nightmares* was my pleasure in relating personally to a Beat book for the first time as a woman reader. I realized instinctively that di Prima's courage to be herself stemmed from being a woman. Later, Joyce Johnson ironically characterized herself as a "minor character" in a man's world, but it seemed to me that di Prima had no need to take refuge in irony. At home in the

1950s bohemian world of Beat writers, painters, actors, and dancers in New York City, she had stepped so far outside the conventional world that she was free of it. Di Prima was so hip that she had found a way to exploit her "minor" status and gain strength from it. She possessed the necessary strength of character to go her own way and invent her own domestic space so that she could function as an artist. With her talent she was generous and hard working enough to create a three-dimensional world in *Dinners and Nightmares* that could be brought alive in the imaginations of her readers, responding to the good dreams/realities of the Dinners section and the bad dreams/realities of the Nightmares pages of her book.

Diane di Prima's writing epitomizes the achievement of all the women discussed in this anthology, who for more than a quarter century have had the courage to be themselves and write Beat. For the past decade there has been a need for a collection of critical essays examining the writing of women in the Beat generation. *Girls Who Wore Black* explores the literature created by di Prima, Elise Cowen, Brenda Frazer, Joyce Johnson, Hettie Jones, Joanne Kyger, Janine Pommy Vega, and Anne Waldman in greater depth than has ever been done before, helping us to appreciate the unique evolution of their diverse voices during a dynamic moment of profound and far-reaching cultural change in the United States.

Ann Charters

Acknowledgments
and Permissions

Women writers of the Beat generation charted an existential and artistic course for which there were few models and sometimes too few rewards. Yet many women after them took this same exhilarating course to define their own lives, in part because the presence of women Beat writers had made it possible. So we would be remiss if we did not first extend our special thanks to all the living Women Beat writers for their perseverance, inspiration, and generosity: Joyce Johnson, Hettie Jones, Janine Pommy Vega, Anne Waldman, ruth weiss, Joanne Kyger, Diane di Prima, and Bonnie Frazer. We thank as well the late Helen Adam and Elise Cowen, and many others who chose this same path.

We are especially grateful to Leslie Mitchner, our editor at Rutgers University Press, for helping us to conceive this project and keeping faith with us. We thank Susannah Driver-Barstow, our copyeditor, for her meticulous work, support, and professionalism as the book moved through publication. We also thank Theresa Liu, our editorial assistant, and Brigitte M. Goldstein, our production editor. We thank as well Linda Wagner-Martin, who recognized the timeliness of this project, and we extend special thanks to Jennie Skerl, whose imprint can be felt in the final shape of this book. We are grateful to all of our contributors for their willingness to develop the new scholarship needed to recognize and understand women Beat writers, and, in this, to risk redefining Beat.

This volume benefited greatly from the generous support of The College of Wooster. Through its Henry Luce III Fund for Distinguished Scholarship, the college provided support for the purchase of permissions and photographs, and for the indexing of the volume. The book would never have reached final form without the technical assistance of Kathie Clyde at The College of Wooster. Her calm and reasoned approach to many technical problems eased us through the publication process. Several talented and adventurous students at The College of Wooster also provided valuable assistance: Mary Neinaber, who has a deep love of Beat literature and the library, aided our efforts to track down many obscure resource materials; Timothy Drouhard and Emily Schadler assisted with the construction of the selected bibliography and with proofreading.

Many others have been helpful as well, not only assisting us with the research of the book but by providing continued encouragement for the project. We acknowledge Bob Rosenthal, Peter Hall, and Bill Morgan, of the Allen Ginsberg Trust; Hilary Holladay at the University of Massachusetts-Lowell; Ann Douglas of Columbia University; Regina Weinreich; Belinda Buie at the University of Louisville; and Robert J. Berthoff of the State University of New York at Buffalo. Our thanks go as well to Stella Johnson, Larry Volk, and Matt Dilyard for their contributions to the photography in this volume.

We are especially indebted to Ann Charters, who pioneered the study of the women Beat writers with her work for the *Dictionary of Literary Biography* and who has been extremely supportive of this volume. We are grateful for her wisdom and her welcoming spirit. Ronna Johnson thanks her friends and colleagues Sandra R. Joshel, Alan Lebowitz, Nancy Reisman, Eric Rosenberg, Eve Sandberg, Kathleen Weiler, Peter Weiler, Jonathan Wilson, and Sandra A. Zagarell for their interest in and strong support of her Beat studies, both at Tufts University and beyond. She thanks her summer community in Provincetown, Massachusetts: Tim Barry and Dorian Gardner of Tim's Bookstore, Maggie Cassella, Guy and Liza Marinello, and especially Allene, Nancy, and Donald Thibeault for humor, camaraderie, and respite. Her deep gratitude and affection go to Paul and Louise Bernheimer, who have been part of every project, as has the indispensable Malcolm O. Slavin, without whom there would be no work. She is grateful for the confidence of her sister Stella Johnson and for the love of her sister Pamela A. Johnson. Special thanks go to the students from her Spring 2000 Beat Seminar in Tufts's American studies program, especially Sarah Aibel, John Beck, Megan Burke, Daniel de Wolff, Rina Eisenberg, Pierce Kilduff,

Jack Levner, Luke Meixner, Hillary Tinsman, and Jess Wells; challenging and endlessly interested, they warmly and intelligently welcomed Joyce Johnson and Hettie Jones during their extraordinary campus readings. The curiosity and commitment of many classes of Tufts students have energized Johnson's studies of the Beat and of women's studies, making the work in this volume possible. Finally, to Girard Nakagawa-Mabe, her husband, she gives proud thanks for his intelligence, wit, and cool; from the beginning, his support and faith in this and all projects have made all the difference.

Nancy Grace thanks The College of Wooster for supporting a research leave in 1997 and 1998, which allowed her to begin work on this volume. Thanks go as well to her friends and colleagues Deb Shostak, John Gabriele, Peter Havholm, Tom Falkner, Joanne Frye, Henry Herring, and Marcia Holbrook, all of whom have given generously of their time and wisdom over the years. She is particularly grateful to Carolyn Durham, who has always understood the importance of the scholarly life and has been the most generous of friends. She thanks her sister, Marianne Bowden, for her friendship and willingness to listen. To Tom Milligan, her husband, she extends special gratitude, for his confidence in the merits of the project and for the intellectual and emotional partnership that is necessary for the sustenance of her work. His fine critical eye, his ability to praise and motivate, and his wry humor supported this project from start to finish.

Women Beat writers have waited too long to be recognized and appreciated, considering their work's significance to and influence on both the Beat literary movement and the emergence of women into social and civil equality. Beat women writers are a pivotal enclave of American individuality and self-sustaining community. These women and writers are the soul of this book, and this book is tribute to their accomplishments, courage, and vision.

Permissions have been generously granted for use of the copyrighted works listed below. Passages from the prose and poetry of Helen Adam are printed with the permission of The Literary Estate of Helen Adam. Excerpts from "For Joe" copyright 1975 by the Estate of Jack Spicer are reprinted from *The Collected Books of Jack Spicer* with the permission of Black Sparrow Press. Reprinted from *San Francisco's Burning* 1985 by Helen Adam by permission of Hanging Loose Press. Passages from *The Complete Naropa Lectures of Allen Ginsberg* Allen Ginsberg Trust. Excerpts from an unpublished interview of

Diane di Prima copyright 1989 by Tony Moffeit, poet-in-residence at the University of Southern Colorado in Pueblo. All works by Diane di Prima copyright Diane di Prima and used with her permission; all rights reserved by the author. Excerpts from *Come and Join the Dance* reprinted by permission of Joyce Johnson. Portions of "What I See in *How I Became Hettie Jones*" by Barrett Watten first appeared in *Poetics Journal* and are reproduced with permission of the author. Two untitled poems from *How I Became Hettie Jones* used by permission of Grove/Atlantic, Inc., 1990 by Hettie Jones. Excerpts reprinted from *Drive* 1998 by Hettie Jones by permission of Hanging Loose Press. Lines from the poem "Am/Trak" by LeRoi Jones/Amiri Baraka from the book *The LeRoi Jones/Amiri Baraka Reader* by Amiri Baraka copyright 2000 by Amiri Baraka appear by permission of the publisher, Thunder's Mouth Press. Elise Cowen's poems are printed with the good will of Leo Skir and the Estate of Elise Cowen, 1992 in the name of Leo Skir and the Estate of Elise Cowen. Excerpts from *Troia: Mexican Memoirs* are used with permission of the author copyright 1969 Brenda Frazer. Excerpt from *Helen in Egypt* by H.D. (Hilda Doolittle), copyright 1961 by Norman Holmes Pierson reprinted with permission of New Directions Publishing Corp. Excerpts from *The Tapestry and the Web* reprinted with permission of Joanne Kyger. Passages from an unpublished interview of Ebbe Borregaard and Joanne Kyger by Lewis Ellingham printed with permission of the Poetry/Rare Books Collection, University Libraries, State University of New York at Buffalo. Excerpts from "Thoughts" reprinted with permission of Joanne Kyger. Excerpts from *Poems to Fernando* 1968 by Janine Pommy Vega reprinted by permission of City Lights Books. Excerpt from "Altogether Another World" reprinted with permission of Anne Waldman from *Baby Breakdown*, 1970. "How the Sestina (Yawn) Works" and "The Revolution" from *Helping the Dreamer* 1989 and excerpts from *Iovis: All Is Full of Jove* vol. 1 1993 and vol. 2 1997 used by permission of Anne Waldman and her publisher, Coffee House Press. "Fast Speaking Woman" and "Eyes in All Heads to Be Looked Out Of" from *Fast Speaking Woman: Chants and Essays* 1975, 1996 by Anne Waldman. Reprinted with permission of City Lights Books and Anne Waldman.

GIRLS WHO WORE BLACK

Under the street lights only the eccentric stands out garbed in the costume of his game. Streetwalkers, showgirls, perverts . . . poets with pale faces, girls dressed in black beside them.

—John Wieners, *707 Scott Street*

The "cool" (hipster) today is your bearded laconic sage, or schlerm, before a hardly touched beer in a beatnik dive, whose speech is low and unfriendly, whose girls say nothing and wear black.

—Jack Kerouac, "The Origins of the Beat Generation"

I see the girl Joyce Glassman, twenty-two, with her hair hanging down below her shoulders, all in black like Masha in *The Seagull*—black stockings, black skirt, black sweater—but, unlike Masha, she's not in mourning for her life. How could she have been, with her seat at the table in the exact center of the universe, that midnight place where so much is converging, the only place in America that's alive? As a female she's not quite part of this convergence. A fact she ignores sitting by in her excitement as the voices of the men, always the men, passionately rise and fall. . . . Merely being there, she tells herself, is enough.

What I refuse to relinquish is her expectancy. It's only her silence that I wish finally to give up.

—Joyce Johnson, *Minor Characters*

Visions and Revisions of the Beat Generation

Ronna C. Johnson and Nancy M. Grace

Since its advent in the mid-1950s, Beat generation writing has been only partly seen. The category is typically equated with the three men considered to be the movement's principal literary figures—Jack Kerouac, Allen Ginsberg, and William S. Burroughs—and what they are made to stand for: iconoclastic, freewheeling, masculinist community and dissent from both literary convention and conformist "lifestyle." Even those who have not read *On the Road*, "Howl," or *Naked Lunch* recognize this romantic configuration, in which Beat is equated with iconic male figures and their legendary literature. Most critical discussion has preserved this narrow identification of the Beat movement with its white male practitioners, rehearsing the worn dogma of their iconography or attending primarily to autobiographical interests, following the clichéd notion recycled by David Halberstam in his mass market history *The Fifties* (1993) that how Beat writers lived was more significant than what they wrote. [1] But this familiar approach is misleading and instantiates an incomplete account of Beat. It excludes numerous women Beat writers, who were radical exponents of Beat aesthetics and who collaborated in the cultural reforms and resistances

Beat engaged.[2] Although recent literary studies and anthologies of Beat have admitted a wider range of writers, most have not exceeded minimal recognition of those outside the well-known group of males.[3] The exclusion of female Beat writers diminishes understanding of the Beat literary and cultural movement, creates insufficient representations of the field of Beat literature, and distorts views of the era during and after the Second World War when Beat emerged.[4]

The lacunae in representations of the Beat raise concerns about how to constitute the category of Beat; or, how to decide who are Beat writers. Identification as a Beat writer would seem to depend on style, technique, aesthetic, and philosophy. A consensus about these might run thus: Beat is spontaneous composition, direct expression of mind, no censorious revision, jazz-based improvisation; or factualism, cut-up, surrealism; or first-thought-best-thought, cataloguing piled-up images, following breath line, prophetic utterance. Yet, these literary processes and philosophies are as heterogeneous as the works of Kerouac, Burroughs, and Ginsberg that they represent. So, too, not only does the work of most women Beat writers diverge—technically, stylistically, aesthetically—from that of the principal male Beats, it is also heterogeneous in itself, with considerable deviation in aesthetics, ranging from performance-based, spontaneous jazz poetics, to revolutionary, mystical, vernacular poetics, to traditional approaches to composition. From another perspective, Beat writing can be designated by its social and literary iconoclasm, freedom of sexual expression, drug use and experimentation, existential questioning and questing, but these elements also describe most Anglo American bohemias of the twentieth century. What is distinctively Beat is the historical moment and social context in which its iconoclasms were practiced, and the specific communities from which Beat praxis took shape: the way denizens of postwar—that is, post-Hiroshima, post-Auschwitz—Beat bohemian enclaves in Boston, New York, and San Francisco rejected cold war paranoias, button-down corporate conformities, consumer culture, sexual repression, and McCarthy-era gay bashing when it was far from common or safe to do so openly. Who are Beat writers was in significant ways decided by interpersonal associations and common experiences of the postwar, cold war zeitgeist because Beat writing is stylistically and technically too diverse to constitute a homogeneous aesthetic or literary philosophy. Beat writers are united fundamentally by their challenges to conservative postwar consumer culture and by their formative mutual associations; commonwealth and personal relations are integral to writers' identification as Beat. That is, social, artistic, personal, geographical links—literary camaraderies and life relations—underlie most writers' identification with Beat.

The Beat generation literary movement formed out of the postwar bohemian communities of Greenwich Village in New York City and North Beach in San Francisco. Writers, painters, and intellectuals of postwar New York have been linked to bohemians of the 1920s in Greenwich Village. The underground of hipsters Kerouac noticed in New York during the war (1959, 361) brought a harder-edged, existential element to the free sex and art scene in the Village. Beat has been called the New Bohemia (Gruen), the underground (Sukenick), and, simply, bohemia (Gold); but Kerouac, who recognized the hip tenor of the New Bohemians in the late 1940s, shows that cultural Beat is a hybrid of Greenwich Village bohemia and Times Square hipsters; of painters and poets, musicians and philosophers. The Beat literary movement emerged from and drew on this cultural hybridity. It arose concurrently with late abstract expressionism in painting and with bebop jazz, as well as with other literary schools of the fifties and sixties with which it overlaps. Writers associated with Beat, the Black Mountain College school, the San Francisco Renaissance, and the New York school knew and influenced each other, shared work, techniques, publications, galleries, lovers, lofts, bars, and world views while still maintaining specific aesthetic approaches and cultural stances that gave each movement a distinct identity.[5] The postwar New Bohemia was characterized by a heterogeneous collection of artists, writers, and intellectuals, some of whom loosely sorted themselves—or have been sorted subsequently—into schools according to aesthetics and practices. Yet, identity with a school arises from and is sustained by bonds of community as much as by adherence to artistic principles or agreement on social and political matters; Michael Davidson's point that the "San Francisco Renaissance was diverse, relying for its unanimity on a spirit of camaraderie and fellow-feeling more than on shared aesthetic beliefs" (4) applies to bicoastal postwar literary and art movements across the board.

The criteria of camaraderie and community connection to identify artists' affiliations helps to name those Beats who have been elided from the category or even those who deny it, as do, perhaps not surprisingly, many women writers whose alliances and aesthetics otherwise strongly place them as Beat. Ginsberg saw the Beat generation literary movement as "a group of friends who had worked together on poetry, prose, and cultural conscience from the mid-forties until the term became popular nationally in the late fifties" (Waldman 1996, xiv). His genealogy lists well-known male Beats, as well as writers from the Black Mountain, New York, and San Francisco schools; he counted only two women, Diane di Prima and Joanne Kyger, among the working "friends." Later Ginsberg reiterated that Beat artists are recognized by confraternity; he used the phrase "guilt by association" (Weinreich, 268), which suggests de facto belonging by way of confederation. In another instance, Ginsberg pointed to the social to identify Beat writers: they are "the group of people we knew at that time" (Peabody, 1).[6] He revealed the relevance of the shared historical moment ("at that time"), the cold war era; of an association or "group" of individuals with common beliefs and interests; and the somewhat self-serving standard for inclusion, his recognition ("people we knew"), a subjective measure limited by sexism, for although they were there, in this assessment, Ginsberg did not find any women writers of "such power as Kerouac or Burroughs" (Peabody, 1) except di Prima, repeating the elision that has marked Beat women writers' beat condition. [7]

Beat has in common with its affiliated literary schools and with the dominant culture from which all emerged unexamined assumptions of women's intellectual, creative, even sexual inferiority, and, in particular, the supposition that women could neither originate nor help to advance the aesthetic and artistic breakthroughs and innovations that galvanized the schools. Although Ginsberg was confident that "where there was a strong writer who could hold her own, like Diane di Prima, we would certainly work with her and recognize her" (Peabody, 1), this grudging concession rationalizes Beat's failure, except in a few, isolated instances, to support women writers or welcome them as movement artists, and perpetuates the patriarchal concept of the exceptional individual, which entails the use of specious standards of merit or "genius" to limit acknowledgment of persons outside the white male hegemonic norm. Ginsberg's assumption that there were no meritorious women Beat writers, or only one or two, underlies the chronic marginalization of women artists, which is so extreme that few if any have been recognized in rosters of postwar literary schools; Davidson finds that "American bohemia of the 1950s lacked all but the most perfunctory recognition of women as artists" (174). Moreover, Ginsberg places the burden for evincing literary significance onto the women themselves, refusing to be "responsible for the lack of outstanding genius in the women we knew" (Peabody, 1), as if genius was innate and personal, a matter of an individual's luck or diligence in cultivation, rather than a judgment produced by hegemonic social constructions and preferences (Battersby). Indeed, the Beat movement is notable for the considerable number of women writers who were part of the community yet obscured or ignored, for the degree to which women went unrecognized for their literary and cultural contributions, and for Beat's indifference to the kindred spirit of rebellion implicit in bohemian women's protofeminism: even as they did write, both privately and for publication, women Beat writers continued to be unacknowledged and excluded from historical concepts and literary considerations of the movement.[8]

Yet, in Beat literature, social judgments are betrayed by linguistic play, for although the movement has been artificially confined to a restricted set of writers, "beat" is a famously contingent signifier, characterized by a diversity that is consistent with its wide range of practitioners. The variousness of the signifier charts another kind of narrative of Beat emergence. Kerouac gave beat referents ranging from "poor, down and out, deadbeat, on the bum, sleeping in subways" (1959, 363), which derived from the wartime and postwar 1940s, to "beaten down" and "sympathetic," which reflected a fifties resignation, to, in its late phase, "beatific" and other spiritual associations, which anticipated sixties spiritualities. Beat was also used to designate hip and to identify hipsters, the wartime Times Square underground known for drug use and fringe associations, antecedent to those Kerouac called the subterraneans. The subterraneans were postwar bohemians or "cool" Beats characterized by Kerouac as "hip without being slick . . . intelligent without being corny . . . intellectual as hell . . . without being pretentious" (1958, 2). Diversifying the signifier, Kerouac claimed that "beat" had been "stretch[ed] to include people who do not sleep in subways but have a certain new gesture, or attitude . . . a new *more*" and that "Beat Generation," having been elaborated to a discourse, had "become the slogan or label for a revolution in manners in America" (1959, 363). Yet, according to Kerouac, the "new *more*" was personified only by a singular few; he differentiated between scene makers and writers, women and men:

> .. two distinct styles of hipsterism: the "cool". . . your bearded laconic sage . . . before a hardly touched beer in a beatnik dive, whose speech is low and unfriendly, whose girls say nothing and wear black: the "hot" . . . the crazy talkative shining eyed (often innocent and openhearted) nut who runs from bar to bar, pad to pad looking for everybody, shouting, restless, lushy, trying to "make it" with the subterranean beatniks who ignore him. (1959, 362–363)

As Kerouac goes on to insist, "most Beat Generation artists belong to the hot school." In this defining scenario, Beat cannot even be applied to women; they are figured to be so "cool" as to be barely there, and they do not figure at all in his account of Beat artists. It is the "hot" male hipster who embodies the "new gesture," the "new *more*"; the women appended to hipster men only furnish or service the set on which Beat is performed. In an image that is the Beat archetype of hipster women, Kerouac's "girls" who "say nothing and wear black" are accessories for cool hipster men, indispensable to the scene, but meant to be unseen and unheard as they render their essential but subsidiary functions. In Kerouac's schema, literary Beat is "hot"—vivacious—and active, gendered male; cultural Beat is "cool"—inert—and passive, gendered female. Women, allowed only a decorative, auxiliary function, are "cool," a state of being beaten aside that is overdetermined by gender to preclude literary accomplishment, which requires the "hard gemlike flame" of the hot hipster (1959, 363), who is explicitly figured as male. For Kerouac, beat and Beat literary prowess are virtually essentialized conditions constructed on the binary of gender difference, distinctions that have persisted and have made Beat literature narrowly synonymous with men's production of it.

Notwithstanding their de facto exclusion from discourses of Beat art and creativity, women were integral to Beat's development and indispensable to expressing its signature disdain of and challenge to establishment culture and conventions. Women Beats alter and augment Beat's significations of nonconformity, the "wild self-believing individuality" that Kerouac and others saw as fundamental to Beat (1959, 361). Beat women's version of

American individuality was a revolt for personal freedom enacted by and in their writing. This revolt led to a body of woman-centered Beat literature that anticipated second-wave feminism. Radical feminist and Beat fellow traveler Alix Kates Shulman suggests in her historical novel, *Burning Questions* (1978), that women Beats were a protofeminist vanguard. Antecedent to women's liberation of the 1960s, they were those who, advancing "From Silent to Beat to Revolutionary," had suffered a paralysis of expression — "some of us felt we had nothing to say and the rest had no one to say it to" (8) — which, related to gender, was alleviated in the antiestablishment Beat movement, but finally dissipated only by sixties feminism. Beat novelist Joyce Johnson also identifies dissident cultural enclaves of the Eisenhower era such as the New Bohemia or Beat as germinal spaces for protofeminist women who, rejecting fifties mandates for conformity (1983, 53), became "somehow more a part of the Beat Generation than of the Silent one we'd been born into chronologically" (75). So pervasive was the postwar acquiescence to cold war conformist gender and political ideologies that precocious nonconformist white women in the fifties had to jump a generation to the older Beats to find a remotely sympathetic reflection of their unconventional aspirations to think for themselves. Beat poet Diane di Prima speculated that by the mid-fifties such a community numbered only a couple hundred, "forty or fifty" in New York City, "another fifty living in San Francisco and perhaps a hundred more throughout the country," meaning in Chicago and New Orleans (1969, 126). Havens for bohemian dissidents of the 1950s were few; female denizens and exponents were fewer. But women Beats were there, and they gave Beat literature a transformative character, rending speech from their socially mandated silence, presence from their invisibility of gender, and literary works from their subordinated status as literature's objects.

Although the Beat generation incubated feminism and offered women refuge from the stifling silent generation, this aspect has remained invisible because the Beat generation was also, nevertheless, complicit with mainstream gender codes of female silence and subordination. In addition to broaching mainstream fifties social constraints, women Beat writers had to reckon with Beat's masculinist assumptions. Di Prima explains that the hipster "code, our eternal, tiresome rule of Cool" entailed stoic self-repression; displays of feeling risked "blowing our entire scene, retrospectively even" (1969, 94).[9] While male hipsters were also ruled by the code of Cool, for them it was an affectation, a style that did not diminish status, agency, or power, as in John Clellon Holmes's hipster portrait in *Go* (1952), where the impassive "'cool' man" (209) nevertheless signifies: "He's gone to the end of everything" (211). For hipster women, the code of Cool did not convey a subject's "desperation of disbelief" (Holmes 210), but duplicated female powerlessness and objectification, the gendered silence under the reign of which the majority of women of the 1950s suffered politically and socially, individually and as a caste. As di Prima, Johnson, and Shulman attest, hipster women, tyro Beats, sought to escape convention's constraints, not recodify them. The Beat code of Cool had further ramifications for Beat's women writers, undermining literary voice and seeming to endorse the men's indifference to their work (Jones 1990). Yet, though Beat dissidence reproduced establishment gender codes and hierarchies, which subordinated women, Beat, as a cultural discourse and domain, was conducive to the self-assertions of the marginalized, and this embrace of nonconformity included even the women on whose marginalization the Beat movement, like the rest of the patriarchal structure, rested. In fact, second-wave feminism—women's liberation—was by definition the kind of rebellious, antiestablishment impulse Beat endorsed, at least when such an impulse was embodied by men. It is an ironic paradox, then, that canonical Beat literature was so conventional with regard to women and their subaltern place.

Beat's selective inconsistency as an antiestablishment movement that abetted nonconformity but only for certain of its adherents was a contradiction expressed and embodied by women Beats, whose emergence as writers was aided as well as impeded by this disparity. With respect to sexual politics, women Beats, although they exceeded limits imposed on women in mainstream culture, helped give voice to what Betty Friedan famously called the 1950s "female malaise," but with the crucial difference that they struggled to dissipate it. Indeed, for bohemian women, Beat is the hallmark of that struggle. Because of their defiance of convention and because they were artists with a certain level of self-awareness, women Beats occupied an ambivalent position: they were or became cognizant of, on one hand, resisting and, on the other hand, participating in their own marginalization by forces of social construction in both Beat and establishment cultures. Some women Beat writers accepted the marginalization of being female explicitly or in effect by promoting men's art in place of their own. Others, as di Prima's *Memoirs of a Beatnik* suggests, displaying their fitness as hipsters, colluded with their own effacement, for, subscribing to the "rule of Cool"(94), they internalized the code's prohibitions, policing themselves in a process of social control that Michel Foucault has explained as panopticism.

Thus, although frustrated by the inequity of their status, Beat women participated in the pervasive gender binary that figures women's subordination to men, a binary which was, before women's liberation, nearly irremediable. Women's contribution to Beat as expressed in their lives and writing is this liminal state: a recognition of their oppression, the extent of their personal responsibility for it, and the opportunity for liberation presented by the unconventionality of bohemian enclaves like Beat. Women Beats' resistance to marginalization in the Beat movement as well as their reluctance to perform the inhibiting roles assigned them in mainstream postwar culture gave rise to critiques that were instantiated in second-wave feminism, which aimed to be an antidote to the stifling gender binary that represses women. Women Beat writers identified the problem of their oppression, their female malaise, and helped to invent its solution. Their writings both directly address Beat's ambitious obligation to self-reliance and individuality, and enact the self-reliant nonconformity which the liberation of women would require.

Beat women's protofeminist ascent, albeit fostered unintentionally in Beat bohemia, exemplifies the way Beat interventions in aesthetic and cultural hegemonies anticipate postmodern advances in U.S. arts, culture, and politics. Women Beat writers were forerunners of women's movements of the postmodern, post-1968 era; their literary inventions and expressions gave rhetorical shape and urgency to the social freedoms necessary to women's viability as literary producers. Women Beats and their efforts to express literary and social subjectivity emerged at a crucial juncture. Beat writing came to public attention as a countercultural phenomenon at exactly the same postwar moment as the massive redeployment of conformist ideologies of home, family, and normative heterosexuality. Historians and sociologists trying to recuperate the fifties from its bland, conformist repute and to comprehend the decade's role in the social change of the sixties, cite hipsters and Beats, among people of color, closeted gays, and daring middle-class white women, as anomalous strains in the postwar, Levittown gender ideal, the binary of female homemakers and male wage slaves (Meyerowitz). Beat writing critiqued this reactionary postwar reconstruction, articulating discourses that could intervene in or interfere with the heterosexist gender binary (Breines). Focusing on sexual politics and gender difference, the works of women Beat writers problematize the gender binary, elucidating incipient postwar American feminisms. Beat women's writing proves that second-wave feminism and other activist claims for female sexual agency and subjectivity did not emerge ex nihilo in the late 1960s, but were produced—by Beat women, among others in the vanguard—in a protofeminist interval of transition. Edward Halsey Foster notes that Beat's concern with self-knowledge and interest in the discovery or recovery of a true mode of perception are "objectives obviously equally important to feminists" (24). Thus, in spite of its exclusivity, Beat's masculinist, Emersonian insistence on individual truth would paradoxically include feminism in its reach. And, in this, it would include and nurture, if unevenly and inconsistently, female dissidents and artists, the distaff, too-often-unseen exemplars of Beat.

Beat's Literature of Female Transgression

Critical inquiry into Beat literature has been restricted to that by men. But there were numerous women Beat writers producing during and well after the Beat heyday of the early 1950s to the mid-1960s, women who were part of or connected to Beat communities on both coasts. In this group were women who wrote and considered themselves writers, and women who produced literature that may or may not have been published at the time it was written, or that, if published, has not been integrated into standard discussions and constructions of Beat generation writing. The virtual elimination of the women writers who constituted Beat communities from accounts of the Beat school exemplifies the way that those who Johnson has termed "minor characters" are required to underwrite literary legends (1983). Just so, the suppression of women Beat writers created the field of Beat writing as it is known, advancing the male writers' works as the essential Beat arts—at the expense of the women's subjectivity and authority as writers, and with the result of greatly foreshortening understandings of what is Beat. The debased condition of writing by Beat generation women is not a matter of what Ginsberg called a "lack of outstanding genius in the women we knew" (Peabody, 1), but a product of widely held, unproblematized assumptions about gender, literary production, and artistic authority. These have perpetuated Beat women's distaff status and restricted

the scope of Beat culture and the Beat oeuvre. Recognizing the women writers of the movement, understanding the female subjects inscribed in their
writing, and restoring this writing to the Beat canon is an essential project
that illuminates postwar sexuality and discourses of the masculine and feminine in Beat culture and literature as well as in those of the mainstream.
Beat women writers bring to Beat literature women-centered subjects and
themes from the domestic to the sexual to the existential, and by this
modification to Beat's exclusionary masculinism expand what it means to
be Beat.

Studies of women Beat writers have been encouraged by the publication
of two anthologies assembling their biographies and collecting their poems,
fiction, and nonfiction writing. In *Women of the Beat Generation: The Writers, Artists and Muses at the Heart of a Revolution* (1996), Brenda Knight offers
a three-point theoretical construct (writer, artist, muse) to establish a canon
of women Beats and provides biographical introductions to the selected
works of each writer included in the volume. Richard Peabody's *A Different
Beat: Writings by Women of the Beat Generation* (1997) downplays the artists'
life stories in favor of their fiction, poetry, and nonfiction writing. Peabody's
book includes writers such as Bridget Murnaghan, Barbara Moraff, Sheri
Martinelli, and Margaret Randall that Knight's does not, but not Helen
Adam, Jane Bowles, Mary Fabilli, and Mary Norbert Korte, which Knight's
does. Clearly the canon of women Beat writers has not been definitively established, but is transitory and subjective, with debate about the constitu-
tion of the group manifesting itself in editorial choices conveyed through
the publishing industry. Although the Knight and Peabody volumes raise
unanswered questions of standards for Beat inclusion and exclusion with
their diverse and often nonoverlapping lists of women Beat writers, the material included in these volumes has been vital to expanding Beat studies
and scholarship. Yet, in addition to filling a long-troubling omission of
women from concepts of the Beat generation, both *A Different Beat* and
Women of the Beat Generation, by their very presence, ironically illuminate
another lapse, the lack of vital attention given to the literary production of
women Beat writers. The anthologies have helped generate discussion of
the nature and value of the art produced by women associated with the Beat
literary movement, and have led to the critical insight that women Beat
writers form three distinct generations, and, thus, so does the Beat literary
movement.

THREE GENERATIONS OF BEAT

Women writers who contributed to and participated in the Beat movement form a three-generational cohort. Some are closer to Beat bohemia
than others; some practice a more familiarly Beat aesthetic; most engage in
formal experimentation and innovation; all, one way or another, directly or
indirectly, express a rebellious, antiestablishment critique of women's assigned place and value in patriarchy, claiming self-reliant individuality as
the signature of their social and literary production of subjectivity. Women
Beat writers coincide with the well-known male Beat writers' first and second generations and extend beyond them to a third generation. Women
writers who were part of the postwar New Bohemian beat—that is, those
contemporaneous with the first male Beat writers—were, like them born
in the 1910s and 1920s. Included in this group of Beat writing's progenitors, although not associated with the birth of the Beat in conventional accounts, are such women writers as Madeline Gleason (1903–1979), Helen
Adam (1909–1992), Sheri Martinelli (1918–1996), ruth weiss (1928–),
and Carol Berge (1928–). Writing at the same time as Kerouac (1922–
1969), Ginsberg (1926–1997), and Burroughs (1914–1997) and, like
them, part of the first generation to live with the trauma of the Final Solution and the awareness of the possibility of global destruction through the
atomic bomb, these women writers sought to revise or work free of academic or traditional literary models, or innovate new ones for their post-
bomb, cold-war-era experience.

In this interval of Beat formation, bohemian women writers situated
themselves, or could be found, in diverse literary enclaves, for example the
Maidens, the eccentric and insular San Francisco poetry and performance
troop begun by Helen Adam in 1957 to which Madeline Gleason also belonged. The Maidens were antecedent to and contiguous with the San Francisco Renaissance and Beat literary movements. Jane Bowles (1917–1973),
who had affiliations with Ginsberg and Burroughs, epitomized Beat's em-
bryonic connections to and departures from experimental modernisms,
while Denise Levertov (1923–1997), whose first book was published by
Beat poet Lawrence Ferlinghetti's City Lights Books, evinced Beat's pivotal
likenesses to and differences from the intellectualized formations of the
Black Mountain and New Critical schools. Bowles and Levertov, as well as
other first-generation women Beat writers, were initially connected to Beat
aesthetics and interests and then proceeded to other movements. They de-

marcate a Beat cusp, exemplifying the liminality of early Beat writing, and clarifying the way that Beat emerged contemporaneously with several other avant-garde literary communities.

In fact, it required a generation for women Beat writers per se to materialize in any numbers. Born in the 1930s, this younger group comprises the first full generation of women Beat writers. It shared community and the cultural zeitgeist most directly and fully with the established male Beat writers, especially Kerouac and Ginsberg, Philip Whalen (1923–), Lew Welch (1926–1971), Ted Joans (1928–), Gary Snyder (1930–), Gregory Corso (1930–2001), Michael McClure (1932–), and LeRoi Jones (1934–). Second-generation women Beat writers include Joanna McClure (1930–), Bobbie Louise Hawkins (1930–), Lenore Kandel (1932–), Elise Cowen (1933–1962), Kyger (1934–), di Prima (1934–), Hettie Jones (1934–), Johnson (1935–), and Brenda Frazer (Bonnie Bremser) (1939–). In addition to this main group of women Beat writers, who each produced a distinctive body of work or important individual pieces, the second generation includes Brigid Murnaghan (1930–), Margaret Randall (1936–), Rochelle Owens (1936–), Diane Wakowski (1937–), and Barbara Moraff (1940–). These latter writers are, for various reasons, contiguous with rather than Beat per se, but they suggest the range of writers comprising the second Beat generation. This strong showing of women writers with important work evinces a generation gap with the male Beat writers which speaks to material contingencies in the progress of a marginalized constituency: women's greater latitude during the Second World War and the beginning of more widespread secondary education for white women after the war created the material context for bohemian women writers' emergence.

While women Beat writers of the first and second generations predate the contemporary feminist movement, which came into being in the late 1960s, their representations of women as artists and themselves as members of the Beat generation return time and again to gender. There is among them no consistent articulation of feminist principles—a few even seem reluctant to pursue the ways in which gender can affect art or even deny that it can, even as they are cognizant of themselves as women writing. But, taken as a whole, members of the group display a persistent understanding of the importance of asserting themselves as women in the alternative communities in which they lived, and which denied them, during the fifties, and even to some extent today, value as artists specifically because of their sex. Their recognition of this condition exemplifies their protofeminist impulses.

If the second generation of women Beat writers is a vanguard of the sixties women's movement, the third generation, born in the 1940s, comes of age in the sixties counterculture, and in this clarifies Beat's precedence of hippie. Members of the third generation express a security about their freedom and integrity as women writers that profits from the antecedence of second-generation Beat women, the empowerments of sixties counterculture, and second-wave feminist demands for women's civil and economic rights and sexual self-determination. The third Beat generation appoints itself Beat on its own self-evident terms, which are ironically like Ginsberg's exclusionary terms, but expanded to include women like themselves: writers who worked with, lived with, formed literary or spiritual common cause with, and were nurtured and recognized by the established Beat writers. On these terms, there appear to be two women writers in the third Beat generation: Janine Pommy Vega (1942–) and Anne Waldman (1945–). With the noted exception of di Prima, of all women Beat writers, Pommy Vega and Waldman are closest to the idealistic and confrontational sixties counterculture which fostered the women's movement, and they practice a Beat aesthetic distinguished by emphases from that turbulent and liberated era. Born during the Second World War, Pommy Vega and Waldman were adolescents in the suffocating Silent Generation 1950s, and, as young adults during the sixties, they were shaped by the escalating Vietnam War, the undiluted sexual revolution, the unapologetic drug counterculture, and the rage against the "masters of war" decried by fellow third-generation Beat Bob Dylan (1941–). Pommy Vega and Waldman had the opportunity to be influenced by progenitive Beats, but as is the case for most women Beat writers who emerged with or only slightly after the male Beat advent, they evince wide-ranging extra-Beat influences, bringing a fitting variousness to Beat's already hybrid literary heritage.

Indeed, with respect to aesthetic influence, the traditions from which the three generations of women Beat writers work are more diverse than those of the men. The genealogy of the principal male Beat writers seems linear— a clean path back through British and American modernists (e.g., Wolfe, Williams, Joyce, Faulkner), with branches extending into the British and American romantics (e.g., Shelley, Keats, Melville, Emerson, Thoreau, Poe, Blake, Whitman) and the French surrealists and symbolists (e.g., Apollinaire, Rimbaud). This tradition of influence is staunchly male, while female predecessors are very much present for women Beat writers. Their influences are diverse and far less diagrammatic than the men's: there are loci of commonality, but no sharp, discernible path of influence joining them in a neat or familiar literary curriculum. Among the women writers one recurring pattern of male literary influence is the triumvirate of Charles Olson, Kerouac, and Ginsberg. These three artists are significant precursors for writers such as Frazer, who consciously modeled *Troia: Mexican Memoirs* on Kerouac's prose; Kyger, Jones, di Prima, and Waldman, who cite Olson as influential; and di Prima, Waldman, and Pommy Vega, who acknowledge Ginsberg's central role in their artistic development. The prominence of major male Beat figures, as well as Olson, in part results from the fact that so many of the women Beat writers—those who are second-generation Beats—were at least a decade younger than the men and came into the movement after it had coalesced. Because of their seniority and reputation, charismatic literary innovators such as Kerouac and Ginsberg, and the Black Mountain poet Olson, became artistic mentors and models to emerging second-generation Beat writers, the cohort in which there are the most women.

With literary lineages and aesthetic influences that vary dramatically among them, women writers of the second Beat generation additionally bring to bear on the field considerably different sets of antecedent texts and writers than have figured in the men's narratives of artistic formation. Johnson, for instance, was inspired by her reading of Henry James to write novels of psychological probity. weiss acknowledges Rainer Maria Rilke, Edgar Allan Poe, and film director François Truffaut as significant artistic models. Jones credits LeRoi Jones as being the major influence on the development of her poetry, and Pommy Vega praises Herbert Huncke for providing her with an artistic vision. Di Prima acknowledges her indebtedness to Ezra Pound, and Waldman discusses the early, formative support she received from teachers Howard Nemerov and Bernard Malamud. However, the most significant influence women writers of the Beat generation cite comes from literature by women of the nineteenth and early twentieth centuries. Both weiss and Pommy Vega marvel over the impact of reading Djuna Barnes; weiss also acknowledges the importance of Gertrude Stein, Anaïs Nin, and Virginia Woolf. Waldman notes the significance of reading Charlotte, Emily, and Anne Brontë, Woolf, Jane Austen, and Edith Sitwell. Several of the women, including Waldman and Ann Charters, refer to di Prima as an important Beat literary and cultural influence. The juxtaposition of the disparate and eclectic influences cited by women Beat writers with the male modernists and romantics cited by the male Beats provocatively complicates conceptions of a Beat aesthetic, which is evidently not monolithic and consistent, but multiple and divergent and more experimental than has been thought. Beat's women writers show the complexities of the movement's literary heritage and its indebtedness to a wider array of art forms than is usually recognized; even the academy, along with its literary representatives, plays a role in Beat's heritage. Thus, Beat is an avant-garde whose sources are as diffuse, unpredictable, and innovative as its practitioners.

Just as the literary influences of women Beats diverge from and expand the field of the men's, so too do their approaches to artistic production. A few follow a model of spontaneous composition, with Frazer and weiss being the most active proponents of this approach. While Frazer admits to currently using a more controlled technique, weiss believes in the creative power of the unfettered mind. Most women Beat writers revise their work; they are careful crafters of their texts, in contradistinction to popular clichés of Beat writing as well as famous statements by Kerouac and Ginsberg, in particular, which disavow revision for the purity of the unmodified literary utterance. They also depart dramatically from what has become known as standard Beat poetics, the Kerouacian mandate for spontaneity employed by Ginsberg, Burroughs, and other male Beat writers (Belgrad). Women Beats appear to feel no need to follow a Beat "party" line, and, instead, stand by the composition practices they develop and implement. Exhibiting a categorically Beat independence, they buck the directives of many of their male colleagues about the process of literary production, to the point of complying with more conventional and less innovative methods of composition. The women are unapologetic about using more conventional poetic techniques, which many of the male Beats also employ at times but do not freely acknowledge, perhaps because the men are inhibited by their own mystique of Beat iconoclasm.

Similarly, the work and writing lives of women Beats represent divergent conceptions of art's purpose and of the artist as individual, although their artistic praxis is intricately linked to an existential, Sartrean authenticity. Jones and Pommy Vega subscribe to the political and didactic nature of art; weiss espouses a life lived for the pursuit of art as a fundamentally mystical and apolitical praxis; Frazer speaks of having been a young artist who wrote out of tortured and isolated heroism. Di Prima positions herself on a continuum with all women artists reaching back to the cave painters, naming all of them "the leavening of life." For women writers in the Beat movement the act of writing, whether poetry, novels, or, in the case of the critic Charters, literary history and biography, has required personal courage and sacrifice, a considerable degree of nonconformity, antiestablishmentarianism, and a rejection of or separation from the mainstream values, beliefs, and practices of their eras.[10]

Thus, just as male Beat writers defy homogenization, so do women writers of the movement. The effort to generalize, to abstract, and to reduce the cohort to commonalities, is thwarted by the women's artistic divergences and their reflections of the disparate social contexts in which each developed as female. Yet, they are also united in their common experience that so much energy and talent remained locked away, the private secrets of so many women. Perhaps most poignant is the repeated confession made, without rancor, that during their formative years as artists, many of the women were writing alone, without extensive support from male or female friends or mentors. This reality differs dramatically from the experiences of the male Beat writers, whose tightly knit community was not only a group of friends but also a powerful vehicle for developing and promoting each man's writing. Yet, Frazer suggests that such creative isolation also protected artistic individuality; she notes that during her formative years as a writer "not talking was probably more meaningful than conversation could have been. I was able to let my imagination answer all the questions" (Charters 1992, 380). This private, interiorized process of evolution sharply contrasts with the very public group-camaraderie model for writing enacted by male Beats. It is a figure of self-reliant artistic individuality that exemplifies ways in which women writers augment Beat discourses: some of them transformed the adversities of sexism's double standards and Beat's inconsistencies with regard to women into an Emersonian self-reliance, nonconformity, "genius." The fact that so many women Beat writers did shed their silence and secrecy and emerge as public artists is a significant achievement—ultimately, perhaps more daring and consequential than making the mythic Beat road trip.

On Women Writing Beat

This volume seeks neither to produce a formula for Beat writers and Beat writing nor to prove that certain writers are Beat in a formulaic way. Similarly, not all of the most important female writers associated with Beat are covered by the essays here. Those included in this volume represent some of the more well known and some of the more obscure, but essays on, for example, weiss, Levertov, Kandel, Frazer, or McClure would have been equally appropriate and desirable to clarify the limits and reach of women writers of or associated with the Beat movement. Other writers now deemed peripheral may eventually come to be seen as forerunners or significant contributors, and new interpretations of central women Beat writers such as di Prima and Waldman will no doubt emerge as well. The intent of this volume is not to suggest a new canon, but to show that the domain of Beat has fluid, even arbitrary, boundaries, and that those identified as its writers have been so designated by gender assumptions and biases rather than by the application of literary standards, theories of art, and processes of literary assessment. The negation of women Beat writers by critics exemplifies the way a literary school and the roster of its adherents are usually recognized after the fact and founded on exclusion. The Beat generation literary movement is more accurately defined by taking a more inclusive approach to its practitioners, and by examining aesthetics and methods brought to bear on Beat by diverse, even divergent, but related women writers.

Similarly, no single critical perspective binds the essays in this collection. While the focus is critical reading of *women's* work, the collection is not bound to or by a sustained and specific feminist methodology, but, instead, is comprised of diverse critical approaches to the writers and their texts. The study of women Beat writers is nascent in terms of literary scholarship, and the act of criticism—which is an affirmation of the value of the work produced, and therefore of the woman as artist—is significant in itself, regardless of the particular theoretical stance the criticism deploys. Several essays pursue their critical inquiries through various feminist lenses, but others focus more specifically on or integrate historical interpretation, formalism, poststructuralism, and cultural criticism in their approaches.

The essays are arranged according to the three-generation concept of women Beat writers in order to suggest layers of development and influence in the Beat literary movement. The volume's first essay discusses the Beat precursor Helen Adam, who, as a practitioner of the ballad form, worked in a tradition distinctly non-Beat, but also rendered a hybrid form that predicts the emergence of women writers producing fully within a Beat ethos and aesthetic. Kristin Prevallet's essay, "The Worm Queen Emerges: Helen Adam and the Forgotten Ballad Tradition," introduces Adam's modifications to and experiments with the ballad form, connecting her poetry with the appreciation for native languages and bardic orality found in Beat and in folk movements. Prevallet also grounds the work of Scottish-born Adam in the San Francisco poetics of Jack Spicer and Robert Duncan, both of whom knew Adam as a colleague.

This discussion is followed by essays on second-generation women Beat writers, arguably the strongest cohort of women Beats. Di Prima, the one female writer who managed early on to make a name for herself as part of the Beat movement, exemplifies the extent to which patriarchal displacements of women in literary history can be resisted. Anthony Libby, in his essay "Diane di Prima: 'Nothing Is Lost; It Shines in Our Eyes,'" addresses the range of di Prima's poetry from the 1950s to the present day, emphasizing its changeable connections to both prefeminist discourses of hippie-Digger culture and the later women's movement. His overview of di Prima's formidable body of work, much of which is still in print but neglected in Beat studies, as well as in studies of postwar American poetry, emphasizes her iconoclastic heritage, its impact on her politics and poetics, and the way in which di Prima has continued an evolutionary, if not always revolutionary, poetic practice that reflects and resists both establishment and bohemian cultural values.

Ronna C. Johnson provides the first extended discussion of novelist, memoirist, and editor Joyce Johnson's *Come and Join the Dance,* the first Beat novel written by and about a Beat woman, published in 1962 and long out of print. In "'And then she went': Beat Departures and Feminine Transgressions in Joyce Johnson's *Come and Join the Dance,*" Johnson explores Joyce Johnson's "Beat move," that is, her use of Beat themes such as dropping out, sexual experimentation, and the trope of the road tale, to argue that *Come and Join the Dance* challenges the central Beat discourse of male freedom. The essay's attention to the discursive components of the novel illuminates parallels with and departures from Johnson's memoir *Minor Characters,* as well as the transformative possibilities inherent in both fiction and nonfiction, the way that the elision of women in patriarchal accounts may be remedied by narrative's revisionary power.

The poet and memoirist Hettie Jones presents a complementary yet divergent story of the female artist. Jones came of age in the same exhilarating bohemian/hipster Greenwich Village art scene as did her friend Johnson and colleague di Prima, but unlike the latter two, who knew from an early age that they wanted to write—and broke with family and social mores to do so—Jones began to write somewhat later in life and for much of her early adulthood squelched her own literary impulses, composing poetry surreptitiously and sporadically. Barrett Watten's essay, "What I See in *How I Became Hettie Jones*," assumes an epistemological stance, exploring the false split between poetic form and content. The essay suggests ways in which Jones's poetic development was thwarted but also stamped by her Beat connections and how her work, including her memoir and her recent first collection of poems, *Drive* (1998), emerged in competing discursive as well as material relations with her former husband, the African American Beat and Black Arts Movement/Black Nationalist poet LeRoi Jones/Amiri Baraka.

That Beat derived its literary and cultural identity through a tight community defined by bonds of friendship is exemplified by the story of Elise Cowen. Cowen, who was a close friend of both Johnson and Ginsberg, produced poetry with a cold war paranoid intensity that aligns her work most closely with the early prophetic utterances of Ginsberg. It is this symbiotic link that is the subject of "Who Writes? Reading Elise Cowen's Poetry" by Tony Trigilio. Using Michel Foucault's theory of the author function, Trigilio explores the voicing of self and other in Cowen's poetry, some of which was published in small literary magazines of the period, such as *Fuck You: A Magazine of the Arts, The Ladder,* and *El corno emplumado,* while most, although privately circulated in manuscript form, has languished unpublished and unread since her death in 1962.

Second-generation women Beats' experimentation with memoir, or the genre of life writing, expands the limits of Beat literary discourses. Complementing critical attention to the literary art of this generation of women writers is Nancy Grace's discussion of the memoirs, "Snapshots, Sand Paintings, and Celluloid: Formal Considerations in the Life Writing of Women from the Beat Generation." These memoirs comprise the single group of texts by Beat women writers that has received the most critical attention (primarily through book reviews); most of them remain in print, and three have been revised and reissued. The memoirs not only articulate the histories of many Beat women but also demonstrate the women's recognition of the memoir as a genre through which the/a self is constructed. Grace's analysis, which includes *Minor Characters* (1983) and Jones's *How I Became Hettie Jones* (1990), as well as di Prima's *Memoirs of a Beatnik* (1969, 1988, 1998) and Frazer's *Troia: Mexican Memoirs* (1969), elucidates this authorial awareness, and, by utilizing feminist theories of autobiography as a genre of creative nonfiction, the essay explores the formal techniques with which some women Beat writers critiqued their lack of female subjectivity, and created it.

The intersection of Beat with other contemporaneous and concurrent poetic schools marks the work of Kyger, who was for a short time married to Beat poet Gary Snyder, but was much more profoundly influenced by the poetics of Black Mountain founder Charles Olson and the San Francisco Renaissance poets Jack Spicer and Robert Duncan. Much of Kyger's work is now out of print, including her first book of poetry, *The Tapestry and the Web* (1965), which, by re-visioning Homer's *Odyssey,* presents the female poetic project as an attempt to find a place in which the self can be explored through telling that is instinctual, frenzied, creative, and delicate. The essay by Linda Russo, "To Deal with Parts and Particulars: Joanne Kyger's Early Epic Poetics," constructs a feminist understanding of Kyger's methods in her early myth-based poems.

The third generation of women Beat writers, born in the 1940s and coming of age in the feminist sixties, signals not so much the end of Beat but rather the transformation of Beat into a range of aesthetic and social movements, and the continuation through realignment and refraction of Beat ideals such as sexual freedom, nonconformity, and spiritual transcendence. Both Janine Pommy Vega and Anne Waldman represent this turn, especially with regard to female subjectivity; they claim Beat themes and forms to express the sixties counterculture's new-found power to reconceptualize gender as it relates to the woman artist. This foregrounded female subject in the work of Pommy Vega is the focus of Maria Damon's essay "Revelations of Companionate Love; or, The Hurts of Women: Janine Pommy Vega's *Poems to Fernando.*" This collection of love poems, Pommy Vega's first book, published in 1968 and now out of print, reveals an elegiac romantic speaker who echoes early Beat influences but who is positioned clearly as a female subject. Damon discusses the collection's first section, Pommy Vega's love poems to her deceased husband, Fernando, in terms of female asceticism, mysticism, and emerging sixties feminisms.

The poetry of Anne Waldman, cofounder with Allen Ginsberg of the Jack Kerouac School of Disembodied Poetics at Naropa Institute (now Naropa University), evinces a similar trajectory. Her work is more readily available than that of many of the other women Beats, but that has not spared her their same fate, to have seen her poetry dislocated from Beat history. Yet, Waldman's early poetry reveals concerns that not only incorporate Beat perspectives but extend through and beyond Beat into a woman-centered, countercultural idiom with an emphasis on mysticism, political commentary, and the rewriting of patriarchal myths. Peter Puchek addresses this history of the poet's development in his essay "From Revolution to Creation: Beat Desire and Body Poetics in Anne Waldman's Poetry," which draws on the cultural philosophies of Fredric Jameson, Slavoj Zizek, and Judith Butler to read the evolution of Waldman's poetry out of sixties and Beat ethics and customs.

The volume closes by turning from literary criticism to critical speculation with Tim Hunt's essay "Many Drummers, a Single Dance?" which reflects on the impact on Beat studies of the emergence of Beat women writers as a viable locus of critical inquiry. This essay usefully places the women writers of Beat within not only the Beat tradition as exemplified by the male writers, but also within a much broader American literary tradition of outriders and romantic individualists encompassing Emerson, Whitman, Melville, and Olson. Just so, this volume as a whole is intended to encourage scholars to continue and augment the project of re-visioning the Beat through the contributions of women Beat writers. Female Beat discourses of desire—sexual, intellectual, artistic, civil—depict white women's postwar emergence into subjectivity, into social or theoretical, or, in this case, artistic significance. The majority of writing by Beat women focuses on women's lives and existential concerns in postwar bohemia, unseating the masculine reign over definitions of female sexuality, hipsterism, and Beat literary innovation, to contend the Beat movement's male hegemony for a more descriptive and critically nuanced view of the school.

Three generations of women writing Beat have brought women's voices and subjectivities to bear on its patriarchal, experimental literary forms and discourses, constituted some of the breakthrough work preceding second-wave feminism, and yielded in turn to Riot Grrrls and female outriders of the 1990s, later heirs of women Beats. Although it is formally diverse, most writing by women Beats is what second-wave feminists termed woman centered: it takes (mostly white, mostly middle class) women as its point of departure. It focuses on women's lives and existential concerns in postwar bohemia; on challenging stereotypes of white women's passivity and sexual frigidity in the fifties; on the liberation of women's sexuality and self-expression. These characteristics of Beat women's writing provided one context for the emergence of second-wave feminism; feminist writers like Shulman, Kate Millett, and Jill Johnston, for example, had contacts in Beat bohemia, although they found their voices in the more oppositional hippie counterculture. Just so, with more frequency than the male Beats, women Beat writers found a haven in sixties countercultures and radical politics; both di Prima and Kandel were part of the anticapitalist, grassroots peoples' group the San Francisco Diggers. Younger and often more nonconformist than the founding generation of male Beats, women Beat writers, fluent in Beat, hippie, and women's movement idioms, partook of and bridged two important countercultures of the American midcentury. Persistently foregrounding female experience in the cold war 1950s, the counterculture sixties, and every decade up to the millennium, women writing Beat have brought nonconformity, skepticism, and gender dissent to postmodern culture and literary production in the United States and beyond.

Notes

1. See Tytell, Charters (1983), Foster (1992), Cook, Bartlett (1981), Krim, Wilentz, Gruen, and Halberstam; also newer studies such as those by Belgrad and Watson and the collection *Beat Writers at Work,* edited by Plimpton.

2. See Watson for a recent version of this inaccurate Beat history. He cites women as assistants to, not architects of, Beat and relegates women to the lifestyle rather than the art aspect of Beat bohemia. Savran confirms the stereotyping of women Beats in the masculinist literary discourse: "Women, when they appear at all in these [Beat] narratives, function as girlfriends, whores, wives, mothers— figures defined almost exclusively by their relationship to men. Often they are completely erased" (44).

3. See Skerl (2000), Waldman (1996), Charters (1992), George-Warren, Lee. The noted exceptions are French and Davidson.

4. We are aware that the prominent African American male Beat writers LeRoi Jones/Amiri Baraka, Ted Joans, and Bob Kaufman are also frequently excluded from the well-known accounts of Beat culture and the Beat literary movement. This book, however, focuses on gender and on women of the Beat and does not discuss or explore race-based exclusions from and constructions of the Beat generation, except as they apply to women on the scene and to women Beat writers.

5. It's worth recalling that the Six Gallery, where Ginsberg first read "Howl"

publicly, in a 1956 reading that also included Philip Lamantia, Michael McClure, Philip Whalen, and Gary Snyder, was a space for showing the work of visual artists. In an expansiveness characteristic of this period of artistic transition and exchange, this art gallery also hosted poetry readings, in this case a reading more famous and important to (literary) art than any one of the exhibitions of visual arts in its history. See Natsoulas/ Novelozo Gallery Press.

   6. Ginsberg is quoted in Peabody as follows:

   "Yes, it's all right to blame the men for exploiting the women—or, I think the point is, the men didn't push the women literally or celebrate them. But then, among the group of people we knew at the time, who were the [women] writers of such power as Kerouac or Burroughs? Were there any? I don't think so.

   "Were we responsible for the lack of outstanding genius in the women we knew? Did we put them down or repress them? I don't think so. . . .

   "Where there was a strong writer who could hold her own, like Diane di Prima, we would certainly work with her and recognize her." (1)

   7. *Beat* has two forms that will be used with conscious intention in this essay. The first, *Beat* with an uppercase *B,* designates a historical, cultural phenomenon, the Beat generation. The second, *beat* with a lowercase *b,* is the signifier *Beat* derives from; it refers to many states of being and is used in phrases such as "Man, I'm beat."

   8. For example, see Holmes's essay "The Beat Poets: A Primer 1975," in which he cites two women poets—Denise Levertov and Emily Dickinson—out of a multitude of male writers. While Levertov was tangentially connected with Beat, Dickinson was not at all connected.

   9. Shulman also notes the hipster's code: "According to the strict code of Cool by which we lived, only weakness moved anyone to extend a relationship beyond the initial passion of the moment. Once a passion peaked, you were supposed to let it go like a poem that had found its form"(105). Here, she suggests that the "code of Cool" enjoins both men and women to a macho stoicism, the avoidance of emotional "weakness." Rather than the feminization of American culture, as Douglas argues (xiv), Beat is in this view a sweeping masculinization of both sexes to a canonical standard of emotion, the withholding—of feeling, of reaction—that is famous in late high modernist male writing.

   10. This survey of women Beat writers' literary influences derives from Grace's interviews with the writers in question. The interviews were conducted from 1999 to 2001, and at this writing are as yet unpublished.

The Worm Queen Emerges

Helen Adam and the Forgotten Ballad Tradition

Kristin Prevallet

Helen Adam was sitting in the front row when Allen Ginsberg read "Howl" for the first time, on October 13, 1955, at the Six Gallery in San Francisco. She was an active participant in the San Francisco literary scene during these formative years, and yet she is infrequently mentioned in historical or anecdotal accounts of either the Beat generation or the simultaneously occurring San Francisco Renaissance. After all, she primarily composed ballads, a literary tradition that is rarely situated within the modernist canon of contemporary American poetry. Because of her adherence to rhyme and her reliance on narrative, Adam is often overlooked in what Michael Davidson calls the "'enabling myths' of origins—in which women are seldom the subjects" that perpetuate the "privileged narrative" of literary movements (198). If she is mentioned in the narratives of either the San Francisco Renaissance or the Beat generation, she is usually referred to as an eccentric traditionalist when compared to the other poets with whom she was associated. However, she is one of four women included in *The New American Poetry,* Donald Allen's seminal anthology that presents the work of poets attempting to rejuvenate poetic forms as a living tradition by rejecting qualities typically associated with academic verse (xi). Adams adheres to regular meters and rarely varies her rhythmic structure or rhyming quatrains, making her presence in the anthology seemingly contradictory to its focus. Yet rather than being a stubborn refusal to embrace modern forms, Adam's work (which aside from ballads includes hundreds of collages, two films, ghost stories, and an opera) reflects many of the formal and social concerns shared by the New American Poets. As Allen writes, "Adam, chiefly through her superb readings, has helped establish the ballad made new as an important trend in the poetry of the Bay area" (xii). Adam may have resisted free verse, but her presence in San Francisco helped to rejuvenate modern poetic forms.

Although it seems contradictory, it was precisely because Adam rejected modern forms that she became the authentication of an ancient literary heritage that many writers in her literary circle sought to rediscover. Because of her insistence on asserting the ballad form, she was respected by, and inspirational to, writers of both the San Francisco Renaissance and the Beat generation. Ginsberg, introducing Adam at Naropa Institute in 1976, recalled with admiration her resistance to contemporary forms. While Robert Duncan was teaching at Black Mountain College in 1956, Ginsberg filled in for him at his poetry workshop at San Francisco State University's Poetry Center. Ginsberg remembered that

> I beat Helen Adam over the head with my idea of what modern poetry should be after William Carlos Williams' forms. But fortunately, she resisted my malevolent influence and continued writing the ballads and songs, which she does so exquisitely, so that finally, many years later, I find myself writing rhymed ballads and songs and look to Helen Adam for encouragement and advice. (1976a)

Likewise, Duncan embraced her as the authentication of the Scottish ballad tradition, which complimented his own search for poetic sources. He came to respect Adam for having "opened the door to the full heritage of the forbidden romantics. Her ballads were the missing link to the tradition" (Allen 435). According to Davidson, "the Romantic tradition represents more than a historical period or canonical body of texts. It represents an ancient quest for knowledge that, for a variety of reasons, has been suppressed or marginalized" (127). Many poets of this time perceived rhymed verse, fairy tales, and folk songs not as dated, but as essential to the living community that they were creating through their art and writing. By reconceiving poetic formulas, these poets were seeking not only to rescue poetry from academic readings but also to assert themselves into the trajectory of genuine poetic practice.

As with romanticism, the ballad tradition was absorbed into the work of poets writing in San Francisco in the 1950s. Even before Adam arrived in San Francisco, the poet Jack Spicer was appropriating and researching his own connections with ballads and folk music. The son of an Industrial Workers of the World (IWW) union activist, Spicer had grown up hearing the stories of workers' struggles through those of ballad heroes such as John Henry and Joe Hill. While an undergraduate at the University of California, Berkeley, in the late 1940s, Spicer had assisted Harry Smith in tracking down old recordings for his *Anthology of American Folk Music* and subsequently brought this folk history to the San Francisco poets.[1] As Kevin Killian writes, Spicer went on to use these sources in several of his serial poems, including "The Holy Grail," "Golem," and "Book of Magazine Verse." Always with a satirical edge, Spicer's appropriation of folk sources was criticized as nongenuine—particularly when he attempted to subvert them in a KPFA radio show in which he improvised his own words for the classic songs. But improvisation is central to the ballad form, as is evident with Adam who, appearing to be working genuinely with the ballad tradition and adhering to formulaic rules of prosody, was, like Spicer, reinventing the tradition as she wrote. As Susan Anderson observes, Helen Adam's use of the ballad "cannot be easily categorized as 'folk' or 'literary' ballad, but constitutes an important opening of possibility in contemporary poetics: a fusion of traditional composition methods with a content that challenges the artistic properties of twentieth-century academic poetry" (2). The ballad form was not revived simply because it represented an ancient poetic tradition—it was revived because implicit within that tradition is a complex history and a malleable form.

Ballads originate within an oral tradition of songs and folk tales passed down through generations, their tunes and stories changing the longer they survive. In the eighteenth and nineteenth centuries, ballad collectors roamed the hills of Scotland and England, writing down and publishing these songs. As Susan Stewart writes, these collectors "saw the reproduction of past forms as a way of animating a continual and illustrative history of the national literature" (112). In constructing this history, the collectors had to pick and choose from multiple versions of the ballads, adding and editing their rhythmic structure and content in order to produce solid literary examples. Given that poetic language was being used by writers in the 1950s to subvert the dominant power structures and create alternative communities, the ballad tradition presented a form that had been used for many centuries by people working to assert their own histories, language, and communal structures, in spite of the political forces working to control them.

Ballads are written to be sung aloud. Adam herself explained that she wrote "chiefly by sound because all my things, even unrhymed ones are meant to be spoken. I chant them aloud before I write down a word" (Adam and Duncan, 162). The inner rhymes and sounds of the ballad form were in her ear as she composed—and by giving many performative readings around the Bay area during the fifties, she provided opportunities for ballad sounds and narrative structures to enter the consciousness of other poets as well.[2]

To use a term coined by evolutionary biologist Richard Dawkins, the ballad tradition is a "meme." It is a "unit of cultural transmission" that is carried from one poem to another, much like a virus traveling from body to body (Dery 49). Writers associated with the San Francisco Renaissance were exposed to the ballad meme, incorporating certain ballad measures, traditional tunes, and narrative motifs into their own work. In his collection *After Lorca,* for instance, Spicer called nine of his poems "ballads." Similarly, Duncan integrated the form into many of his poems, including "Often I am permitted to return to a meadow," which he composed in 1956.[3] During this time, Adam and Duncan corresponded, and he sent her drafts of many different ballads that he was composing. Out of this correspondence, Duncan assembled a manuscript of ballads titled *Homage to Coleridge.* In the introduction to the manuscript, he writes, "these imitations of Romantic forms have roots. Roots first in first hearing poetry: which was story telling, weaving of fairy scenes. This recalled by Helen Adam, extraordinary Nurse of Enchantment, who read her ballads of evil passions and old lore" (undated, n.p.). Other less-discussed writers including James Broughton and Madeline Gleason wrote and published numerous poems that they also considered to be inspired by ballads.

Adam's ballads bring the intratextuality of the ballad tradition up to date—she tells the same story repeatedly, but uses different dialects, diction, and formal strategies to do so. The theme that Adam repeats throughout her work is the exhilarating monstrosity of desire; desire becomes a monster when it is inhibited or threatened in any way. Love in Adam's ballads is possession; once possessed by love, the object of desire is overcome. For example, her ballad "I Love My Love," which is included in *The New American Poetry,* tells the story of a wife who loves her husband so passionately that her hair weaves around him, enslaving him to "Love's hot smothering hold" (1974, 20). Desperate to be rid of her, he strangles her with a strand of her own hair and buries her body. But her golden tresses emerge from beneath the ground and stalk him, repeating over and over their sweet-sounding declarations of love. The harder the husband tries to free himself from the hair, the harder he is pursued, until finally the hair surrounds his entire world, taking over the grass, the rooms of his house, and the bed on which he sleeps, suffocating him and then devouring him to the bone. Although the ballad can be read as an exaggerated portrayal of feminine desire contrasting with masculine rationality, the ballad also reflects and resists the conservative gender politics of the 1950s. In other words, the woman is constrained and needs to—and finally does—achieve freedom: The hair is characterized as feeling gleeful about its new home, and, although a dark metaphor, the grave represents a room that is all its own. The woman's desire is transformed into an entirely new creature, one that cannot be contained or identified with traditional notions of female seduction and beauty.

As in many of Adam's ballads, "I Love My Love" depicts an oppressive system that is replaced by one that is less secure but ultimately liberating. This ballad's surreal spiraling into the insanity of a world dominated by hair is one way that Adam has resurrected the ballad form for a new era: the irrational mid-twentieth century. During this time, American culture fervently embraced an homogenized status quo, which did not allow much room for imaginative freedom. Alicia Ostriker reads "I Love My Love" (as well as many other angry poems written by women) as a "revenge fantasy. . . a striking example of the volcanic return of the repressed" (1987, 127). This "volcanic return" indicates the emergence of a woman who is aware of her oppressed state, but is simultaneously powerless to change it. The imagination becomes its own agent, freeing the female poet to construct scenarios of vengeance. This is what Anderson calls the "mind 'run amuck'" that Adam manifests by complicating the ballad form to match the madness of her postwar times.

Like common speech, ballads manifested the importance of shedding class, upbringing, and social values in order to join in the human struggle to fight oppression. As in the case of Adam, ballads and folk songs enabled popular artists like Bob Dylan and Joan Baez to critique the social order. In commenting on Baez's resurrection of old ballads such as "John Riley," "House Carpenter," and "Railroad Boy" at the beginning of her career, Kenneth Rexroth described the love that is represented in the ballads as "radically subversive" because it cannot be assimilated by society (54).[4] Such a love is dangerous because its lawlessness represents the possibility of heightened social consciousness through imaginative freedom. Soon after Adam began publishing, the old ballads that were at the center of her poetics were being sung by Baez and Dylan before large crowds, influencing a generation of countercultural activists.

Adam did not go to San Francisco intending to assert her particular poetic focus. But, in 1954 she chanced to take Duncan's workshop at San Francisco State University's Poetry Center and found herself in the company of young poets such as Michael McClure. At this time, Adam was fifty-four years old and had spent the majority of her life reading Victorian and romantic literature and writing poems that aspired to imitate their motifs. At the workshop, she recited Blake and brought in her rhymed poems to share with the group. Duncan immediately saw something in her work for which he himself was searching—the link with the forgotten romantics. Later, in 1956, when Ginsberg filled in as workshop leader, Adam discovered a new way to incorporate new forms and subjects into her work. Ginsberg's reading of "Howl," along with his presence in the workshop, inspired her to write a free-verse poem, something that she had long been hesitant to attempt. Shocked at the protesters who walked out of the now-legendary Six Gallery reading, Adam was irate when one of them, who happened to be in the workshop, attacked Ginsberg for writing "garbage." In a letter to Duncan, Adam described the woman as a "suburban protester" and wrote that "something in the dense dumbness of this remark, because, of course she meant it as an insult, brought home to me how important it was for poets to accept garbage and never to feel superior to it" (Adam and Duncan, 162). The poem, called "After Listening to Allen Ginsberg" (1956), serves as both a document of the evening and a statement of Adam's own developing poetics:

> Let words be naked,
> As Yeats said, walking
> The streets unashamed.
> Let the boast and chatter
> Of shop and office,
> Somehow disclose,
> Through some poet throwing
> Forked lightning
> The essential secret
> All language hides.
> 　(Adam and Duncan, 164–165)

In this poem, Adam articulates her belief that there are essential truths and secrets that are only accessible to visionary artists. What she heard in Ginsberg the night he read "Howl" was "forked lightning," an ecstatic and ingenious manifestation of "the essential secret all language hides." However, in spite of her belief in the entitlement of visionary poets, Adam was clear that this higher state of awareness came only after the poet muddled in the filth of the world:

> Let that prophet of beauty
> Live with ugliness.
> The wise may see
> From the city dump
> The world of Blake,
> The blazing sunflower.
> 　(Adam and Duncan, 164)

In locating "the city dump" as the source of Ginsberg's visionary genius, Adam exposes a critical element of modern art: its struggle to find form in what Ekbert Faas calls "the demons which loom so frighteningly in our contemporary consciousness" (252). These demons came to modern consciousness from the horrors of World War II and the alienating effects of the cultural and social climate of the conformist 1950s. To Adam, the truly visionary artist has joined company with these demons of modern consciousness and is not afraid to be found "grubbing in garbage / Among the outcast, enraged, scab-tongued, / Who howl in the dark their wings broken" (Adam and Duncan, 165).

Adam never published "After Listening to Allen Ginsberg" in any of her books. She would have dismissed it entirely except that one of the workshop participants sent it to Duncan. When he wrote her with suggestions for revision, she replied saying that the poem is "more a comment than a serious attempt at a poem" (Adam and Duncan, 162). While it is not at all characteristic of any of her other poems, it shows how Ginsberg's reading was an epiphany for Adam. This poem is both an homage and a bold declaration of the poetics she too would attempt to embrace in her ballads.

Inspired by Ginsberg, Adam went on to write a series of what she called "blues ballads." These are a very loose adaptation of the blues, not conforming to the twelve measures, the repetition of lines, and the terminal rhymes characteristic of the form. In fact, Adam's blues ballads do not even convey the mood of the blues: if they were not called blues, they would little seem to resemble this musical form. However, they are different from most of her other ballads in that she uses them to depict socially relevant issues and concerns. These ballads are about the atomic bomb, Haight-Ashbury junkies, and real estate want-ads. "They are still English ballads in disguise," she wrote in a letter to Duncan (Adam and Duncan, 162), but they incorporate call-and-response choruses, Beat prosody, social satire, and folk songs. Although the blues ballads repeat the rhyme and meter familiar to most of her work, this blending of diverse forms enabled her to begin experimenting with social themes relevant to the times. Like Kerouac taking inventory of everyday details and incorporating them into the mythical setting and bebop rhythms of *Mexico City Blues,* Adam's blues ballads used a combination of musical and literary forms to comment on the violence of social reality.

In "Evil Spirit Blues" (ca 1956), Adam creates two female misfits named Silk and Luck, raucous predators who wreak havoc on the social order. To personify the murder and mayhem of urban myth, like the evil fairies in so many Scottish ballads, Silk and Luck possess a magic touch which enables them to exert complete control over their victims. Their sexual charms cause men to become obsessed with desire, driving them to leave their families, spend their savings on booze, and pine their lives away. The town's preacher does what he can to purge the community of the "Devil's snare." But no one can cross Silk and Luck because there's nothing the salacious twins like more than murder:

> Every good man for miles about
> Felt his guts turn inside out.
> Evil Spirit's spoilin' for fun
> Pantin' to see some murder done.

> "Touch them gals there'll be murder done."
> Knives hunt late in the thunder dark
> One loud cry and a man's left stark.
> Preacher's stark on the river sod.
> Gone like thunder to meet his God.
>   (Helen Adam Collection, Box 24C, Folder 102)

There have been numerous female villains in the murder-ballad tradition, from Pretty Polly who pushes a thief into the ocean before he can kill her, to the possessive maid who murders her "little Scotch-ee" with a pen knife when he threatens to see another woman. But Silk and Luck differ from their predecessors, who are punished for their crimes: Silk and Luck are never caught.[5] Although extreme, they are only two of several femmes fatales in Adam's ballads. These "lethal women," as she once referred to them, are empowered and indestructible. They get their vitality from all the repressed desire that has accrued in acceptable society. In her study of representations of monstrous women in Victorian literature, Nina Auerbach concludes that characters such as Ayesha from Ryder Haggard's *She* and Lady Arabella from Bram Stoker's *Lair of the White Worm* embody a shift in women's roles as they move out of nineteenth-century domesticity (43). Adam, writing in the 1950s when the social roles many women were expected to play resembled being fettered to a Victorian home and family, created monsters who also reflected women inventing themselves outside of acceptable social mores.

Although she does not call them blues ballads, Adam wrote other poems that would fit in this category. Two of the most satirical are "Cheerless Junkie's Song" and "Jericho Bar" (ca. 1970s). In "Jericho Bar," a young boy walks into a bar and is transfixed by a junkie playing an electric guitar. Like the young girls in Christina Rossetti's "Goblin Market" who get hooked on the goblins' forbidden fruits and eventually die from their craving, youngsters who stumble upon the Jericho Bar will never go back home:

> I drank milk, Mother, in my sheltered home.
> I drank milk, and I ate honey-comb.
> Now I'm eating goof balls, drinking rum and gall,
> Wine, and gin, and vodka, and wood alcohol.
> Give me ten Tequilas, a jigger full of stout,
> And a little lap of Pepsi before I freak out
> In the reeling Jericho Bar.
>   (1977, 99–100)

The Jericho junkie believes that drugs will satisfy his desire. Drugs transport this sheltered child to another plane of reality decidedly outside middle-class social boundaries, like the world the monstrous women Silk and Luck inhabit. The Jericho Bar symbolizes the dark side of the imaginative freedom which Adam depicts in "I Love My Love." Drugs may provide a temporary breakdown of boundaries, but ultimately they destroy the imagination. Those who find freedom through drugs are simply entering another world that mirrors the oppressions of the one they are fleeing.

The junkie's pride in a carefree life dramatically contrasts with the self-destruction produced by the life depicted in "Cheerless Junkie's Song":

> Goodbye transcendent Thompkins Square
> I haven't long to stay.
> A double jolt of heroin and I'll be on my way.
> Let rats and roaches bury me.
> They'll bury me in state,
> As they march from Verrazano Bridge
> Down to the Golden Gate,
> Clear across the continent.
> Yonder let me lie,
> In the gutters of Haight Ashbury,
> To freak the passers by,

Till all the tourists gape, and say,
"Brother! He died high!"
Let rat tails write my epitaph.
"Brother! He died high!"
   (1977, 103)

This junkie wants all those gawking tourists who walk through the Haight district as if it were Disneyland to recognize that he is a radical nonconformist. He puts himself on display, thinking that the suburbanites will envy his freewheeling lifestyle. Presenting the junkie's pathetic monologue as sincere, the poem simultaneously critiques him. The singsong tune for "Cheerless Junkie's Song" emphasizes this irony, making the poem sound partly like the refrain to an old ballad and partly like a Broadway show tune. Adam makes an appearance in Ron Mann's 1982 documentary film *Poetry in Motion,* singing this ballad about heroin and rat tails so energetically that she tosses off her turban and lets her gray hair shake free.

While her ballads reflect social tensions between conformity and nonconformity, and Adam later embraced marginal aesthetic forms as powerful means for expressing disgust at the status quo, her ballads also reflect a conflict between colonial and postcolonial attitudes. Adam and her sister Pat were tutored from an early age and received an education that considered English literature, art, and customs to be more civilized than those of their native Scotland. Strong ethical obligations were instilled by her father, a strict and intolerant Presbyterian minister whose preference for golf over preaching strained his relationships with the poor rural farmers of his congregation. Adam despised her father and felt that the stray golf ball that hit him in the head and caused a fatal concussion was karmic retribution for his elitist pretensions. But the lasting effects on his two daughters of his Anglocentric, highbrow attitude took many years to shake. Born in 1909, Adam began writing poetry when she was two years old (her mother took dictation); when she was twelve, the British publisher Hodder and Stoughton published a collection of her poems entitled *The Elfin Pedlar and Tales Told by Pixy Pool.* This book gave Scotland a prodigy poetess whose Anglicized, genteel verses depicting fairies, mountain brooks, and butterflies in spring were officially touted in an effort to boost Scotland's morale in the midst of the political restructuring and post–World War I economic depression. Adam finally renounced this early verse as "dreadful doggerel" and moved to London in 1932 to pursue a career in journalism. In 1939 she, along with her sister and mother, attended a cousin's wedding in Hartford, Connecticut, and never moved back to Britain. After living in New York City for ten years, the three Scottish ladies moved to the Bay area in 1949.

Although Adam began composing ballads while living in New York City in the 1940s, the workshops she took at The Poetry Center led her to experiment with different stylistic techniques. Unlike much of the "doggerel" she had previously composed, the blues ballads incorporate several regional accents —"Evil Spirit Blues" is written with a rural twang ("Flashin' fire and spoilin' for fun, / Spoilin' to see more murder done") and "Jericho Bar" is written in urban slang ("a little Pepsi before I freak out"). Coming from Scotland, where regional dialects clashed with the standardization of English in schools and churches, Adam had developed a good ear for picking up on a variety of accents and speech patterns, and was comfortable incorporating American dialects (from African American vernaculars to hipster diction) into her work. As she began to be more open to these influences, she also began to investigate the Lallan dialect of her native Scotland. Although she had grown up in a literary household and been in college when Hugh MacDiarmid was asserting the political necessity of claiming Scottish literature and dialect as distinctly separate from English, all the poems Adam had written while she lived in the United Kingdom followed English rules and diction.[6] It was not until she got to America that she began investigating her own native Scots language and incorporating Lallan dialect into her ballads. Similarly, Ginsberg encouraged his students at Naropa Institute, on a day when they were studying Helen Adam and the ballad tradition, to remain true to their own regional American dialects (Ginsberg 1976b).

Adam's rediscovery of Scottish vernacular is nowhere better manifested than in the ballad "The Queen o' Crow Castle." Written in 1957, the year in which Kerouac published *On the Road,* the ballad was one of the first in a series of White Rabbit chapbooks illustrated by the artist Jess. It tells the story of a young man named Castallen, who falls in love with a queen possessed by the devil. A female Bluebeard, this queen feeds all of her husbands to the devil residing in her chamber. But the smitten Castallen is determined to free her, and with help of the castle's crows he sets out to slay the evil captor. These crows, however, have a mind of their own, and gradually take over the ballad structure with their wild caws, much like the crows that replace Ginsberg's voice in part five of "Kaddish"—"Lord Lord Lord caw caw caw Lord Lord Lord caw caw caw Lord" (1984, 227). Adam's crows echo the story as a sinister chorus eager to move the plot along:

"Weesht, Wheesht, the dead went before.
Seven dead husbands ha' opened her door.
Kra!
Wheesht, wull ye wheesht. We'll drink o' his gore.
Sharpen your beaks,
Kra! Kra!
If he opens her door."
    (1977, 43)

Castallan and the crows manage to send the Devil back to Egypt and free the Queen from his possession of her. But as the naked lovers frolic on the moors, a sinister subplot becomes clear: the whole liberation was part of the crows' elaborate plot to seize the castle for themselves. In a dramatic ending, the crows attack and eat the fair Castallan, and announce their domain:

Smoke reeking black on the blue morning sky.
Over his ashes her gorged corbies fly.
Mair than the Deil must a man overthrow
Wha weds wi' the Queen o' the Castle o' Crow.

"Greaf" cry her corbies. They reel as they go.
Great is the Queen o' the Castle o' Crow.

Great is the Queen. Kra!! Ha! o' the Castle o' Crow."
    (1977, 44)

The caw of the crows that overtakes the ballad language replaces the love story of the knight and the queen with a screechy cry that points to an entirely different reality. No longer the Queen of Crow Castle, the queen is now enslaved in the Castle of Crows.

As in "The Queen o' Crow Castle," many of Adam's ballads blend Anglo-Saxon literary conventions with oral folk traditions. Although these ballads adhere to certain structural strategies common to the ballad form, Adam's blending of literary styles complicates rhythmic and narrative expectations. Adam's theatrical use of the chorus of crows (as with the echo that runs through "Evil Spirit Blues") reflects the question-and-answer dialogue found in popular ballads such as "Lord Randall." But it also reflects the call-and-response popularly associated with Southern Baptist church services and the Greek choruses which comment on the drama as the plot unfolds. As Anderson notes, Adam's "occasional deviations from form seem all the more unsettling because they appear out of character with her poetic voice. But, in truth, Adam often torques the form in her ballads to create an eerie effect of a sense of mind 'run amuck'" (20). Utilizing a variety of compositional strategies from literary and cultural history is one Adam's most significant contributions. Adam modified the ballad form in a way crucial to its perpetuity, for undermining the rules of composition is a part of the history of the ballad tradition.

Adam's subversion of traditional forms, however, also revises traditional content with regard to gender. In most ballads, women, no matter how strong, are rarely positioned outside of domestic space. Even if they are traveling, they are still traversing a passage between one form of bondage to another. In Adam's ballads such as "I Love My Love" and "Evil Spirit Blues," women are often the active protagonists. They are the ones who seek out their rights of passage, even if they are aided by supernatural powers. Although Adam did write other ballads which portray women as enslaved—such as "The Queen o' Crow Castle" and "Kiltory" (ca 1958)—these exaggerate the woman's captivity so dramatically that the male character is portrayed as a freaky masochist. In "Kiltory," the eponymous protagonist is an innocent huntsman who while riding happens to pass a bored and lonely lady, whose husband, Lord Rand, is away. The lady falls madly in love with Kiltory, and although they never actually meet, she constructs sexual fantasies about him: "if I were a falcon tae come at your call / From the ramparts o' heaven tae your fist I would fall" (1974, 56). Lord Rand returns to finds his wife proclaiming her desire for Kiltory. Mad and jealous,

Lord Rand hunts down the huntsman and kills him, placing his slain body on Lady Rand's bed:

Tae the dead man he flung her, He nailed up the door.
"Kiltory, I wish ye the joy o' your whore!"
Awa in the woodlands the wild throstles cried,
And the waters ran red on the brant mountain-side.
   (1974, 57)

The image of Lord Rand flinging his wife at the corpse of her (imagined) lover exemplifies the woman's oppression by her domineering husband. Unlike the wife in "I Love My Love," Lord Rand's wife is not able to imagine herself into a different world where she is the mistress of her own fate.

As a woman artist working within a community dominated by gay men, Adam found herself in a world in which female identity was often conflicted. At one level, the women who were part of this literary community were limited by the social roles they were expected to play. On another level, these roles enabled the women to exist as artists, giving them the freedom to live their own lives without having to conform to the social expectations of the mainstream culture. This contradiction is not unlike that of the women of the surrealist movement, for example, who felt that being reduced to "femmes-enfants" or muses was preferable to what they could become if they conformed to the mores of bourgeois French society (Chadwick 67). As in the surrealist movement, women in the San Francisco Renaissance were looked upon as muses, priestesses, or, as Robert Duncan called Helen Adam, "nurses of enchantment." Duncan admitted that he saw them as "strange women; they are the priestess figures which we all allow" (Ellingham 1982a, 25). But although these roles are reminiscent of some secret society where priestesses and wizards conjure up ancient rituals, it is important to acknowledge the positive ways in which they may have functioned to liberate women from the less creative social expectations of the 1950s. Duncan's romanticizing of Adam as a priestess who represented the ancient ballad tradition gave her an identity which she internalized and incorporated as a part of her persona. She began reading tarot cards and developed a unique spiritual philosophy based on a mixture of Buddhist karma, Christian judgment, and Egyptian magic. She began singing her ballads, which before her arrival in San Francisco she had lacked the confidence to attempt. Adam internalized her role as the "priestess," reshaped her image, and directed it back at the male-centered community, which was all too willing to receive her in this form.

Sometimes, however, this acceptance was withdrawn. For example, at a book party and reading in 1957 celebrating Denise Levertov's and Helen Adam's White Rabbit chapbooks, Spicer read his aggressively misogynist poem "For Joe" :

> People who don't like the smell of faggot vomit
> Will never understand why men don't like women
> Won't see why those never to be forgotten thighs
> of Helen (say) will move us into screams of laughter.
>   (Spicer 1975, 62)

Adam, who worked as a bike messenger, had a dream that night that she delivered an envelope to one office after another, saying "I'm sorry, but I'm a woman" (Killian and Ellingham 124). Levertov, on the other hand, countered with her now famous poem "Hypocrite Woman," which reflects "how much of women's self-deprecation came from macho male attitudes" (Killian and Ellingham 126). Unlike Levertov, who confronted Spicer, Adam seemed, according to her dream, to be taking the passive role by refusing to address the male community, allowing herself to be defined by its expectations and preconceptions.

However, this would not be a fair assessment of Adam's complex role in this community. By allowing herself to be essentialized, Adam inadvertently became the means of her own transformation, culminating in the development of her alter ego, the Worm Queen. This figure first appeared in Adam's opera *San Francisco's Burning,* where she resides in the back room of a sleazy waterfront saloon, waiting for lost sailors to stumble in for a drink. She slithers out from her lair, a slimy nirvana that represents total possession and the fulfillment of desire, and challenges the sailors to games of Patience. This is her refrain:

> My crown is crusted with carrion flies
> And my head is bald and wet

But the loveliest women of living flesh
With me you will quite forget.

I am the Fair forgetfulness
Whom men seek only in pain
Who sleeps in the bed of the Worm Queen
He will never weep again.

Follow me, Sailor.
   ([1964] 1985, 18)

Once she has possessed him, the Worm Queen separates the sailor's body
from his spirit, keeping the flesh and leaving the lonely spirit to wander
aimlessly around the docks. The man's body, once enveloped by the Worm
Queen, has no desire to return to the real world. The dead body speaks in
a "burbling murmur" to his spirit: "Young maids may be faithful while the
flesh it is fair. / But the Worm Queen will love till the bones are stripped
bare" (100). The body's realization is macabre, but read in the context of
Spicer's "For Joe" ("Send us no letters. The female genital organ is hideous.
We / Do not want to be moved" 1975, 7–9.62), the Worm Queen's dark
slippery lair, the gynocentric void that swallows male flesh, connotes
female genitalia. Adam's manifestation of revenge is an exquisite monster.
Although she may have been perceived by her male contemporaries as little
more than an enchanting priestess, Adam sought vaginal power and transformed it into her own intellectual and artistic persona.

   The Worm Queen's role is not limited to devouring men. She also acts as
the primary overseer of the wild, orgiastic docks where the seediest characters gather for their nightly drink. As Davidson suggests, the opera, set in
the early twentieth century, is both a mythical rendition of the actual San
Francisco community of artists and writers, and a depiction of the riotous
gold-rush and mercantile history of the Barbary Coast (184). Although
there are no direct references, *San Francisco's Burning* presents a caricature
of the San Francisco poetry community, from the bad-boy Ginger Jack
who always talks out of turn and continually causes trouble (Spicer) to Neil
Narcissus who obsessively analyses himself using mirrors and Freudian psychology (Duncan). The Worm Queen also brings together many different

references from Adam's love of gothic literature and horror films: Madame Blavatsky, Edith Sitwell, Orson Welles's *Macbeth,* Victorian fairy queens, and she-monsters. Moreover, the Worm Queen is an exaggerated pastiche of all the otherworldly characters of Adam's ballads, ranging from Silk and Luck to the omnipotent hair. She is inhuman like the crows and asserts her strange alien presence in what is otherwise a Western-style opera. From the act of asserting what Davidson calls "gynocentric authority" (179), the Worm Queen is the creator of her own world.

At the end of the play, the earthquake of 1909 hits San Francisco and destroys both the seedy waterfront and the wealthy mansions. This is reminiscent of the ending of Bram Stoker's *Lair of the White Worm,* in which men construct an elaborate system of dynamite that forces the caves of the snake Arabella to collapse, suffocating the monster. But social order is not restored to San Francisco just because the earthquake buries the diverse parts of the city. In a chilling ending, the Worm Queen emerges from the rubble, twice as big as she was during the play. She is cast in a red light, and one black-laced arm carries a gigantic ace of spades. The chorus chants "San Francisco is burning, burning. / Crackling to the sky and burning" as the Worm Queen brandishes the tarot death card across the stage. Presumably, San Francisco is now hers. Matriarchal authority is asserted, but it is ultimately revealed to be something different from this singularly dark power. The Worm Queen's alter ego from the wealthy side of town emerges to have the last word. In satiric form, the society matriarch Miss Mackie Rhodus pushes the Worm Queen aside saying:

> Out of my way, Trollop!
> Troublesome fire and earthquake,
> But we know that whatever comes,
> We'll still have Grace Cathedral,
> And crumpets and cream at Blum's.
>   ([1964] 1985, 163)

Miss Mackie Rhodus is a representation of Adam's sister, Pat, who wrote many of the opera's songs. She is the antithesis of the Worm Queen, but at the same time she completes her. The conclusion of the opera displays both the bond shared between the two Scottish sisters, and the way in which layers of magic and reality are used to build the poet's ideal city. Through this convergence, *San Francisco's Burning* makes a theatrical world out of the world of poetry. Apparently, however, few San Francisco Renaissance poets attended the performance. Spicer and Duncan, perhaps the two muses who inspired it, regarded the opera as theatrical fluff and an abasement of Adam's pure poetic gifts.[7] They didn't see that the play, although written in rhymed couplets, presents a complex melding of the poet's experiments in structure and content. Adam fuses all that she had absorbed from her male counterparts with her own experiences, knowledge, and personality. This assimilation of sources cannot be explained entirely or positioned by literary history's "enabling myths."

If the fluidity of contemporary poetry is emphasized over canons and movements, then it does not matter if the "enabling myths" of the San Francisco Renaissance or the Beat generation did not articulate Helen Adam's life and art. Adam found her company outside, inside, and around these movements, slipping between their myths of origin and creating art that reflects a wide range of traditional and social influences. By working within the ballad tradition, seemingly antithetical to postmodern form, Adam revealed that that very tradition is a prime example of how pastiche, revision, and meme work to create both poetry and community.

Notes

1. Now hailed as a major cultural influence, *The Anthology of American Folk Music* is divided into three volumes: *Ballads, Social Music,* and *Songs.* A compilation of recordings from the 1920s and 1930s, *Ballads* includes a mixture of both Scottish ballads from the Child collection brought to America by Scottish immigrants and North American ballads that had been passed down in the form of spirituals and folk songs. Smith's anthology provided the roots for an alternative cultural history of North America. As Kevin Killian writes, "In the early 1950s, when this *Anthology* was released, it had the same kind of impact on the music world as *The New American Poetry* did among poets a decade later. . . . funny to think of Spicer as being at the center of both anthologies, which served him so differently, and funny to think of the sixties as bearing the fruit of two such different efforts" (n.p.). In her revival of the ballad form within the context of *The New American Poetry,* Adam had a particular connection to both anthologies.

2. Anderson calls this "the ballad consciousness" and traces it through several poems of the time including Duncan's "My Mother would be a Falconress" and Spicer's "After Lorca" (24–37).

3. Other poems that Duncan did call ballads are "The Ballad of the Forfar

Witches' Sing," "A Country Wife's Song," "A Ballad of the Enamourd Mage," all from *Roots and Branches;* "A Man at the Crossroads," "The Green Lady," "The Master of Mandrake Park," "The Grue of Mandrake Park" (also called "The Return, a ballad"), and "Thomas the Rimer," all from *Homage to Coleridge.* For more information on the connection between Adam and Duncan, see the author's essay "An Extraordinary Enchantment: Helen Adam, Robert Duncan, and the San Francisco Renaissance."

4. Joan Baez began her career singing American, Spanish, English, and Scottish ballads and folk songs and *The Joan Baez Ballad Book* was released in 1972. Correspondence from 1964 indicates the possibility of Baez recording one of Adam's ballads but apparently this was never done. The old ballads Baez sings are what Greil Marcus calls the tales "of murder and suicide in which love is a disease and death the cure," which Harry Smith collected in the ballads volume of the *Anthology of American Folk Music* (105).

5. This ballad was rewritten and published as "Ginger Jack's Warning" in Adam's 1984 selection of poems, *Stone Cold Gothic.* When she revised it, she toned down the violence of the original, edited out the chorus, and introduced a character from her 1964 opera *San Francisco's Burning,* Ginger Jack, who saves the town.

6. Beginning in the early 1920s, Hugh MacDiarmid formed a movement called The Scottish Literary Renaissance. Its goals were to mobilize Scottish poets to begin experimenting with writing in their own dialect—called Lallan. This was a nationalist movement that sought to assert a distinctly Scottish poetry, removed from English verse culture.

7. Duncan wrote an attack of *San Francisco's Burning* called "What Happened: Prelude," in which he asserts that "she who had been the Poet now denies the inspiration of her tunes and next, influenced by certain poetasters and know-betters of the town, seeks to improve the play to suit the dictates of the Stage" (1962, n.p.). Duncan believed that Adam's involvement with the production of the play ruined her as a poet.

Diane di Prima: "Nothing Is Lost; It Shines In Our Eyes"

Anthony Libby

I

Two poems give us a snapshot of the mind of Diane di Prima as it was for a moment in 1973. "For Pigpen," composed in 1974, celebrates the now-mythic blues-master of the Grateful Dead, himself dead at twenty-eight that year, by recalling the early Acid Tests organized by Ken Kesey, at which the Dead were the musicians. Di Prima remembers the momentous quality of the event, the sense of the future looming "[a]t the edge of history"; she describes the synesthesia of the drug—"Sound was light"; and she experiences the distant archetypal past moving into time present: "Like tracing / ancient letters w/yr toe on the / floor of the ballroom" (1975, 31). Such strange visions are what we expect of di Prima. She is the rebel who was immersed in the three major American cultural revolutions of the century: modernism, through her association with Pound, the Beat movement of the fifties and early sixties, and then the explosion of LSD and protests of the sixties and seventies, when romanticism hit the streets. Three revolutions, with wildly different political polarities, each created the future in a different way; few writers or public figures lasted as long as di Prima in the difficult terrain of the counterculture without burning out.

But "For Pigpen" looks across the facing page of *Selected Poems* to a very different poem. "Backyard," a Ginsberg/Whitman-accented memory poem of Brooklyn written the same year, shows the child still in the poet, fighting her battle on the terms established in childhood, but remembering that difficult childhood with affection. She recalls the sexual child in a desexualized culture, a landscape of lawns "eternally parched beneath red gloomy sunsets." But the child feels the touch of something eternal, which gives her power to fight for her own vitality:

> where angels turned into honeysuckle & poured nectar into my
>   mouth
> where I french-kissed the roses in the rain
> where demons tossed me a knife to kill my father in the stark
>   simplicity of the sky
> (1975, 320)

Always there would be a tension between the Italian girl from a traditional family, struggling with traditional values and even against the sexual abuse suggested in later poems like "To My Father,"[1] and, on the other hand, the acid revolutionary creating (among the boys) a new voice of sexual power for women. Sex is the burden of the past, but sex is the way to the opening future.

Di Prima is fully aware of the ensuing tensions and contradictions, which often appeared most dramatically in the area of sexual politics. As she says about the problems of writing autobiography, "maybe you didn't look so good . . . God knows, maybe you weren't 'p c' about something" (1995). In fact, di Prima is not always "politically correct," which is hardly surprising given that the term has developed an increasingly negative connotation, suggesting obedience, often superficial, to contemporary progressive fashion. Even allowing for the radical changes in the definition of progressive values over the period of her life as a writer, di Prima was not one to fit general patterns. She went her own sometimes contradictory way.

Di Prima was one of the heroic precursors of second-wave feminism, and her poetry achieved its own unique vision. She is perhaps best known for *Revolutionary Letters* (1971), much of which is a mirror of the violent paranoia of the late sixties, and for *Memoirs of a Beatnik* (1969), which blurs countercultural biography with pornographic improvisation. These texts do provide a fascinating glimpse of the underlying contradictions that animate a writer riding the waves of a new consciousness while still deeply immersed in the struggles of the old. Living the revolutionary life, but aware of its limits, di Prima herself gives the clearest definition of her internal tension between old and new: "for every revolutionary must at last will his own destruction / rooted as he is in the past he sets out to destroy" (1975, 206). Considering the ways that tension produces contradictory or even destructive conclusions, one can see that di Prima's best poetry is not finally about conclusions. Rather it records what she calls "the process, the bloody process" (1975, 57) of a life lived on the edge, in times when the edge, especially the sexual edge of the future, was in many ways destructive to all but a few. The area of sexual politics reveals how rooted in the past the poet can be. Today di Prima is often considered a feminist, but she was always one to elude boundaries. When she strays from the progressive fold, she does so with a vengeance. Though she is often understood to be "deconstructing patriarchal definitions of gender" (Friedman, A., 204), di Prima represents herself as male defined both personally and aesthetically. Almost by definition, to live as a woman Beat poet in the fifties was to be defined by men; coolness and the cool mode of rebellion were at the time primarily masculine attributes. According to her life chronology at the end of *Pieces of a Song,* the various boundaries di Prima wandered were drawn by men, from Ezra Pound through Ginsberg and Kerouac, to Timothy Leary, finally to Chogyam Trungpa Rinpoche (1990, 198–199).

Di Prima seems to have gone further than most to enact the traditional notions of gender she also distrusted. The mother of five children herself, she is defiantly the poet of reproduction, opposed not only to abortion, but even to birth control. Even more disturbing is one presumably fictional passage from *Memoirs of a Beatnik* (successive editions of which now carry different LCN numbers identifying them as nonfiction and fiction) in which "Diane" is quietly raped by the patriarch of a dysfunctional family and says she ends up enjoying it.[2] Here di Prima seems to be guided more by the conventions of pornography than by convictions about gender. But as in the passage in "Revolutionary Letters" when she includes "rapists" along with women in her list of "political prisoners" (1975, 218)—presumably unfairly punished—her apparent sympathy for the perpetrators of the most unambiguous violence against women may come as a stumbling block to sympathetic readings of di Prima. For the di Prima of *Memoirs of a Beat-*

nik, however, nothing sexual is unambiguous; nothing sexual is wholly destructive, and even destruction is never wholly negative. In any case, *Memoirs of a Beatnik,* written in the exhilaration and rage of 1969, is intent on
the smashing of "civilized" taboos, all taboos, that obstruct the sacred
energies of women or men.

   This in fact is di Prima's strength. She values experience that breaks out
of the usual categories, as she values a conception of self that breaks out of
the usual groupings, groupings which form the basis of progressive politics
now. She wants to live on the margins, not in the group, and if she feels
solidarity with women, it is primarily solidarity with a sisterhood of outsiders. This is most conspicuous in another of di Prima's deviations from
more recent progressive notions of what is politically acceptable or desirable. As a political propagandist, she reveals the distance between sixties
radicalism and the contemporary left, often in a way that suggests the conceptual limitations of both periods. In the increasingly sensitive area of
identity politics, the politics of race, she has done so in a way that is both
controversial and on its own terms admirable. She was one of the few white
radicals to complain about the violations of friendship and solidarity, the
arbitrary essentialism, involved in the black separatist movement. Of
course she was in an unusually good position to complain without being
accused of being racist, since she had had a daughter with Amiri Baraka,
when he was LeRoi Jones, and had been very close to Audre Lorde since
they attended Hunter High School together. Her tone about Baraka tends
to the wistful, but when she writes about Lorde she lets her anger show.
"Narrow Path to the Back Country" "for Audre Lorde," written in 1974, is
a protest against racial identity politics and the artificiality of defining self
in terms of group origins rather than individual experience:

> You are flying to Dahomey, going back
> to some dream, or never-never land
> more forbidding & perfect
> than Oz. . . .
>
> . . . .
>
> And I will not bow out, cannot see
> your war as different. . . .
>   (1975, 311)

This is an outcry in favor of friendship, for fidelity to one's friends over agreement with what is politically fashionable. Always suspicious of group mentality, the poet rejects the narrow, tribal self-righteousness of identity politics which is, like all forms of nationalism, implicitly the politics of hate, or at least solidarity against the Other. But di Prima was also arguing for the solidarity of women as being stronger than race and in this she may have been more radical than many radicals dare to be now.

In any case, any accounting of di Prima's political excesses in the fifties and sixties risks oversimplification and must confront the problem of accounting for the difference between the present more cautious time and a period which brought out the excesses in almost everyone. Di Prima has received comparatively little critical attention for several reasons: maybe gender is still an obstacle, as well as the admitted unevenness of her work as whole, to say nothing of her identification with the still not academically respectable Beats. But perhaps there is also the perception that she is a difficult case. The writer who deliberately positions herself as an outsider, preferring marginalization, is still in some sense positioned against the academy, which has moved away from the romance of the rebel. Examining her progress as poet and revolutionary, the outsider voice she has consistently chosen, her life lived on the margins, her desire to "stand clear," creates a progressive vision which remains powerful even in its sometimes shocking divergence from the later progressive visions which di Prima herself makes possible.

II

But a closer look at her own sexual politics—in her poetry as well as the calculated shocks of *Memoirs of a Beatnik*—will indicate that critical ambivalence towards her work is not solely a function of changes in liberal values. The heart of the di Prima dilemma—her refusal to fit neatly into the progressive assumptions she herself played a major part in creating—is also the source of her strength as a poet in her most productive years. This is evident especially in her treatments of sex and anger, frequently blended. As she said in a 1989 interview, "I can see that I was triggered a lot by a subterranean stream of anger that I think, considering everything, I used pretty well. I could have used it in a much more destructive way than to write books and have babies." (Moffeit 1989, 2). To have babies out of anger: perhaps an odd displacement of the function of love. But in her early poetry, especially in *This Kind of Bird Flies Backwards* (1958), di Prima freely blends love and anger, in habitual imagery as well as general themes: "Your tongue / explodes / like jailbreaks / in my head" (1975, 11) and "the fine edge of my love / cuts thru your ribs / like a buzz saw" (18).[3] The having of babies itself became rebellious, an act against the oppressive father, when the babies were biracial or, in the quaint term of the repressive fifties, when respectable single motherhood was not yet an option; single motherhood was "illegitimate." As di Prima said later, "I decided I wanted a baby, but I didn't want any man around" (Moffeit 1989, 1).

But rebellion through motherhood can also be a capitulation to the very forces that provoke her anger. Her opposition to all forms of birth control is most notable in the "Fuck the Pill" section of *Memoirs of a Beatnik*. There she advocates more or less constant childbirth, which she suggests "takes less time, trouble, and thought than any of the so-called 'modern methods of birth control.' And to support the baby? Get welfare, quit working, stay home, stay stoned, and fuck" (1969, 106). She may well be amusing herself here: the will to be provocative partly explains such statements. But her poetry of reproduction also dramatizes an extreme passion to bear children. In what is probably unique in the nature of its angry complaint against a man, her poem "I Get My Period, September 1964" actually reproaches a lover for not making her pregnant: "How can I forgive you this blood?" (1975, 132). Indeed, blood is the issue, a sort of blood mysticism, reminiscent of D. H. Lawrence, embedded in the mysteries of the flesh, the sacred processes of the body. As with Lawrence and other modernists, the term for this is not *conservatism* (though di Prima wrote in the gender-conservative fifties and early sixties)—the term is *primitivism*.

The great sin against this primitive mysticism of the body is abortion. Di Prima omitted "Brass Furnace Going Out: Song, after an Abortion" (1960) from her *Pieces of a Song,* the 1990 revision and updating of her 1975 *Selected Poems,* and it has been a problem for some critics, who tend to evade its literal subject. For example, Amy L. Friedman, who considers di Prima "overtly feminist," describes the poem as di Prima's "Howl": "In Di Prima's [poem] the lost generation is the aborted child, the sense of fury the product of the emotional aftermath. . . . Both poems are enunciations of the torment of bearing witness" (206). Possibly, but much more obvious is the torment of not bearing a child. This is one of her strongest poems, and one of the strongest of all abortion-regret poems because it is genuinely pro-life, not legalistic or moralistic.[4] There seems to be very little that di Prima would make illegal, certainly not abortion, but her account of its painful emotional consequences is powerful. In the jungle terrain that often embodies di Prima's primitivism, "Brass Furnace" imagines the aborted child drowning, ironically dissolving in water like the amniotic fluid that sustained its life: "your face dissolving in water, like wet clay / washed away, like a rotten water lily / rats on the riverbank barking at the sight" (1975, 93). The poem's surreal imagery here has a perverse beauty, as it suggests the vision of dreams, or late-night remorse. As the (male) child's death and dissolution keep repeating, mirroring the obsessive repetitions of guilt, the dream landscape grows denatured to echo the dreamer's anguish. The poem began with two dogs playing the trumpet ("there is something disturbed / about the melody," [92]) and now it is the rats who are "barking," giving surreal voice to their unreal dismay at the vision of the dissolving child. As his death continues to reverberate, the mother imagines his life; the aborted child grows beautiful in her mind. She asks him to "forgive, forgive / that the cosmic waters do not turn from me / that I should not die of thirst" (95). But his fetal death has warped the world.

Di Prima's poem "Moon Mattress" is even more blunt about the degree of evil involved in abortion, though its images make it sound like a fairy tale for the dead child. As Anne Sexton would demonstrate a decade later, all fairy tales verge on nightmare, their transformations often suggesting or enacting the ultimate human transformation, death. With its strange dislocated imagery, "Moon Mattress, for the child we didn't have," also composed in 1960, again creates a surreal landscape of guilt:

in the act of murder we are interrupted,
what kind of feast is this?
where are the maidens

a woman has slipped off her shoes, they dance by themselves
disconsolately, at the end of the path they dance
    (1975, 105)

The image of the dancing shoes tempts one to read the poem against its logical sense; the flowing rhythms of di Prima's lines are interrupted by the flat "disconsolately," but before and after that word the rhythms still dance. As George Butterick has noted in his discussion of di Prima's "incipient feminist consciousness," "[i]ndeed, without the qualification 'disconsolately,' there would be no way of knowing whether this is a joyful image or one of desperation" (155). Di Prima is both the free-living beatnik, defiantly celebrating a life of sexual freedom beyond any rules, and, contrary to the voice in "Brass Furnace," the fierce judge of that life, the righteous old-country moralist. The crevasse between the two selves fills with anger.

III

This combination of opposites is not unusual in di Prima's poetry. In fact, it could be said to be the defining characteristic of her work, both in aesthetics and in more general habits of mind, from her earliest publications onward. In the poems' treatments of anger, rage is cut with comedy, just as their treatments of love blend romance with squalor, appropriately voicing these mixtures in language and imagery that themselves mix radically different tones, figures, or levels of style. The anger comes early, in the prose poem sequence that comprises the "Nightmares" section of *Dinners and Nightmares* (1961). The poems can be harrowing, because di Prima does not shy away from the unpleasant results of anger. Some of these unnervingly realistic bad dreams read like the types of sixties horror movies shot with hand-held cameras: no fancy European settings, all human weakness. In "Nightmare #4," the speaker, living in squalor and hungry, hits her cat with a frying pan when the cat steals her "raw chopped questionable meat probably edible hope so . . . Motherfucking bitch I said and flattened her with the frying pan squashed her bones practically dead and left her for tears" (1975, 4). The cat does die, but not before (as the trails of blood indicate when the speaker can bring herself back to the killing room) catching a mouse for the speaker in trade for the meat. This domestic gothic scene is made grimmer by the surrounding squalor: "on bug-jumping bed I cried screamed and then cried" (4). But the horror movie is immediately preceded by poems reminiscent of cartoons in which animals behave comically like humans. "I saw a line of sleek roaches was marching the worm away and singing *Onward Christian Roaches*" ("Nightmare 2," 1975, 3), and an "uncool" moth "doing herself in" in a candle flame is followed by another who "raced, and screaming 'Dido' followed her" ("Nightmare 3," 1975, 3). "Nightmare 6," which follows the cat revenge killing, reads in its entirety, "Get your cut throat off my knife" (1975, 5), its ironic humor conveying grimmer implications about human relationships.

The most striking combinations of opposites in di Prima's early work appear in poems about what would become for a time the work's primary subject: the complexities of love. These opposites are both conceptual and stylistic; elements of both exist in one of the poems' dominant tendencies: the mixture of high styles (or tones) and low. The high is higher than one might expect from a writer too often stereotyped as beatnik; di Prima frequently experimented with rhyme and iambic tetrameter. And the low is not just a question of her use of hip slang, such as "cool," "dig," "pad," and "chick," which does not wear well. The use of such self-consciously in-group jargon troubles the surface of the poems; it now seems more reminiscent of the Rat Pack than the Dharma Bums. But the less specifically marked colloquial language is an effective counterbalance to the ancient high style of romantic utterance. In "More or Less Love Poems," the first version of which appeared in *Dinners and Nightmares,* "he pins with amorous wing the struggling / moon" (1975, 19) coexists with "shit man / you think its easy / opening doors" (17) and "for you / i'd kill my favorite roach" (15). The juxtaposition is comic—di Prima's sense of humor is constantly lurking beneath the grubby surfaces—but it also grounds the romantic fights in a convincing ordinariness.

Another sort of di Prima reversal involves the substitution of the literal for the figurative, or vice versa. A simple extension of this play with logical opposites produces di Prima's style of surrealism, which is often simply figurative language presented as if it were literal, as in "The Window" (composed in 1956), which uses personification to make the abstract concrete: "I think / tomorrow / turned you with his toe" (1975, 28). This passage has the restraint of the most austere surrealism, but even when di Prima's surrealism blooms into more extravagance, there is usually some sort of logical comparison at its root, like a metaphor with the tenor suppressed. In "Monochrome" (1957 or 1958), the almost impenetrable line "at the smell of a nail grey hammers fall to pieces" (1975, 35) suggests the mysteries of Neruda, but the sea, mentioned elsewhere in the poem, clarifies the referent of "grey." Given the poet's typical blending of contraries, her surrealism can function in the service of her ash can realism, as in a poem written in 1960, "The House":

the house was waiting, quite a number of bats
eating bananas
floated too close to the ceiling
    & had their brains dashed out by icicles
the floor was slimy with them
(1975, 77)

When di Prima is in full voice, her surreal passages rise above all these dichotomies, because they rise above logic into a visionary space illuminated by something other than the gleams of reason. "December, 1961" begins "love would not be so simple if there were not chunks of you in the air," and rises at the end to "the sidewalk is slowly crumbling into diamonds / in the sky over central park a mouth is opening / to take you finally in" (1975, 115). To observe how this ending somehow reasonably completes the first line, to observe the buried metaphor which turns literal in the mind as we imagine lovers' mouths—all that fails to do credit to the way the poem soars above the limiting interpretations of reason.

IV

This tendency to combine opposites, sometimes incongruously, is also a primary characteristic of the prose of Diane di Prima's middle period; as usual the formal oppositions reflect a basic authorial ambivalence toward the constant subject of sexual interactions. *Memoirs of a Beatnik* is a text divided by many oppositions: most conspicuously the genre opposition between convincingly recounted memoir and pornography. The latter usually reveals itself in the degree of described physical detail. Pornography depends on an obsessive rendering of the minutia of bodily movement, of the sort that seldom comes from the pen of the autobiographer. So passages of luminous memory alternate with passages of fairly lurid sex, in which di Prima is—as she later explained—fantasizing for the money of Olympia Press, her publisher. Even here, though, in serving one of the least respectable needs of the patriarchy, she is also progressive in her own way, introducing unusual elements into the usually rigid genre of male-centered pornography, elements that threaten the neat gender hierarchies that form the basic pornographic conventions.

For instance, many of the early sex scenes (even, indirectly, the acquaintance rape scene) depend on the close friendship of a sexually linked group of bisexual women. Unlike most of the sex in the Olympia series in which *Memoirs of a Beatnik* was published (along with *Lolita* and *Candy*), di Prima's narrative includes liberal accounts of homosexual activity, though usually between women. The male connections are either routed through the narrator ("You are a veil, through which we make love to each other" [1969, 27]) or just sketched in very quickly ("Allen [Ginsberg] was lying full out on the bed, and Leslie was fucking him in the ass" [184]). The lesbian scenes are themselves a little unusual because shaped by female desire, rather than fetishized for a male spectator. Di Prima's occasional use of a novelist's verisimilitude is also threatening to the suspension of intellect required by pornography, for instance in the description of the sublimely dysfunctional family that produces the rape, as well as a scene of incest. So is the surreal metaphor that sometimes brings her bordello tableaux alive in ways more imaginative than erotic: "Against my cheek Petra shuddered and came like a great, alien mammal, and my hand in Matilda's cunt ached . . . " (62). The empathy of the body on which pornography depends, the reader's flesh tumescent at the sight of words like "tumescent," can easily be compromised by too much imagination, by deviation from the most conventional metaphors, especially when great alien mammals disrupt the erotic theater of the mind.

Di Prima has mentioned that while writing *Memoirs of a Beatnik* in the sixties she constantly listened to Miles Davis's 1954 recording *Walkin'*, the title track of which is a great jazz/early-funk-blues, which sounds as unblue as one can get. It begins with an exuberant fanfare, heraldic and assertive, then goes on to the more personal meditation suggested by title, but it remains oddly cheerful, in the way of early fifties jazz, and luminous. One of its solos even quotes from "When You Wish upon a Star." Di Prima's *Memoirs of a Beatnik* picks up some of that quality from the music, often capturing the exhilaration of breaking out of the rigidities of the fifties. But the "Dinners" sections of her 1961 *Dinners and Nightmares* captures more of the fun, although with much less of the sex. *Memoirs of a Beatnik* often reads as a record of the anxiety or gloom that accompanies life on the edge; even if enthusiastically consensual, its sex is often depressing. A later cut in the album is "You Don't Know What Love Is," and di Prima's ambivalence about men and sex is the book's powerful subtext. At times, as if in a gloss on the line from her poems—"an unloved woman is a gnarled, misshapen thing" ("Song of Black Nana," 1975, 156)—sex with a man is the essence of being. "I felt his cock in my cunt, coming home, like the most natural and only complete state of being." And in one pastoral idyll, when she lives in the country for a while, three men are even better to have sex with and to cook and clean for: "Yes it was good, being a chick to three men" (77). Again the intent may be shock or humor, but di Prima here manages to turn the Beat chick into a sort of super-hausfrau.

However, her explanation of the desirability of her barnyard ménage is that such arrangements avoid the "regular one-to-one relationship," which di Prima describes as "claustrophobic and deadening." For all of her celebrations of loving sex, there is also a harshness in her descriptions of it, especially in her poems of Beat squalor, which tend to emphasize filthy beds, roaches, and more bodily fluids, especially "spit," than are entirely consistent with either soft pornography or its more respectable cousin, romance. Rather than romance, di Prima presents us with a sort of love under erasure. About childbearing, her tone is usually reverent; about sex, sometimes her matter of factness is bitterly cold: "the / juice of all those balls pumped into me" (1975, 40). Under the surface of the libertine, there is a traditional puritanism. But an older di Prima gives us a way to understand the ambivalence: she describes herself as having been torn between the "pre-Classical" belief "that the universe is basically good, fertility is good, the natural sexual rhythm is good" (1978a, 29), and a gnostic anti-materialism: the suspicion that "*this is not our home*" (29). As she noted in the late seventies, "There is the belief, in most forms of gnosticism, that the spirit stood somewhere outside of this matter universe, and had fallen into it, that the universe itself was a trap" (29). The more recent di Prima seems to have moved away from this belief, but "*this is not our home*," with its opening to a sort of puritan alienation from the flesh, seems the much more powerful side of the dichotomy for the young, angry di Prima.

V

If di Prima's accounts of sex can be marked by anger, her anger also found more direct outlets. Rage drives much of her poetry of the sixties and early seventies, a time of anger often misremembered and romanticized simply as a decade of love. Consonant with her times, di Prima herself romanticizes the anger, as when in "April Fool Birthday Poem for Grandpa" (written in 1968 for her beloved anarchist ancestor) she describes "young men with light in their faces / at my table, talking love, talking revolution /

which is love, spelled backwards" (1975, 196).[5] Much of *Revolutionary Letters* (1971) seems simple, an almost involuntary reaction to the events of the sixties. In fact, it dramatizes the dichotomy between love and revolution, often speaking out of emotions far from love.

Though *Revolutionary Letters* is not di Prima's best work, it may have been her most influential, and it is, certainly when historically considered, a fascinating text. It is of its time in the best and worst of ways, sometimes revealing what seems from certain contemporary perspectives not just inclinations that are no longer fashionable on the left, but reactionary and destructive tendencies. Yet those counterprogressive attitudes form part of a stream of thought leading to the gentler (on the whole) progressive attitudes of today. But of contemporary American political groups that di Prima on revolution evokes, it is not the left but the extreme right wing: survivalists and gun lovers. As in right-wing fantasies today, government conspiracies are everywhere, especially in schools and the media, and violence has a powerful appeal, as do fantasies of the apocalypse. As di Prima writes as early as 1960 in "The Jungle":

> to drop the fucking thing & watch it burn
> if it were in my hands, the atomic war wd be past history.
> how cosmic chill
> passes from one to other as we kiss.
> I walk with every beast that walks in me
> more catfooted than they
> but at the kill, exultant, . . .
>   (1975, 70)

But this early poem rhymes joy in the kill with an awareness of the corresponding chill that comes over the lovers, as it balances the crude "drop the fucking thing" with the more nuanced and graceful language of the later lines. By the time of *Revolutionary Letters* in 1971, radical celebrations of mundane violence had become habitual, even to the point where in one of the many admonitions offered by di Prima she advises avoiding those opposed to violence:

> avoid the folk
> who find Bonnie and Clyde too violent

who see the blood but not the energy form
they love us and want us to practice birth control
(12)

The language of the poem is prosy: the stiff "practice birth control" has neither the colloquial immediacy nor the counterbalanced elegance of the passage from "The Jungle." And the reference to the film *Bonnie and Clyde* (1967), in which Hollywood made romantic revolutionary sentiments heroic by combining rural nostalgia with unprecedented amounts of slow-motion violence, hardly dignifies the attempt to justify violence as "energy form."

The letters attack not only birth control, but also a wide range of other targets, including most meliorist and nonrevolutionary programs for making things better for people: "if what you want is jobs / for everyone, you are still the enemy" especially if you imagine those jobs as connected with "degrees from universities which are nothing / more than slum landlords, festering sinks / of lies" ("Letter #19," 1975, 206–207). Since di Prima later attacks pasteurized milk and peanut butter and jelly ("Letter #54," 1975, 214), the cities that she obviously loves (e.g. "my love affair with Manhattan"), "not western civilization but civilization itself," ("Letter #32," 1975, 210), and equations ("Letter #22," 1975, 208), perhaps she is not entirely serious. Or maybe one should just ignore the excesses of an extreme and paranoid decade—not all of these poems were included in the definitive *Selected Poems,* and only six remain in the 1990 *Pieces of a Song.* But the rhetorical stance di Prima takes, along with the romantic primitivism found in much of her poetry, may shed light not only on the desperation of intellectuals in the sixties, but also on the larger problem of modernism, the problem exemplified by Ezra Pound. How could the apparently progressive aesthetic revolutionaries of modernism come to sound so reactionary, even fascist in Pound's case?

Di Prima refers with approval to her mentor Pound's economic ideas in *Revolutionary Letters,* and he still echoes in some of her poem's language, not only in the habitual Pound-like abbreviations ("wd," "w/," "&"), but in some of the basic theorizing, such as this passage from "Letter #12" which recalls Pound's vorticism: "the vortex of creation is the vortex of destruction / the vortex of artistic creation is the vortex of self destruction / the vortex of political creation is the vortex of flesh destruction" (1975, 206). Once either poet decides that destruction is the only answer, because he or she is fundamentally horrified by modern civilization, perceived as a "cancer," and convinced that the ideal existence was lost somewhere in the distant past, the temptation of extreme political ideas is obvious. Such ideas provide a violent actuality to match the violent rhetoric of the poetry, but that rhetoric has already elided the distinction between the destruction of ideas and the destruction of flesh. In post–World War II American politics, extreme political ideas seem to exist not on a line reaching from left to right, but in a sort of circle, extreme left meeting extreme right in the romance of violent revolution or anarchy. Di Prima writes "SMASH THE MEDIA, I said, / AND BURN THE SCHOOLS" (1971, "Letter #11," 23): like long hair for men, such ideas as these have now migrated from the Weatherman left to the militia right.

The irony is that for both Pound and di Prima, the furious hatred of the status quo that lies behind their extreme statements began as a hatred of the violence of war. Di Prima speaks from a generation revolted by the war in Vietnam. But as World War I was the fundamental trauma for Pound's generation, what di Prima remembers with particular anguish is the end of World War II. The bomb fell on Hiroshima on her eleventh birthday, she remembers. Unlike most Americans her family was grief stricken, possibly because of the anarchist background she celebrates when she talks about her grandfather. And she recalls with a still-fresh nausea the festival of hate and revenge on the streets of Brooklyn when the war ended (1995). But underneath di Prima's revulsion at the activities of ordinary people, there is a characteristically Euro-American modernist nostalgia for ordinary people at some safe remove in a preindustrial society.

Di Prima's primitivism provides a vision of the future as well, postrevolutionary or perhaps postapocalyptic. "Rant, from a Cool Place," written in 1968 and preceding *Revolutionary Letters,* is the ultimate poem of sixties paranoia presented as, in the words of the poem, "cold prosaic fact." The title implies that di Prima may have anticipated the ironic tone "Rant" would acquire over the years, but most of its lines have a prose-like directness that suggests total conviction: "I don't know if I will make it somehow nearer by saying this / out loud . . . / . . . . they're waiting to get Tim Leary / Bob Dylan / Allen Ginsberg / LeRoi Jones. . . ." (1975, 168). But the hope expressed in the poem rises above paranoia to longing for a time beyond "bloody, heartrending revolution": "How long before we come to that blessed definable state / known as buddhahood, primitive man, people in a landscape / together like trees, the second childhood of man" (168). Here the speaker is romantic in the old style of the movement that produced di Prima's poetic hero Keats, the style of noble-savage romanticism. The problem is not really political in any ordinary sense—the problem is "called Western man / Called individual consciousness, meaning I need a refrigerator and a car" (168). It may be difficult to accept "individual consciousness" as the root of evil, but the poet means civilized consciousness, corrupted by culture. Behind the self-confessed ranting in *Revolutionary Letters* lies a belief in the essential goodness of uncivilized human nature. As "Letter # 4"—retained through all the different versions—puts it:

> Left to themselves people
> grow their hair.
> . . . .
> Left to themselves they make love
> sleep easily
> share blankets, dope, & children
> they are not lazy or afraid
>   (1975, 204)

Again di Prima is very much of the sixties counterculture, with its own particular cultural imperatives. No historical manifestation of romanticism includes dope and long hair among the inevitable attributes of "natural man," but the dream-vision of "natural man" existing without fear in a state of communal innocence is a staple of European romanticism and, to a large extent, American modernism.

The children here, to retain their blessed state, must avoid the dark and bloody engines of civilization, especially schools. Why should they learn "equations, philosophy, semantics . . . merely history of mind of western man"; what "your kids" really need to know is the practical stuff: "to trap a rabbit, build a raft" ("Letter #22," 1975, 208). Such Huck Finn romanticism, based on a fantasy of premodern rural life (for which some Beats searched in the hidden places of the Third World), would be claimed by the right wing during the next American "revolution," the one led by Ronald Reagan. The poet, moving beyond her focus on urban life, would take it even further, looking forward to the "American aborigines / who will inhabit / this continent" who may include "your grandchildren" and who will sell "artifacts" "to the affluent / highly civilized Africans" (1975, 208). Given the negative valence "highly civilized" carries at this point, this dream of African sophisticates may be somewhat inconsistent with di Prima's respect for African Americans, with the poet's inclination toward Black Power defined as "killing / the white man in each of us" (1975, 210). But consistency is not the aim of *Revolutionary Letters*. Revolution is. But even that is not presented consistently: "Letter # 7," after urging that its readers acquire proficiency not only with "a gun / or knife," but also "molotov cocktail, flamethrowers, / bombs," suddenly changes tactics: "the guns / will not win this one" (1975, 14). Here, the intelligent (and highly civilized) poet overcomes the radical who mouths the slogans of the era.

VI

Though fascinating as the semifossilized remnant of an ancient time, *Revolutionary Letters,* written when, for instance, even the editors of *The New York Review of Books* thought it was cool to run a diagram of a Molotov cocktail on their cover, is ultimately a somewhat deforming mask for di Prima. But the habitual romance of the primitive that dominates the poems of revolution is also evident in her poems of ordinary existence. Jungles are everywhere in her poetry. In "Goodbye Nkrumah," an antiwar poem, she imagines us judged and condemned by the jungle and its denizens:

> we are burning the jungles, the beasts will rise up against us
> even now those small jungle people with black eyes
> look calmly at us out of their photographs
> and it is their calm that will finish us, it is the calm
> of the earth itself.
>   (1975, 154)

The tone of this poem is quieter than that of much of di Prima's poetry of anger, and more chilling, as the speaker imagines another apocalypse. Di Prima uses jungle imagery with a different multiplicity of affect in her ambivalent celebrations of the city, as seen in "The Jungle":

> the beasts cry out:
> lushpadded, making it, the growth slimy

they walk, paths never crossing, like dancers
their tails erect, or swishing, or they droop
. . . .
. . . tenderfooted they walk, tendergrowling, all of love
in their deathspring
   (68)

The ambiguous joy in primal vitality here, reflected in the exuberance as
well as the customary paradoxical duality ("tendergrowling") of the images,
is edged with the customary violence. The poet, alternately grim and joyful, describes a dark city again waiting for the apocalypse it deserves, as
jungle beasts are transformed into archetypal ones:

I walk with every beast that walks
      to take the dragon
thru the city gates
      neck with the cyclops
   (70)

In this passage, the romance of the primal, shading into the mythic, has a
resonance that predates the apocalyptic politics of the sixties. As early as
"Howl" or later in the darker fantasies of William Burrroughs, a tendency
toward nihilism was one of the markers of Beat consciousness, not opposed
to but in some sense complementary to the lust for beatitude, since both
are marked by a passionate revulsion against the mundane.

Di Prima's poems embrace wildness, which is one reason their political
outcries can be disturbingly ambivalent. Before the poet's ultimate epic,
Loba, di Prima's most direct statement of this wildness is not in her own
voice, but in the first-person voice she creates for the saint in "Canticle of
St. Joan." This poem, written in the fall of 1968, presents the Maid of Orleans not as maid at all but as a companion of dragons and a powerful force
who mates with dark forces in the "darkling wood":

I stand in its breath, that fire, and read love
in its eyes like crystal balls which mirror gore
of the burning, pillaged cities I set free.
O brew me mistletoe, unveil the well

I shall lie down with him who must be nameless
and sink my strong teeth into unhuman flesh.
   (1975, 223)

The pagan blood mysticism here is Joan's, but it seems close to the heart of
the creator of this passionately imagined poem, perhaps released by the assumption of the other voice. The line "GRAIL IS BLOOD IS HOLLY" (1975,
225) dominates section three of the four-section poem, and an initial
misreading fits the line into the familiar boundaries of the traditional Chris-
tianity in which both Joan and di Prima were raised. The grail was presumed to have contained Christ's blood, and both were holy. But "HOLLY,"
the marker of European pre-Christian rites, subverts the equation as the
poem has subverted the image of the child saint, now converted to witch-
craft and what has been mistaken as devil worship, the dark side where di
Prima finds the spiritual sustenance of blood and earth.
   Di Prima's primitivism, however, can also be suffused with light, in a
very different ancient spiritual tradition that became increasingly a recourse
as her poetry moved out of the violent sixties and seventies. The concluding stanza of "The Bus Ride" illustrates: "coming upon you in morning
meditation / I find in your eyes the light of the first man / greeting the winter sun at the edge of the world" (1975, 145). Here the Buddhist practice
("morning meditation") and a more radical sort of primitivism ("the first
man") converge in a powerful statement of the strength of the perception
that precedes ideas. The light is internal ("in your eyes") but also external,
subjective and objective, the substance of direct perception, almost unmediated by abstractions. "It seems to me," di Prima said at Naropa Institute in 1975, "more and more as I get more and more deeply into poetry
that the actual stuff that poetry is made out of is light" (1978a, 27). She
means this almost literally because of the power of the visual image in all
the poetry she finds most intensely real. But it suggests the light of Beat
vision, not just the blue light of acid hallucination, but the white light of
traditional mysticism, associated with St. John of the Cross, or—to choose
an example more directly connected with the more recent di Prima of *Seminary Poems* (1991)—with the final enlightenment of Buddhism.
   Some of di Prima's most elegant poetry, poetry that reveals the spiritual
world that ultimately displaces political obsession, is full of images of such
internal and external light. Often they are enriched by the same jungle im-

agery that was used to deepen the darkness of the angry poetry. "Ode to Elegance," a vaguely surreal catalogue of praise of the physical, composed in
1964, begins by comparing hands to "thin giraffes / raising themselves in
the sun on distant plains," and proceeds through a free association of natural and jungle animal images to images of death, treason, murder. But the
light, here, rules the darkness, even of death: "with light inwoven / the elegance of the skull / the phosphorescence of the ending body" (1975, 134).
The subject that slowly forms itself through the images is the beauty of life
even in the face of, under the condition of, death:

> in this white light
> under this rush of wind
> all things teem forth like dust motes in the air
>
> that all things send forth love, inanimate
>   (135)

The metaphor of the dust motes beautifully reinforces the exaltation of
"white light." While suggesting the dissolution of all things, the metaphor
also shows the motes to join into oneness, a physical oneness, but aspiring
to the condition of light, which itself exists on the border between particles
and waves and something more abstract, something as immaterial as love.

   To examine the sometimes contradictory political implications of di
Prima's poetry is to emphasize one central aspect of di Prima, the passionate revolutionary, but there is still another aspect that moves toward a Buddhist renunciation of contraries (including the simplistic us vs. them of
Revolutionary Letters). This is the poet devoted not so much to Malcolm X
as to Keats, the poet who happily quotes Keats—"What shocks the virtu-
ous philosopher delights the chameleon poet"—and goes on to praise "that
openness, that negative capability, that letting it come through you. Leaving behind opinion and judgement—the first requirement for tuning the
instrument in poetry" (1978a, 27). Di Prima seems herself to be inconsistent here, to forget the torrent of blunt opinions that dominates so much of
her poetry. But the fact that her poetry, even the heavily ideological *Revolutionary Letters,* is best read as the record of life ongoing, not as consistent
philosophy, implies a resistance to critical categorization. While di Prima
has been identified as a minor Beat revolutionary, much of her work is more

fully illuminated by comparison with the button-down rebel Frank O'Hara, the poet of whom she said "you my big brother brought me up" (1975, 163). George Butterick finds in di Prima's "poetry as day-to-day engagement" what he describes as "the sense of a journal's freshness, the varieties of daily experience that Frank O'Hara would perfect" (151). Di Prima was close to O'Hara in her intellectually formative years when they worked together in her New York Poets' Theater. O'Hara, the prophet of "impure poetry," was also a neoromantic poet of life ongoing, capturing its textures and its radiance, rather than any fixed conclusions. Though her Buddhism provides a spiritual rationale that O'Hara lacked, like him di Prima values the incidental music of existence; she stresses the primacy and sometimes the transcendent beauty of individual experience, beyond all rules, beyond all political groups.

Not that di Prima can be fixed to any ultimate claims, even the ones made in this discussion. But sometimes the bloody process achieves a moment of intensity that lasts like a final statement. For instance, "The Clearing in Autumn," a poem of meditation on place composed in 1975, begins with immersion in the details and rises to a high-romantic transcendence through a series of haiku-like steps to abstraction: "Tart sweetness of time / white butterfly." Near the end, there is the outward leap:

That tree my angel. Wisps of cloud
his dance. Fogbank explosion of light in which
white egrets lift & fall, pelicans tumble.
Infinity of fog-mirrors in moonlight, mirrored back
by the Bay. Splintering universes.
you are blue, you are golden, you fall on me
    (1990, 124)

Here, as in Ginsberg's "Wales Visitation," the carefully observed distinctions finally disappear in union. The process ends simply, with di Prima's beautifully evocative metaphors collapsing difference into a sequence of resemblances, illuminated by white light, and by blue. Again the linkage of objects through metaphor embodies the spiritual joining. "Angel" links "tree" to "Wisps of cloud," which are linked by angel wings and color to "white egrets," which are linked by their falling movement to the tumbling pelicans. All are reflected in the "fog-mirrors," themselves "mirrored" no longer by metaphors but by the actual physical mirroring of "the Bay." As the "infinity" of resemblances threatens to fall apart, they reach a sort of visionary critical mass and implode on the poet: "intangible Lovers I open my body to / inaudible cries as I spin towards / the sun." In the final union, her ecstatic self is ravished by the flow of landscape.

VII

If the early radical di Prima was defined by contraries, the "us vs. them" of the sixties, the late Buddhist di Prima, evident as early as the seventies, moves toward a resolution of contraries, or a sense that the voyage ahead transcends all simple oppositions, divisive categories. This was the burden of the dream that gave birth to her epic-in-progress, *Loba,* according to the account in her essay "Light / and Keats" (1978a). In her fairy-tale dream "rich people" seeking decadent entertainment send a wolf to hunt her and her children, but the wolf turns out to be an ally, the goddess. Di Prima finds herself dancing with the rich people, the enemy, and she thinks "but they're the bad guys" and then her long-dead friend "Fred Herko said to me, 'di Prima, if you go on thinking like that, you're going to be sick for the rest of your life.' and I woke up" (35). So her later poetry, particularly *Loba,* is based on a spirit of solidarity, not opposition, primarily solidarity with women, though she still challenges our general conception of what is appropriate for a feminist and a poet. In fact she may illuminate the limits of that conception. She may be engaged in a rebellion deeper than that of her critics.

Especially given the current power of identity politics, politics has become a way of understanding the group, but di Prima's spiritual poetics is a way of understanding the individual. Even in statements of solidarity, she valorizes the individual, as she did in protesting the loss of her friends to the racial exclusiveness of the Black Power movement. She wants "for us as women, that sense of absolute self-reliance" (Moffeit 1989, 32), not reliance on the group. Di Prima values the marginal above all. As early as *Memoirs of a Beatnik,* she registered distress about any movement of the left to the center. There she even admits a sort of disappointment about gay liberation: "the social stigma has gone out of homosexuality, and with it the high, bitter romanticism. . . . Gayness can no longer be used to hold the world at bay, put down the society around you, signal your isolation and help you stand clear"(1969, 14). That is her final value: to stand clear.

Influenced still by the anarchist light of her youth, she wants that clarity, isolation, the outlaw stance. It may well be difficult to remember the allure of the old radical idea of the outsider, the individual riding the waves of history and culture but still able to achieve a perspective beyond both, answerable to no rules. Di Prima's poetry suggests that she wanted to be "true," even if it took her in dangerous directions. Robert Creeley uses this term in his 1973 introduction to *Dinners and Nightmares* (repeated in *Pieces of a Song*), characterizing di Prima within her historical context: "Growing up in the fifties, you had to figure it out for yourself—which she did, and stayed open—as a woman, uninterested in any possibility of static investment or solution" (1990, vii). Di Prima stayed open. This has been clear all along, through all her extremes and all her changes. Her solidarity with other individuals is defined by her gendered experience, but not limited by race or gender. It is primarily the solidarity of the artist with other artists; in the eighties she speaks movingly and with great modesty about that: "There have been billions of us making art and in some way we have been the leavening or the thing that made human life possible when it was full of death. . . . being a part of that work crew in some way is a bigger honor than anything that our single work brings us in terms of what we can have or make" (Moffeit 1989, 26). As for her solidarity with women, the vital connection she makes is not with women in general but with a particular group, where "woman" intersects with "outsider," her "companions of the road." Reading from *Recollections of My Life as a Woman* in the 1995 film of the same name, she says "there is something between me and the women of my generation who have truly lived that is stronger than any other connection, any other intimacy. The women, that is, who have borne the children, taken the drugs, traveled the world, smuggled somebody out of the country" (1995). She elaborates, unwavering in her support of the LSD adventure against all conventional pieties about drugs, mentioning "acid megadoses" in the same breath with "the struggles for and with the children." Then she falls into the customary imagery of light: "all these things shine."

So her sisterhood is a sisterhood of outsiders. Among all her blending of opposites, the final paradox, one not unusual among the most creative humans, involves the solidarity of extreme individualists. "Oh lost moon sisters, crescent in hair, sea underfoot" *Loba* describes them, living the forbidden: "you lie with the yeti / you flick the long cocks of satyrs with your tongue" (1990, 169–170). Eagerly embraced here are the dangers of energy, creation, vitality, sexual magic: the irrational virtues at the heart of her life as well as her poetry. Like the life, the poetry is "impure" like O'Hara's, and wildly uneven; its ideological excesses are sometimes extreme. But both life and poetry were never driven by a wish for purity or correct conclusions, but rather the will to explore "the bloody process," a will to test the new, to live on the further margins, that was itself heroic and—for those who would come after her—liberating, despite the radical areas of ideological separation. Through the intricacy of her times, a powerful energy emerges still: "nothing is lost; it shines in our eyes" (1995).

Notes

1. This poem does not appear in *Selected Poems,* but in the later *Pieces of a Song, Selected Poems* (1990, 93). In the video recording "Recollections of My Life as a Woman" (1995), di Prima says of her childhood, "I feel I was abused in some way, I'm not sure how."

2. Not one to hold a grudge, she parts from him with bored affection, thinking "like most vigorous, healthy men, . . . civilized life could not contain. . . his energies" (1969, 66–69).

3. First published in *This Kind of Bird Flies Backwards* (1958).

4. In a recent communication to one of the editors of this volume, di Prima hoped that "Brass Furnace" would not be misread as an anti-abortion poem. Letter to Nancy Grace, March 22, 2001.

5. Di Prima may be remembering Baraka's memorable "In Memory of Radio," which more convincingly reverses love into "evol."

"And then she went"

Beat Departures and Feminine Transgressions in Joyce Johnson's *Come and Join the Dance*

Ronna C. Johnson

In 1962, at the age of twenty-six and under the name Joyce Glassman, the writer, editor, and educator Joyce Johnson published her first novel, *Come and Join the Dance*. The author has signed two names to her books, and this discussion uses both, following her publishing history, to preserve the distinction between the novice and the established writer.[1] Johnson's second novel, *Bad Connections*, came out in 1978 after a hiatus from writing during which she was widowed, then remarried and had a child and began her editorial career. Her third novel, *In the Night Café*, a portion of which won the O'Henry Prize for short fiction, was published in 1987. The three New York novels map key cultural and gender discourses of their eras, portraying adventurous middle-class white women in the Beat 1950s and free-sex sixties. Johnson is best known for her 1983 memoir, *Minor Characters: The Romantic Odyssey of a Woman in the Beat Generation,* which, though it does recount her emergence as a writer, focuses on her youthful affairs with Beat bohemianism and Jack Kerouac in the late 1950s. However, Johnson's significance as a writer surpasses her famous literary connections and bohemian antecedents, for with *Come and Join the Dance* she entered literary history by publishing the first Beat generation novel by and about a Beat woman.

With its female bohemian perspective on sex, cold war existentialism, and the New York hipster milieu, *Come and Join the Dance* stands as a Beat urtext, on par with the renegade declarations of *On the Road* or "Howl" or *Naked Lunch*. But Johnson's seminal novel, in contrast to the male purview of these classic Beat texts, proclaims instead the arrival of the women typically marginalized in them. Just so, *Come and Join the Dance* is out of print and has been invisible in discussions of postwar American women writers, even to feminist critics who have begun to identify and assess works by women Beat writers.[2] Nor has it been studied in analyses of Johnson's work.[3] It has been further eclipsed by the view that women's prose contributions to Beat literature are confined to memoir.[4] This neglect obscures the novel's pivotal emendations of the Beat field, and its signification of a feminist movement in the fifties. Dissipating the silence of Kerouac's "girls" in black, *Come and Join the Dance* brings to Beat literature a model of female subjectivity. It depicts women's transformation from culture's objects to their own subjects by foregrounding them as sexual actors and consumers, attesting to Beat's anticipation of the sixties women's movement. As a literary text, *Come and Join the Dance* enlarges the scope of Beat invention with its hybrid innovation of "hot" self-expression by means of a "cool" restrained style. And, in an illuminating discourse about gender and canonicity, the novel quotes and revises tropes of classic American literature and the genre of the road tale, a double move that decisively and symbolically delivers the Beat female from eclipse by male hegemony. Challenging masculinist discourses of Beat with its heroine's anti-establishment alienation, sexual autonomy, and subjectivity—attributes and privileges reserved for men—the narrative of *Come and Join the Dance* critiques, challenges, and transgresses Beat as well as mainstream gender codes.

Yet, although it focuses on a bohemian woman, *Come and Join the Dance* is not a feminist but, rather, a proto-feminist novel. Its instantiation of women as Beat subjects anticipates, but does not equal in promise or achievement, the second-wave feminisms emerging in the late sixties and the early seventies. Despite the novel's emphasis on white female subjectivity, it makes no claim to address directly the emancipation of women; its corrective discourses are written in a Beat key rather than with the rhetoric that would be familiar from later women's movements. Indeed, *Come and*

Join the Dance is a Beat novel in the usual sense. It recounts the emergence of the individual as counterforce in conformist postwar America; its distinction is to see the white female as that individual, as a Beat subject who, like Beat men, rejects the numerous oppressive overdeterminations of postwar establishment culture. Beat bohemia's inducements are portrayed in the protagonist's efforts to escape conformity, enjoy sexual freedom, and reach existential awareness. Elucidating the decisive role of gender in Beat's formation, the novel calls attention to Beat's reproduction of traditional patriarchal precepts, a recognition which anticipates dialogues of second-wave feminism. The restoration of *Come and Join the Dance* to Beat history and to accounts of postwar women writers illuminates an under-studied continuity between Beat nonconformity and countercultural sixties liberation movements for women.

Set in the mid-1950s, *Come and Join the Dance* recounts ten fraught days before its protagonist, twenty-year-old Susan Levitt of Cedarhurst, a Long Island suburb, graduates from an unnamed women's college near Columbia University and sails to Paris. The novel's principal characters are Susan's college friend Kay Gorman, who, having dropped out of school, resides in a beat hotel called the Southwick Arms and works in the college library; Susan's dull boyfriend, Jerry, whose slavish unrequited love, devotion to upward mobility, and anxiety to conform make him the figure of bourgeois practicality (28); eighteen-year-old Anthony Leone, a self-proclaimed communist, "campus bum" (53) and poet, who has just been expelled from college "for bringing a girl up to his room" (54); and Peter, at nearly thirty a generation ahead of the others, once married, a "perpetual student" who's been working on his thesis for five years, possessor of a 1938 black Packard and the semi-ironic ambition to "be a promising young man as long as possible" (21). The generational divide in this cast of characters suggests the multi-tiered formation of the Beat movement: the moody older hipster Peter evokes Beat's first generation, which includes writers such as ruth weiss, John Clellon Holmes, Kerouac, and Allen Ginsberg (all born in the 1920s); Kay, Anthony, and the protagonist Susan, more than a decade younger than Peter but sharing his disaffection, are akin to the second Beat generation, which includes writers such as Elise Cowen, LeRoi Jones, Joyce Johnson, and Diane di Prima (all born in the 1930s). The novel's generational structure exemplifies Beat's extended influence in the postwar era and Glassman's emergence from an ongoing literary and cultural avant-garde.

However, *Come and Join the Dance* depicts a postwar interval of nonconformity and alienation before Beat is recognized, when the underground
avant-garde was inchoate, and its famous adherents Kerouac and Ginsberg
were unknown. The novel's moment is situated at Beat's emergence from
Greenwich Village bohemian and Times Square hipster subcultures during
and after the Second World War. While postwar bohemians, mostly intellectuals and artists, were linked to the Greenwich Village avant-garde of the
1920s, the Times Square hipsters Kerouac saw during the war formed an
underclass characterized by hard drugs, criminality, homosexuality, jazz,
and revelatory personal vision, and embodied, he felt, the resurgence of a
nineteenth-century American individuality (1959, 361). These New York
bohemians and hipsters served as antecedents and foundation for the Beat
generation, which relished jazz and drugs, writing and sex, nonconformity
and petty theft, confession and hallucinatory vision. Like Holmes's early
Beat novel *Go* (1952), *Come and Join the Dance* represents a bohemian/hip-
ster subculture characterized by the post-bomb alienation distinct to its era.
Johnson recalls reading Holmes's 1952 essay "This Is the Beat Generation,"
which elaborated a "state of mind that, although new, according to this ar-
ticle, was totally familiar to me" (1983, 74); it was the "Bohemian world"
(1983, 44, 55) she knew from Washington Square Park and Greenwich Village. And, as Johnson noted, that incipiently Beat culture was exemplified
exclusively by men (1983, 75). Kerouac's idea that "Beat Generation" had
"become the slogan or label for a revolution of manners in America" (1959,
363) suggests the signifier's elaboration to a cultural formation; a set of discursive conventions and relations, inclusions and exclusions that shape and
are shaped by subjects who participate in and effect the cultural, linguistic
field. Addressing the exclusion of women from Beat representation, *Come
and Join the Dance* clarifies the discursive field of Beat; unlike *Go* and, later,
On the Road (1957) and William Burroughs's *Junky* (1953), Glassman's
novel sees second-generation Beat women in active relation to the postwar
culture of post-bomb alienation.

Yet, while *Come and Join the Dance* challenges and revises discourses of
and assumptions about gender in Beat culture and literature, the novel oscillates between adopting Beat stances and privileges for its female protagonist and abolishing discursive structures and assumptions about gender
that seem central to Beat's construction. The bohemian dropouts Kay and
Susan contest stereotypes of female passivity and conformity; their sexual

desire and nonmarital sexual experience explicitly portray female agency and individuality. However, because these modifications of the feminine challenge Beat's patriarchal politics, *Come and Join the Dance* can also seem to be a refutation of Beat. The focus on Susan allows the narrative to sift through the complicated process for women Beats of dropping out; to problematize and resist the silencing of women by fifties gender codes, which afflicted both mainstream "girls" and bohemian "chicks"; and to depict negotiations for the sexual satisfaction that authenticates female subjectivity. Yet, at the same time, in its renovations of Beat discourses, *Come and Join the Dance* dramatizes the irremediality of gender constructions and roles in the postwar era before second-wave feminism, for the protagonist's arrival into Beat subjectivity depends on emulation and appropriation of masculinist hipster styles and freedoms, suggesting that even radical ameliorist subcultures and bohemias are reactionary and inadequate to accommodate women as subjects.

Just as it both adopts and refutes Beat conventions, *Come and Join the Dance* accomplishes a distinctive double move in its representation of Beat bohemia that attests to its proto-feminism and, in this, its anticipation of the postmodern. Linda Hutcheon has observed that formations of postmodern literary discourse enact an oscillating subvert/install maneuver. *Come and Join the Dance* exemplifies this postmodern discursive move: it subverts Beat's male hegemony by positioning a woman as its protagonist, and, revising essential features of Beat narrative, it installs a corrective or replacement discourse, the narration of Beat female agency, sexual desire, self-reliance.[5] At the level of the plot, *Come and Join the Dance* is further marked by the subvert/install tactic Hutcheon has identified: the novel appropriates and then sabotages the traditional road tale, a fragment of which it samples and refigures in the penultimate two chapters. This double move functionally terminates the road tale's iteration in the narrative, and in this rejects the patriarchal, canonical tradition which masculinist Beat follows even in its iconoclasm. Depicting bohemian women's preferences for nonconformity, their rejection of the confining feminine and the masculine hegemonic, *Come and Join the Dance* inscribes the effaced women of the Beat generation as a presence in its representation of a postwar bohemian clique, entering and perforce altering the male-defined, male-centered discursive field of Beat.

Come and Join the Dance partakes of and simultaneously surpasses Beat's opposition to bourgeois compliance for it reforms Beat's contestatory impulses to fit women. Like other texts of the era of its composition, such as Kerouac's *On the Road*, C. Wright Mills's *The Power Elite* (1956), and William H. Whyte Jr.'s *The Organization Man* (1956), *Come and Join the Dance* contends with the postwar conformity that negates individuality, but with this critical difference: as it affects a young, middle-class white woman. Glassman began work on the novel in 1955,[6] two years before she met Kerouac (1983, 105, 107), so its Beat subject arose from the Greenwich Village zeitgeist. That is, as a neophyte novelist with a book contract in the late 1950s, Glassman was writing amidst many of the same cultural influences as the male Beat writers. Yet, her rendition of the radical sociocultural discourses of her time diverged from both postwar intellectual assumptions about gender, focused mostly on men, and Beat's narrow literary portrayals of women. This jockeying registers the renovation of Beat discourse which its implementation by female bohemians and artists necessitated and effected. Johnson recalls in *Minor Characters* her ambitions for writing:

> As a writer I would live life to the hilt . . . just as Jack and Allen had done. I would make it my business to write about young women quite different from the ones portrayed weekly in the pages of *The New Yorker*. I would write about furnished rooms and sex. Sex had to be approached critically. . . I would not succumb to the lady-like stratagems of shimmering my way toward discreet fadeouts. I'd decided this even before meeting Jack or reading *Howl*. (156)

She recognized that her gender might consign her to "lady-like stratagems" limiting expression and transforming sexual climaxes to fadeouts in more ways than one. Shaping her Beat moment to accommodate female subjectivity, Glassman determined to write "critically" about sex, disclosing its pivotal role in women's experience without condemning or trivializing female sexuality; she would broach her subjects—femininity, female sexual experience, the existential anonymities and liberties of furnished rooms— freely, as a Beat writer. Her novel illustrates that women practicing, personifying, and writing Beat were instrumental in shaping the Beat literary and cultural fields, even as women writers and their texts have been excised from the Beat record.

Come and Join the Dance was conceived and developed in the wake of such early Beat and qua Beat novels as Chandler Brossard's *Who Walk in Darkness* (1952), John Clellon Holmes's *Go* (1952), and Sloan Wilson's *The Man in the Gray Flannel Suit* (1955), as well as women's novels such as Grace Metalious's *Peyton Place* (1956) and Barbara Probst Solomon's *The Beat of Life* (1960), but Glassman's book contends hegemonic gender codes the others accept. Although *The Beat of Life* is today obscure, its author, Barbara Probst Solomon, was said to have considered herself the first woman Beat novelist (Grace 1999b, 114). This is inaccurate, but *The Beat of Life,* also about a restless young white woman, does illuminate the Beat character of *Come and Join the Dance.* In both novels, female sexuality is paramount, contingent not on marriage but desire. The heroine of *The Beat of Life* gets pregnant, undergoes the harrowing process to obtain a "therapeutic" abortion, suffers a four-day hospital stay, and upon release, puts her head in a gas oven, committing suicide. In this defeat of female sexual autonomy and desire, *The Beat of Life* is not Beat, although the legendary Beat figure, the poet Elise Cowen, has a similar history. Rather, like *Peyton Place, The Beat of Life* reinscribes women's subordination to patriarchal prescriptions. *Peyton Place,* a controversial bestseller, subverts the conventional view of women as sexually passive, and portrays the psychological, emotional, and physical abuse women suffer from men, focusing on the sexual double standard and the need for legalized abortion. Yet although *Peyton Place* may have been adventurous about women's sex lives, its suburban setting and characters situate the novel in mainstream bourgeois culture. In contrast, the female Beat discourse of women's subjectivity and sexual agency in *Come and Join the Dance* rejects the immaturity and passivity of the feminine mandated by the dominant culture. Glassman gives her protagonist sexual desire and experimentation, with no 1950s penalty of guilt or pregnancy. At the novel's conclusion, Susan leaves her lovers without regret as she embarks for Paris. Rather than stereotypes of female instability and suicide, which Solomon didactically exploits, *Come and Join the Dance* enacts the male Beat model of flight from convention for its protagonist, rejecting female stereotypes and male hegemony through the same discourses by which Beat masculinism affirms them. *Come and Join the Dance* turns Beat's gender conventions to women's ends.

    The position of *Come and Join the Dance* as a fiction in the discursive field of Beat literature is clarified by the life-stories recounted in Johnson's memoir *Minor Characters.* The memoir shows that the novel is a fiction based on

Glassman's experiences in college and bohemia during the mid-fifties in New York, before she met Kerouac in 1957 and experienced with him the tumultuous publication of *On the Road*. The novel's intersections with and departures from the events recorded in the memoir elucidate the author's development of a Beat fiction; that is, rather than annexing her lived experience, she invented a narrative of bohemian women's experiences and perspectives. Glassman made characters of her college friend, the poet Elise Cowen, and her older lover, a Barnard philosophy instructor she calls Alex Greer (identified as Donald Cook [Johnson 2000]) (1983, 61, 121). But, for example, she does not represent Cowen's hospitalizations and suicide attempts (the last, in 1962, was successful), which might have suggested that a young woman's hunger and capacity for sexual and existential freedoms—her resistance to fifties gender roles—could be only overwhelming and deadly. Cowen's counterpart in *Come and Join the Dance,* Kay Gorman, is cynical and depressed, but the portrait forbids female stereotypes of self-pity and hysteria, and allows the dropout Kay to survive her own defiance.

Similarly, the novel's departures from life in the treatment of the Alex Greer/Donald Cook character transform the young woman whom he cavalierly discarded into a fictive protagonist whose story in *Come and Join the Dance* is commensurate with those of hipster men, the sexual consumers and adventurers of bohemia. In *Minor Characters,* Johnson discloses her plans for the heroine of her first novel: "Just like me, my heroine would have an affair with the Alex character and end up alone. But in my fictional rearrangement of life, it was she who was going to leave him after their one and only night together. I rewarded her with a trip to Paris" (1983, 121).In the novel's discourse of Beat female subjectivity and sexual agency, the heroine's self-sufficiency is not a punishment; she is not seduced and abandoned, but sexually free and journeying into adventure. Further, Glassman did not give her heroine the illegal abortion she herself suffered in the mid-1950s (1983, 110–115), in this avoiding the reactionary sexual politics of contemporaneous norms and novels by women. These moves out of 1950s femininity produce the novel's Beat discourse, while its emphasis on gender roles and conventions problematize the Beat assumption that hipster iconoclasm is normatively male. Indeed, Glassman's fictionalizations of and departures from her life in *Come and Join the Dance,* joined with the novel's self-proclaimed female "outlaw" (62) or bohemian nonconformity, reveal the constructedness of Beat literary discourse so often (mis)taken in the male writers for unvarnished autobiography, and construed and treated as universal.

The contention of 1950s conformity in *Come and Join the Dance* provides a radical answer to what Betty Friedan named in 1963 the "female malaise." The novel prescribes for its dissenting heroine the Beat male ethos: to drop out—of college, of anaesthetized suburban life (122), of "perfect, terrifying blandness" (11). This outcome is anticipated by the novel's opening, which depicts Susan mired in feelings of insubstantiality that she struggles to overcome:

> Her image floated ahead of her like a balloon . . . transparent, ghost-like. . . .What did others see when they looked at her? She would try to study her face as though it belonged to someone else . . . her face cheated her. It had a way of rearranging itself when she looked into mirrors, as though it were giving a performance. (10–11)

Afflicted with not-thereness, Susan is disembodied, disengaged, dissociated, even from herself. A sense of unreality and opacity blends Friedan's malaise with Didionesque dissociation: the age of anxiety meets the silent generation. The novel's starting place is at this intersection, but as it unfolds, its theme of dropping out repositions the novel on the cusp of fifties conventionality, and sixties feminism and sexual revolution. As the novel intimates, dropping out is a complicated move for postwar women, who have been marginalized in or excluded from the institutions only males are privileged to join and scorn. *Come and Join the Dance* depicts the obligatory downward mobility of Beat masculinity, but problematizes what dropping out can mean when the subject is by definition of her gender already excluded from the social, political, and cultural centers of her era. Nevertheless, the novel's valorization of dropping out defines it as Beat. Beat bohemia reverses mainstream standards, for here, dropping out and relinquishing social privilege designates the attainment of subjectivity, the individual's significance in a cultural or theoretical sense.

For the heroine of *Come and Join the Dance,* dropping out signifies her arrival as subject, and entry into Beat culture and community; her instantiation in Beat history. The story's plot to thwart Susan's "particular" gender and class "fate" to be a "good girl" (75) provides an account of how a bohemian is made, how a college girl is transformed into a Beat dropout.

What is thwarted is traditional femininity, which is relinquished for the masculine privileges that secure subjectivity and agency. Susan fields feelings of illegitimacy, convictions of inauthenticity, fears that she "was just a spy, a sneak thief,"[7] a supplicant quartered within the "pink walls" of her mother's house, awaiting rescue. She wants "to be saved from boredom" (70) rather than marry into it (51); she prefers "outlaw" bohemians to her conventional boyfriend, Jerry, for "the terrifying thing about Jerry was that he was someone she could marry—she could marry him and never have to go to Paris—he was only waiting for a signal" (9). Susan rejects the bourgeois destination of sterile conformity in a rhetoric of refusal: "Not me, she thought. She was . . . the odd one. Not me. At last the pain of it was alive inside her. Not me. Not me" (109). Her pain and refusal signify yearning for subjectivity, which she sees as a possibility in bohemian marginality. Coveting the freedom of the "wild girls" who live beyond gender's restraints, Susan would renounce the passive, dissociating silence of femininity—of being "only blank, a spectator of herself, immensely bored" (27)—to claim the connection and power of male Beatness, even if that renunciation is ungendering, as implied in her friend Kay's antifeminine Beat cynicism that "everybody uses everybody. That's the way it is" (71). Thus the college girl is transformed into Beat dropout by the appropriation of male models of sexual agency and subjectivity, which produces the novel's revision of Beat discourse.

This revision is announced in the novel's opening salvo, a challenge to the hegemony of the literary canon. The heroine's capacity for rebellion and resistance is explicit in her inclination to test tests, the vaunted Beat disdain for establishment institutions. The novel begins with the scene of Susan's final college exam as she considers its last question, which is on Melville: she "wondered what Melville would have thought of sixty-three girls concentrating on him at once" (3) and, expecting "freedom to happen" (4) after her last exam, Susan hastens liberty by leaving before she finishes it. Already subversive, the image of sixty-three "girls" "concentrating" on Melville suggests a disruption of the exclusionary conventions and canon that Melville represents: women have broken into the Men's Club. Doubling that subversion, and rejecting rules, customs, and canon as might a male Beat writer, Susan rebels against service to Melville the renegade writer of road tales by refusing to commemorate him with her attention. Susan authenticates her own iconoclasm—that is, her Beat capacity for urgency, restlessness, and flight—by appropriating a male model of agency, the insider's capacity and readiness to reject convention's expectations.

In giving its protagonist the status of Beat subject, *Come and Join the Dance* revises and reinscribes gender codes, particularly the aspect of female passivity which directs that the female function as a mirror reflection, and thus validation, of male power. As Susan J. Douglas argues in her chronicle of the way postwar mass-culture media narratives reify tropes of sexual difference, "boys are cool; girls are their mirrors . . . surfaces whose function is to reflect all this coolness back to them and on them. Girls watch boys . . . they're only spectators," not actors or possessors of "cool" (299). This assessment echoes Virginia Woolf's metaphoric critique of women's reflective role in hegemonic sexual politics: "Women have served all these centuries as looking-glasses possessing the magic and delicious power of reflecting the figure of man at twice its natural size" (35). Just so, Glassman writes against the gender code's consignment of women to reflect men, revising and expanding Beat by making the male bohemian reflect the female. This ironic reversal is accomplished in the novel's depiction of Peter, the mercurial hipster Susan admires. The narration depicts Peter as a reflective existential surface, a mirror returning Susan's gaze to herself, thus enlisting the Beat male to signify female subterraneanism. He is, nevertheless, an ambiguous aid: "There was something about Peter that forced too much knowledge upon her. He was as dangerous, as compassionless as a mirror" (99). In Glassman's Beat narrative, the figure of the male mirroring and measuring female affect is used to register female subjectivity, which is posited as a "dangerous" excess of awareness. This construction comments on women's potential for liberation in the postwar era: knowledge is seen to jeopardize quiescence and conformity, contravening the gender code for women, instigating a revolt. That is, knowledge instigates women's transformation from object to subject, as in the 1960s liberations that effected the empowerment of white women and people of color, whose subordination had been the foundation of white male subjectivity and whose emergence undermined and fragmented that male hegemonic.

For the Beat woman, this transformation from object to subject encounters cultural, gendered resistance in the form that Helen McNeil has named the "chick category." Like most young bohemian women in 1956, twenty-two-year-old Joyce Glassman working in publishing houses and writing her first novel was regarded in hipster precincts like the San Remo, the Cedar

Tavern, or the Five Spot as a "chick."[8] McNeil defines a "chick" as "the at-
tractive, young, sexually available and above all silent ('dumb') female"
(189). The "chick" corresponds to Kerouac's "cool" hipster "girls [who] say
nothing and wear black" (1959, 362), wordless companions immured in
hipster iconography, signifiers of the men's subterraneanism. Johnson recalls worrying about her bohemian status—"How Beat could I actually be,
holding down a steady office job and writing a novel about an ivy-league
college girl on the verge of parting with her virginity" (1983, 216–217).
But, in fact, for postwar middle-class white women, economic self-
sufficiency such as Glassman's was as radical a step as dropping out; and if
it was not hip, it was certainly convenient for the often unemployed male
artists of bohemia.[9] Yet, while these square facts of her life undermined her
Beat credibility, which valorized voluntary poverty, unemployment, and
disdain of establishment culture, the most disempowering dismissal for
a self-aware, discerning woman was to be seen as a chick. For as McNeil
notes, "the 'chick category' does not violate any existing gender codes."
Rather, it provides men more opportunity to have sex with women without
responsibility. Most importantly, "it is sex with those who will—mostly—
not tell their side of the story" (189). That is, the "chick category" is above
all intransitive. It goes only one way: the chick serves male freedom and
narrative while herself remaining a cipher, a "girl" who wears black and
says nothing. Breaching this intransitiveness, *Come and Join the Dance*
breaks a silence; it dissipates Susan's chronic reticence, which Peter, the
novel's Beat hero, mocks: "Susan, I've never heard you say anything before.
You come to my parties with Kay, you sit on the sofa, you listen to someone
very dutifully, and every now and then you tell a story or a little joke—and
that's all" (20). This paralyzed, silent "girl" is posited as the chrysalis of Beat
female emancipation, for she will emerge from this camouflage of reticence
with full discursive powers and unsettling desires.

Susan's alienation and subsequent attraction to bohemia elucidate the
text's expansion of Beat discourse, while its representation of her existential
condition contends the usual Beat erasure or denial of female subjectivity.
Establishing her malaise in the story's opening, Susan is said to be "frozen
into a deadly laziness. If she moved she would shatter like glass" (3). She is
occupied by questions whose rhetoric typifies Beat existentialism as usually
conveyed by men. This discourse elaborates the problem for which drop-

ping out is the solution, the dissatisfaction with convention for which bohemia is antidote:

> What if you lived your life entirely without urgency? . . . spent [hours]
> waiting for something to happen to you; when you were particularly
> desperate you went out looking for it . . . something had made
> [Susan] want the feeling of living a little close to the edge; perhaps she
> had chosen to feel frightened rather than feel nothing at all. (14–15)

To live "without urgency" is to exist as an object—a conformist "girl"—
rather than a subject—a Beat rebel. Susan's dilemma is whether to conform
or to drop out: to wait passively for the future or to seek it out, to shun urgency or whip it up. Dropping out would position Susan on the edge, at the
marginalized field of Beat. Choosing to drop out, she chooses the urgency,
search, and trepidation that signifies being a subject, the rejection of conformity's numb safeness for the hipster alternative. This is the uncharted
territory of desire, selfhood, and individuality; the "underground brother-
hood" (62) of existential adventurers; the bohemian "Outlaws world" (10)
of her friends Kay, Peter, and Anthony. Joining them Susan would forego
her lassitude, for in the "stolen time" gained by dropping out there is "such
a liveness . . . you could really feel yourself exist" (62). The uncertainties of
bohemia preclude anaesthetizing complacency, promoting risk and disaffection, sex, movement, and freedom: subjectivity. The narrative's rhetoric
for this condition is signature Beat: "driven by a restlessness for something
new, unknown" (41), Susan wants "to be set in motion, too, to run mind-
lessly," to ride "into the night and emptiness to a place where all the clocks
had stopped and no one cared" (70). This discourse of nothingness and indifference, of urgings and energy and escape, is reminiscent of the literature
of Ginsberg and Kerouac, but the discourse's articulation and embodiment
by a female subject contradict the male writers' representations of women,
in which females are silent, do not survive the existential trial, or thwart
men's freedom.[10]

Come and Join the Dance strongly suggests that, as opposed to the paralysis of conventionality, Beat's dropping out in its restoration of self-awareness provides for subjectivity, a position reminiscent of Julia Kristeva's
argument that women's social function is to "reject everything finite,

definite, structured, loaded with meaning, in the existing state of society"—
to reject gender discourses and differentiation. This "attitude places women
on the side of the explosion of social codes," Kristeva notes, in alliance with
"revolutionary movements" (1981, 166) to overturn establishment re-
gimes. Just so, *Come and Join the Dance*'s Beat theme of dropping out,
its formulation of a revolutionary alternative, rejects the immaturity, passivity, and spectatorship—the object status—of traditional femininity.
College women of the silent generation, the mass of "replaceable" "pastel
girls" (109) whose "faces were the same semester after semester, the same
things . . . said, thought, done" (8), are countered by the bohemian "wild
girls" who "test limits" (63, 47) and drop out. In this, *Come and Join the
Dance* creates an alternative to traditional postwar femininity: neither college "girls" pursuing the "M-R-S" degree, nor hipster women immured in
black, but the inspiriting step out of both establishment and counterculture
tableaux to a revolutionary subculture that recognizes women's existential freedom. Ultimately, the novel delivers female dissidents from oppressive restrictions assigned to women in both hipster and establishment cultures and consequently renovates masculinist Beat discourse, which, in
being stretched to accommodate women, clarifies its continuity with sixties
liberation movements.

The novel, however, also reveals that for white, middle-class postwar
women, dropping out is a complicated move, since they are denied any
privileges beyond skin privilege by patriarchal codes. While the Beat ethic,
styled on a white male model, is voluntary poverty and downward mobility, for women in the 1950s, a college education and economic self-
sufficiency in the middle class were actually rare and unusual; Susan was to
be the first one in her family to graduate from college (124). Yet, it seems
unreal: "in a way, I never went to college at all. I was just putting in time at
a place that was school, because I'd always gone to school. I was afraid of it
ending" (114–115). But Glassman's heroine does end her education; she
drops out to cure herself of anomie, much as Kerouac's Sal Paradise leaves
college because his "life hanging around campus had reached the comple-
tion of its cycle and was stultified. . ." (1957, 10). Cutting so many gym
classes that she fails to complete the requirements for a diploma (106–
107), Susan refuses to make up the credit, choosing instead to transgress
the "peculiar institution of graduation" (114). This signifier evokes the one
for slavery; from the novel's Beat perspective, attending college is regarded

as institutional servitude, an unjust captivity righteously resisted. With classic Beat contempt, Susan sees graduation as an exercise in obedience and order, a spectacle of three hundred "dressed up. . . already vaguely secretarial" "girls" being "counted off and subtracted" (103–104); they are rendered nameless objects of specularization in their graduation march, voided by their ritual certification into the educated class. In this lies one of the novel's contradictions. Women cannot reject privilege in the male Beat manner or enact the male Beat's downwardly mobile refusal of institutions unless they have attained them. Susan embodies this irony, the way the existential rigors of Beat bohemia require her to reject the unprecedented privilege of college to display her fitness as hipster.[11] In the novel, she would escape slavery by dropping out, whereas historically, and paradoxically, women's escape from the subordination meted out to the second sex, as Simone de Beauvoir named women's caste in 1949, could well be to finish college.

Glassman's adventurous, rebellious, questioning protagonist might be dismissed as a chick but, very un-chicklike, Glassman gives Susan consciousness, voice, desire—in other words, a bohemian life outside the dominant culture as well as an equally bohemian freedom to flaunt the Beat norm. Amy L. Friedman posits that male Beat writers "reified. . . female sexuality into a mode of expectation of the female which privileged her (sexual) subservience and silence" (211). Speaking for silenced women—the "dumb and sullen" "girls" that Kerouac's heroes in On the Road would "make" (30); the "little girls, simple and true and tremendously frightened of sex" to whom they will "prove" sex is "beautiful" (48); the "gorgeous country girl" the men would rouse from her dullness (200)—Come and Join the Dance contests Beat men's self-serving representations of having sex with "chicks." Glassman sardonically limns the double bind of female sexuality, in which, to avoid subservience, insignificance, and exploitation, a woman must feign experience. Susan, for instance, has a "bad reputation": "Probably very few people thought she was still a virgin. No one knew how much she lied, how skillful she had become in making adjustments in reality: inferences, suggestions, a few dark strokes, a laugh she had learned from someone" (62–63). By these means, the virgin intimates that she's a sexual adventurer. The heroine's transformation from the object of the scene to its subject-chronicler, from observer to actor, from prevaricator to narrator, explodes the "chick category." Female subjectivity is effected by narrativiz-

ing the repressed text of women's real sexual and existential experience, de-
claring for women the agency and voice mitigated by traditional femininity. As Johnson remarks in *Minor Characters* about her younger self, "It's
only her silence that I wish finally to give up" (262). The novel defies gender traditions that valorize female self-containment and propriety. The
heroine's self-revelation, the narration that forms *Come and Join the Dance,*
stages and signifies the demise of women's silence and transcendence of
chick status.

Clearly, however, the male existential model was problematic for the Beat
female and *Come and Join the Dance* ponders whether and how to adapt it.
One recurrent trope is a refiguring of the Hemingway code of moral behavior, which at mid-century functioned as an important cultural icon for male
Beats such as Kerouac. Allusions to Hemingway, often derisive and ironic,
appear throughout Glassman's text, inscribing the inadequacy for women
writers of the sexual if not the literary model Hemingway provides, and in
this advance the novel's move toward a specifically female Beat subjectivity.
After losing her virginity, for example, Susan wonders, "If something happened, why didn't it really happen? . . . Where was the moment when
everything became luminous and the earth shook? She could remember being bored and not knowing what time it was" (89–90). In Hemingway's
(in)famous euphemism for orgasm in *For Whom the Bell Tolls*, the "earth
moved" (160, 174, 176) for Maria, implying something seismic in sex that
was taken as prescription rather than metaphor. Yet, this figure is, of
course, the measure of male self-congratulation. As the ersatz Hemingway
rhetoric of Susan's sexual disappointment elucidates, the role assigned to
women in masculinist culture is a source of dissatisfaction, self-doubt, and
the perception of lack. The Hemingway model cannot adequately account
for female subjectivity since it is constructed on female self-effacement, on
female gratitude for earth-shaking male attention. Masculinist constructions may provide a model of subjectivity, and some attributes of the male
model can be emulated, as with Hemingway's style, but the prescriptive
roles assigned to women must be refused.

As the Hemingway trope suggests, *Come and Join the Dance* situates itself
in literary history with a temperamental affinity to modernism, but the
"cool," restrained style is deployed in the service of "hot" self-expression
and modes of subjectivity, a combination which results in a central Beat
contradiction.[12] Rather than the breathless jazzy endless lines and ebullient

emotions of "hot" Beat stylist Kerouac, Glassman's minimalist, succinct prose mannerisms embody Beat "cool" via the elegant restraint of Henry James, Glassman's acknowledged mentor, and the sparseness of modernist stylists like Hemingway and, later, Joan Didion. The language is contained, inert, not an unnecessary muscle moving; the dispassionate, clipped syntax and diction of understated feeling mark Glassman's aesthetic and style. Registering anomie, the narrative has an emotional climate, a gestalt of incipient fragmentation. This climate derives in part from the intellectual existentialism of postwar New York, where hipsters read Gide, Nietzsche, and Kierkegaard, trying to account for the postwar fatigue and sense of dislocation. It also derives in part from, and signifies, a defining state of the feminine, in which the self is atomized by its objectification in the hegemonic male gaze.

Yet, if the novel moves and speaks stylistically with indirection, coolness, and restraint, in contrast, its characterization of Beat female subjectivity appropriates and follows Kerouac's model for male subjectivity, which valorizes "hot" Beat talkativeness and lack of restraint over "cool," "laconic" effeteness (1959, 362–363). This dichotomy is figured in *Come and Join the Dance* as a contradiction of the novel's "cool" style with its "hot" content. Although Hemingway is evoked in injunctions against expressing emotion, and in valorizations of stoic self-containment and Garboesque insulation, the evocations are simultaneously negated: Susan concludes she would prefer "to feel frightened rather than feel nothing at all" (15); silent stoicism is not heroic but "a kind of failure" (17). To refrain from speaking and articulating painful or confusing matters, as in Hemingway, evokes the influential style of withholding masculinity disseminated through modernist literary and popular twentieth-century culture alike. But this model only perpetuates the silence of female repression. Susan, admonished by her lover Anthony to control her feelings, flashes back the novel's credo for its outlaw wild girls: "I think you have to get upset!" (22). Glassman's discourse of female subjectivity insists on disorder, transgression, forbidden excess, volubility: "trouble's better than nothing" (47), better than femininity's "nothing" of repressed desire and conformity. It is, therefore, incumbent on the heroine to narrate, to become by achieving voice. "Telling" is paramount. She must spill out feelings, confessions, histories, even engage in novel-making: Susan observes that "no act ever seemed complete until it had been made public and a little fictitious" (41). As Kristeva notes, the

woman novelist "creates an imaginary story through which she constitutes an identity" (166); and just so for Johnson, who stated that "only the
publication of my novel would transform my existence into what I wanted
it to be" (1983, 122). Affording identity and visibility, invention makes
heroic and exemplary the telling that assures subjectivity. Fictitiousness
here is not the stereotype of female deceit but the female entry into history.[13] The directive to write is the directive to enter literature. Glassman's
novel, providing her voice, bids to install her among the ranks of her peers,
the male Beat writers such as Holmes and Kerouac, Ginsberg, and LeRoi
Jones.

Beat female resistance to both mainstream and hipster gender negations
is also registered and rendered textually and narratively in the matter of ac-
quisition and alteration of voice. The narrative marks shifts in Susan's discourse from passive to declarative constructions: she evolves from "never
really knowing whether or not I mean what I'm saying" (20–21)—from un-
certainty of self-knowledge and a consequent passive self-construction—to
a declarative self-possession, the certain knowledge of "what it meant . . . I
know what it meant" (175). The shift in emphasis here from knowing to
meaning suggests an evolution from understanding to interpretation, from
seeing to naming. Such a shift signifies subjectivity. The intention to find
significance in experience melts the anomie of being gendered female and
silenced. The magnitude of this is evinced in Susan's authorship of her own
subjectivity; her agency is not effected by a Pygmalion makeover, as Kerouac's men would overhaul women to be perfect foils,[14] but, rather, by self-
development. Her patronizing older lover, Peter, deems Susan "worth
saving" but Glassman's Beat move is to refuse to assign him the mission.
Like the prototypical *sui generis* Beat hero, Susan will make herself; she will
be "anything [she] want[s]," "anything" she decides to be (22). She will
cease to be produced by operations of the male establishment or bohemian
expectations of women and instead author(ize) herself, mimicking the story
of this narrative in which she ceases to be the passive object and becomes
the active subject. Thus, the narrative enacts the female agency that is antidote to the symptomatic anomie of its heroine.

Contentions of the "chick category" and resistance to female passivity
and alienation find their most explicit expression in the arena of sexual relations, in Susan's contemplation and arrangement of "a gratuitous act of
sex" (56), a figure inspired by Glassman's reading of Gide (Grace 1999b,

114). The phrase underscores an axiomatic reality, chronicled in *Minor Characters,* that for women in the 1950s the *acte gratuit* of the existential trial to feel in the face of nothingness is to have sex outside marriage in the face of illegal abortion and in the unavailability of effective birth control (1983, 94–97; 110–115; 249). That is, sexual freedom for women is the existential *acte gratuit* at the same time as it is the sine qua non of individuality. Here, the novel embraces for its heroine a Beat (male) sexual ethos. Virginity is seen not as a barter commodity that secures women's cultural survival through marriage, but as a state of infantilization and passive spectatorship: "graduating a virgin was against all her principles. She was sick of being a child, sick of being only a member of the audience" (47). Yet in this rejection of the feminine, Susan attains male equipoise and self-reliance. Kristeva observes that in a "culture where the speaking subjects are conceived of as masters of their speech, they have what is called 'phallic' position," and, although she sees textual language calling "into question the very posture of this mastery" (165), the trope Kristeva uses even for the female subject who writes, the signifier the "'phallic' position," suggests gender's irremediable saturation of constructions of subjectivity. As a subject who must tell or fictionalize, Susan moves into the masculine, the "'phallic' position" of language. This move has the paradoxical discursive potential of erasing Susan as a gendered woman so as to inscribe her as an agent or individual; to figure her as a Beat in the usual (male) sense.

Thus, Susan is rendered a Beat subject by her capacity for masculine privilege, the ultimate expression of this being her (re)positioning as the privileged consumer of sex. In her sexual awakening, Susan expends men: she rejects Jerry, for "when he began to kiss her, she could not shut her eyes" (30); decides to lose her virginity with Anthony; seduces Peter. In *Minor Characters,* Johnson traces "the new self-consciousness about coming or not coming [that made] it a man's duty and triumph that both should come, and a woman's shame if she didn't" (93), which *Come and Join the Dance* explores and critiques in Susan's two affairs. The 1950s pressure on women to "let go" (1983, 99) is, as Johnson suggests, a pseudofreedom that amounts to another way to keep women subservient; to enforce the dissimulations—the faked orgasms—of the powerless. Reversing cultural données that blame women for their sexual incapacity, Susan's sexual relations with immature Anthony and seasoned Peter, supplicants for her favor, focus on both men's failure to bring her to orgasm (93, 175). The novel observes that desirable and desirous men are not necessarily competent lovers, deflating Norman Mailer's promotion of hipsters in *The White Negro* as sexually proficient.

Wryly commenting on women's education and postwar liberalism—"I know everything [about sex]. I had Modern Living as a freshman" (82)— the narrative authorizes for Susan the expectation of sexual satisfaction and makes the men liable for her pleasure, contending the 1950s Freudian discourse which blamed women for sexual failures that were overdetermined by masculinist social norms.[15] Susan's poise and self-reliance unnerve Anthony; he fears that his lackluster sexual performance has estranged her, a male self-doubt rarely voiced by male Beat writers.[16] But, here, male failure provides opportunity for female subjectivity, as Susan tells Anthony, "'It [the sex act] had nothing to do with you. It was an experiment.'. . . she had never been more honest" (93–94). Repositioning the male from his usual superiority to her subordinate object or "experiment," Susan's "honesty" signifies the refusal of femininity's repressive dissimulations in favor of the existential engagement that arrests alienation.

Possibly the novel's most striking bid for Beat female subjectivity is its re-formation and termination of the road narrative so strongly identified with male Beats. Its decline is so pivotal that both penultimate chapters 19 and 20 are devoted to it. The road tale is a foundation and staple of mainstream and Beat American literature borrowed from European archetypes and, beginning with the texts of colonial settlement, extending well into the mid-twentieth century and Beat generation writing by Kerouac and others. *Come and Join the Dance* transgresses the road tale's traditions by making a woman the protagonist of its quest narrative. It abolishes the stock materials of the American road tale—vehicle, travel, escape—by aborting the entire expedition and shifting its focus to the kind of movement produced in women's typically interiorized flights, journeys to existential and sexual revelation, not destinations on the road away from home. These emendations to the generic road narrative exemplify the subvert/install double move which Hutcheon observes characterizes so many postwar, postmodern texts.

It is Peter, Susan's older lover and subterranean hipster-as-cold-war individual, who represents the novel's conventional Beat road hero. He is reminiscent of both Sal and Dean of *On the Road,* which Glassman read during the time she was writing her novel; he is thinker and doer, intellectual and driver, writer and Kerouacian "mad one," a man constantly in motion, making the rounds of cafés and bars and bookstores in the story's six blocks of New York City (13) or driving off in his 1938 Packard (19, 57, 73, 158). Peter's road binges to Chicago and places in New York State (19) inscribe escape from constraint and the way motion is an antidote to frustration and angst: his "car was the place where he really lived. . . a curious desperate joy possessed Peter at the wheel as long as everything went fast, and he always kept the back seat littered with the fragmentary preparations for a journey" (73). This discourse that links Peter to his car to his existential condition evokes the classic road tale as reinterpreted in the postwar era by Kerouac.

The novel's female appropriation of this male mythic genre negates the canon and refigures Beat, as in the novel's opening in which, pinned by the gaze of sixty-three concentrating "girls," Melville, the peripatetic adventurer, is made their captive, a specimen of their scrutiny, his movement thwarted, his road blocked. When Peter embarks on what proves to be his final odyssey in his Packard, with Susan in tow, the novel's closing on this "buddy" image has a sardonic congruity with its opening on Melville: refusing to "work" Melville anymore, Susan, headed for Paris, would take the road herself. She must authorize her own adventure; bringing women on the road with men will not make the Beat journey accessible to them for they are never going to be the archetypal "buddy": "Suppose you wanted to go wandering with him and you knew that he would never take you along and night after night you watched him go—and you were never able to say 'Take me with you'" (150).[17] A central challenge in taking on the quest narrative, which is one way to regard the mission of this novel, is to cancel the gender inequity that shapes the genre, the stipulation that women are hobbled unless escorted by men, or always already Penelopes resignedly awaiting the Ulyssean return. In *Come and Join the Dance,* the Beat female solution is radical: drop Homer and Melville; or, if women cannot take the road, terminate journeying itself. The road tale, the male escape from civilization, is predicated on having women and domesticity to leave. Just so, Susan's presence with Peter negates the road narrative, which, when stretched to accommodate women or forced to integrate the sexes, ceases as itself. Thus, the re-formation of the road tale mandates that Peter's journey come to a stop.

The novel's protofeminist denouement anticipates the second-wave women's movement. With its diminution of male privilege and concomitant augmentation of female status, it sounds impending changes in gender roles. In parallel plottings, just as Susan foregoes her diploma for flouting the college's rules, Peter is denied his car when it breaks down, but the two moves signify differently. Susan has achieved the Beat masculine condition of rejecting institutions, the hipster's antiestablishment disdain, while Peter has achieved the feminine condition of being denied, in this case, tools for freedom or pleasure. This plotting frees the Beat female to the status of the male while the Beat male becomes truly downwardly mobile, reaching the disaffection of the disempowered, which is ostensibly the point of dropping out for white Beat men. When the decrepit Packard must be junked, it signifies the novel's expiration of the road discourse as rendered by Kerouac, Ginsberg, and William S. Burroughs to express iconoclastic male subjectivity.[18] In its obvious metaphoric capacity, this discourse of the machine which equals power which equals mobility comprises and figures male subjectivity; here, the debilitated machine signifies the decline of male power. Concomitantly, the termination of the road narrative that conveys the Beat male discourse serves as a prelude to Susan and Peter's sexual consummation, which requires equality, for in Glassman's Beat discourse, only after women and men are set in horizontal, not vertical, alliance, can they have sexual relations.

It is the termination of the road tale that achieves gender parity for the novel's New Bohemians (Gruen), or Beats, for it resituates Peter at Susan's level by making him a denizen of urban domesticity, the way women are stranded at home by patriarchal prohibition:

> She was thinking about how it would be for Peter now [without the car], how he would wake up in his apartment each day and find that more dust had settled overnight, how he would go out for breakfast because there weren't any clean cups, how he would drift up and down Broadway until he was tired enough to sleep again. (162)

Stalled, trapped, landlocked without his car, emasculated like Melville under the scrutiny of college girls, Peter would drift now rather than race in society like an archetypal Beat hero. Enraged, smashing his broken-down car and junking it (168), Peter is reduced to travel by taxi, passive in the hands of drivers for hire, which provides a clear contrast to such scenes in

On the Road in which, when a burned-out car is abandoned, Sal and Dean simply find another vehicle and continue their journey. The destruction in *Come and Join the Dance* of the determinants of the road tale and the diminution of the road hero provide for the heroine's self-assertion: her enactment of Beat subjectivity and agency. Seated with Peter in the taxi, Susan expresses her desire for and attraction to him: "Suddenly she couldn't bear not telling him in some way that she was here with him, that she hadn't just come for the ride, couldn't bear not touching him. . . . She turned to Peter, put her arms around him, held him close to her" (172). As the sexual aggressor, Susan negates the feminine subordination of the silent, acquiescent chick, a breakthrough which occurs at the cost of male mobility and the viability of the road tale as an existential course. This anticipates the decline of white male hegemony during the women's liberation movements of the late 1960s and early seventies. Just so, Susan proves false the 1950s Freudian view of female sexual incapacity and joins the dance, the Beat life of "kicks" and sex, subjectivity and desire that the women's movement later appropriated for many women, not just Beats.

The novel completes its renovation of Beat discourse by extending to the female bohemian the sexual agency men possess; it tells its scene of sexual connection as an event staged for and judged by the female lover. Satisfaction of perspective takes the place of sexual gratification. Delivered by the taxi to Peter's apartment, the lovers consummate their attraction in the novel's brief last chapter. Susan's imminent but not-reached orgasm does not signify sexual incapacity here, but rather, idiomatically, her empowerment. Glassman renders this unclimactic event with characteristic lucidity: during sex, Susan "felt herself becoming flooded with light . . . float[ing] up, up—toward something she had almost reached" (174), an image of the orgasmic brink. Asserting that the sex "was good anyway. . . . It was what it meant. . . . I knew what it meant" (175), Susan claims the sexual agency of the wild girls, renouncing the passive silence of the "chick category" for the élan and power of the (Beat) male. Leveling but not abolishing tropes of gender difference, the Beat female arrival is evinced in the narrative's denouement when Susan renders Peter the object of her departing gaze; now she "knows" Peter, she "can see" him (172). In Laura Mulvey's lexicon, Susan moves from being the object of the gaze to becoming the subject-gazer. In this scene, her judgment and evaluation are foregrounded, asserting women's subjectivity in this incipient Beat bohemia. In the novel's one-line last paragraph, "And then she went" (176)—out of Peter's apartment, off to Paris—Susan becomes protagonist of her own quest narrative, dropping out of bohemia as well as college. Refusing to be the chick, Susan renounces her assigned role in Beat discourse and authors her own subjectivity. "And then she went": no longer passenger or spectator, her renunciation of submission expands and reconstitutes notions of Beat iconoclasm. With this narrative, shaking off her silence, the Beat female subject emerges, contending and refiguring what it means to be Beat.

Notes

1. Joyce Glassman is the signatory of one novel, *Come and Join the Dance,* while Joyce Johnson is the author of novels, prose fiction, and journalism, and is the Beat memoirist and historian. Preserving the distinction between the two names/two selves calls attention to the author as a young, unmarried writer of her first novel, a habitué of Beat scenes and hip New York enclaves who was working to establish herself in a male-dominated world—both the Beat scene and the world of work—without becoming a chick. The second name, "Joyce Johnson," is that of the established writer, editor, teacher. The subject of this essay is the neophyte.

2. See Helen McNeil, "The Archeology of Gender in the Beat Movement," and Amy L. Friedman, "'I saw my new name': Women Writers of the Beat Generation." In neither of these recent survey essays is Joyce Johnson's first novel mentioned, even as each essay addresses the elision of female writers from the Beat canon; both critics see Johnson merely as a memoirist with connections. As Friedman puts it, "Novelist Joyce Johnson . . . was involved with Kerouac at the time *On the Road* was published and is a Beat memoirist" (201); for McNeil, "Joyce Johnson should be added to the list [of eight women writers out of a total of 67 Beat writers included in Ann Charters's 1979 bibliographical compilation] for her memoir *Minor Characters*" (193). McNeil refers to Ann Charters's 1983 volumes for the *Dictionary of Literary Biography, The Beats, Literary Bohemians in Postwar America.*

3. Brenda Knight mentions *Come and Join the Dance* twice in her survey of Beat women artists, *Women of the Beat Generation: The Writers, Artists, and Muses at the Heart of a Revolution,* but the novel is mentioned by title, not discussed (168, 176); Johnson's two other novels are not cited. The full discussion of Johnson's significance and achievement is shortsightedly confined to her memoir *Minor Characters* and her affair with Kerouac.

4. For example, see Bonnie Bremser, Diane di Prima (1969), Hettie Jones (1990), Carolyn Cassady. All four prose texts are billed as memoir, rarely dis-

cussed, and have not been examined either in terms of feminist theories of the memoir form for women writers—although this lapse is redressed in this volume; see Nancy Grace, "Snapshots, Sand Paintings and Celluloid"—or as texts whose genre should be interrogated with regard to narrative shape and invention.

5. This indubitably Beat gesture or double move suggests Beat anticipations of the postmodern, or Beat pre-postmodernism. For an extended discussion of Beat pre-postmodernism, see my essay "'You're putting me on': Jack Kerouac and the Postmodern Emergence."

6. Johnson recounts in *Minor Characters* that "[i]n the fall of '56 . . . just turning twenty-one . . . I found a new job at another literary agency . . . moved into a new apartment of my own . . . [and] worked on the novel about Barnard I'd begun in Hiram Hayden's [novel writing] workshop" in 1955 (107, 121). This unnamed book is certainly *Come and Join the Dance* and, far from being just a "novel about Barnard," it is consumed by the protagonist's effort to transcend the paralyzing expectations for bourgeois college women of the fifties to marry and conform.

7. See *Door Wide Open* (Johnson and Kerouac 2000) for this same formulation or trope about bohemia and confinement to straight communities. With her mother secretly asking her friends questions about her, Joyce Glassman writes to Jack Kerouac that she's "living in the middle of a spy ring" (104).

8. See Sukenick and Wakefield for detailed accounts of the bars, cafés, all-night cafeterias, and jazz spots that served as nuclei for nascent postwar bohemian writer-artist, abstract expressionist, bebop scenes in which women, when they are noticed at all, serve as witnesses to that history or as scenery framing the really important occurrences, like Jackson Pollock's fights or Dylan Thomas's seductions.

9. See Shulman, Johnson 1983, and memoirs by women of the Beat generation listed in note 4.

10. In Ginsberg, the female archetype of "the best minds of my generation destroyed by madness" is actually of the antecedent generation: his mother, Naomi, commemorated for her madness and self-destruction by fantasized political persecution in "Kaddish" (1961). Kerouac offers more female figures destroyed by countercultural existentialism, especially Mardou Fox of *The Subterraneans* (1958), Mary Lou of *On the Road* (1957), and Tristessa of the eponymous novel (1960).

11. In Shulman's *Burning Questions*, the heroine, Zane, proving her fitness for bohemia, refuses to go to college; instead, she moves to Greenwich Village (from her home in Ohio) and seeks out beat bohemians. Although she is treated as a chick and exploited for sex and rent money, her hopes for agency are nurtured until they can be realized in the second-wave women's movement that began in the late 1960s.

12. See Jack Kerouac, "The Origins of the Beat Generation," in which he makes distinctions between "hot" and "cool," and sees most artists belonging to the "hot school," although some are "fifty fifty" and a few "hot" ones like him "cooled it"

down after encountering Buddhism (363). While Kerouac allows for degrees of "hot" and "cool," and even mixtures, it is Glassman's distinction to develop the combination of a "hot" style of subjectivity by means of a "cool" literary discourse.

13. Shulman's *Burning Questions* provides an account of the early second-wave women's movement in the Third Street Circle cell of the novel, where women meet and endlessly talk themselves to subjectivity. Later in the novel the talk fest moves to the New Space, a café, but the scene exemplifies the same principle.

14. See *On the Road* and Sal and Dean's continual consternation with women as they are; their repeated assessments of what renovations would need to be made in Camille or Mary Lou or Okie Frankie or Inez or Terry or Rita Bettencourt so that the women would better fit with and accommodate the desires of men like Sal and Dean.

15. In *Burning Questions,* Shulman depicts the first bohemian sexual encounters of the novel's eighteen-year-old protagonist in New York. Of her first Greenwich Village encounter with a Beat poet, in 1958, Shulman writes that Zane "was so intimidated, so terrified of Marshal Braine, that [she] ought to have been quite frigid" (70). The expectation of women's fear of sexually aggressive or sophisticated men and their failure to achieve sexual satisfaction is implied and ironized in Shulman's discourse. Here, Shulman mocks but nevertheles confronts the 1950s burden placed on women, the accusation of frigidity if they did not at least seem to reach orgasm.

16. In Kerouac's *On the Road,* there is an understated scene in which the protagonist Sal Paradise seems to imply he has been a sexual disappointment to a woman: Rita Bettencourt "was a nice little girl, simple and true, and tremendously frightened of sex. I told her it was beautiful. I wanted to prove this to her. She let me prove it, but I was too impatient, and proved nothing" (48). As in *Come and Join the Dance,* it is the male who short-circuits the sexual experience, but such admissions are extremely rare in Kerouac or other male Beat writers, and are never ascribed to such sexual heroes as Dean Moriarty.

17. Johnson writes in *Minor Characters* that "I'd listen to [Kerouac] with delight and pain, seeing all the pictures he painted so well for me, wanting to go with him. Could he ever include a woman in his journeys? I didn't altogether see why not. Whenever I tried to raise the question, he'd stop me by saying that what I really wanted were babies" (142). Further on, she recounts a waterfront prowl with Kerouac: "Here and there at the ends of the dead-end streets were dim taverns all brown inside, with dock workers and sailors steadily drinking under yellow lights. There were no women in this nighttime world . . . I'd never seen anything like it before. It was strange to think that because of my sex I'd probably never see any of this again, and would probably never have seen it at all if it hadn't been for Jack" (145).

18. See not only Kerouac's obvious road tales, but also consider that Ginsberg's

Howl is a road narrative in unwinding rhythmic verse—its visions unroll geo-graphically across the United States—and that Burroughs's trilogy of *Junky, Queer,* and *The Yage Letters* (Burroughs and Ginsberg) is precisely a road tale on its most explicit level, for it moves progressively south, geographically and symbolically away from constraint to freedom, moving as it does from New York to the very tip end of South America, a pattern which is evident when the novels are read in the chronological order of the travels given above (as opposed to their publication order).

What I See in
How I Became
Hettie Jones

Barrett Watten

Does poetry have any knowledge, and if so, what? At times one feels as if the blank space of the poetic were a cult object to quantify the unknown. Knowing anything—or more important not knowing anything—in terms of poetry enters one into larger questions of the possibility of the world, and it may be that many who pass through poetry, but do not remain with it, do so for that reason. . . . [But] for us, increasingly, the poetic can only be known as its history. First we were displaced by it, and then we reasoned why. After that, we had knowledge.[1]

I

Does poetry have any knowledge? In poetry, a rigid distinction between knowledge as positive—a concern with the facts of the world and our experience in it—and not knowing as negative—that which exceeds our understanding, which we may desire but cannot know—simply does not exist. If there were such a distinction, we might be tempted to label positive knowledge a matter of content, reserving questions of not knowing to form as a locus of defamiliarization. Such a splitting of form and content in poetry, and the privileging of one over the other, is a commonplace in contemporary discussions of poetics. But even if we were to agree with Robert Creeley's famous dictum that "form is never more than an *extension* of content,"[2] the question would still remain: What is content? Is the form of the poem not also a significant element of its content—as it everywhere is in Creeley's own work? From an opposite perspective, "formalism" has been taken to stand for a privileging of aesthetic autonomy that is insensitive to the content of our lives, and that masks its universalizing claims through modes of defamiliarization and distancing. A pernicious splitting (in virtually psychoanalytic terms) has resulted that permits unexamined modes of identification and ascription—with either form or content as political absolutes—to run rampant. "Formalism" has conventionally come to denote, for both adherents and critics, a separation of signifier from signified that ignores determinants outside the work of art, while an equally blind notion of a poetic "materialism" sees the poem as transparent to the historical conditions that created it. A stability of practice has set in around both conventions.

A significant range of current language-centered poetry, for instance, seems to accept a contextless formalism as the basis of its aesthetic effects.[3] Does such poetry defer knowledge to contexts not yet determined by the poem, an undisclosed futurity or that which cannot be known in the unconscious—thus enacting a primarily "differential" rather than referential function? Is the knowledge gained by an experience of such poetry merely in its separation from experiential contexts, toward futurity or the unknown, and not in terms of anything represented within it? If so, then what is the knowledge gained from the experience of poetry in its nonreferential aspects—or is knowledge, rather, effaced by poetry, what Russian poet Arkadii Dragomoshchenko has called an "eroticism of forgetting"? Is the knowledge of poetry that results primarily a matter of apperception, a "blank space of the poetic," "a cult object to quantify the unknown" that conveys no commitment to the world, even if it is only encountered in specific cultural contexts, at a given point in time? How, then, do we account for the tradition in American poetry, from George Oppen's *Discrete Series* (1966) and Charles Olson's *Maximus Poems* (1983) to expressivist lyrics and the New Sentence, in which poetry is identified with a knowledge of mundane particulars and a belief in their necessity? If poetry contains particulars, is it only to separate them from any claims to ultimate knowledge of them? The experience of poetry, in this radical differentiation of form from content—what kind of knowledge is that?

The essay that follows explores another locus for thinking through the relation of form and content: the divergence of the possibility of poetry as material practice in the writings of Hettie Jones and LeRoi Jones/Amiri Baraka at a crucial historical moment. Their mutual but not entirely acknowledged collaboration, and the destruction of that relationship, identifies a moment of exchange and betrayal that has a great deal to say about the relation between whatever we might think of poetic agency, or "form," and its historical motivation, or "content." The splitting here is gendered, even as it leads to the historic creation of a politicized racial aesthetic in the Black Arts movement. Poetry practice, race, and gender are in their examples obdurate and irreducible, in terms of both form and content: I am not seeking to privilege one aspect over the other. What is more interesting is the baseline historicity of these events, and an ethics that takes into account the kinds of knowledge poetic form generates as it proves how irreducible matters of content are, even as it imagines kinds of agency that transcend them. Agency, too, has its privileges: what has not been recovered yet are the gendered dynamics and material history of forms of poetry that take on political agency but that, in themselves, do not entirely represent it.

II

Roughly seven years (1957–1964) of a life in and around poetry are recorded in Hettie Jones's autobiography, *How I Became Hettie Jones* (1990), a testament to an experience of passing through poetry for one who, in every sense, remains "with it" but who, at the time, wrote little of it. Her memoir not only details the life and times of its author and the literary scene in New York as the bohemian 1950s evolved into the countercultural 1960s, but is an exemplary account of the relation of poetry to knowledge, seen in terms of an historically significant private/public experience of it. The dividing line between public and private is central here; the relation of poetry to knowledge is intimately connected to her marriage with LeRoi Jones as well as to the book's overarching question, Who is Hettie Jones? The problematic of identity is manifold and epochal for both authors: on the one hand, the emergence of "the poet" is depicted in its precise cultural context as LeRoi Jones moves from what he called the "aesthetic" period of his avant-garde work to the Black Arts movement and a new identity as Amiri Baraka; on the other, the "knowledge" of poetry becomes the necessity of Hettie Jones's narration of her transformation from Hettie Cohen, not only through marriage, to Hettie Jones, a shift of identity in racial and cultural terms that is only to be completed with the writing of her book.

The notion of poetry as not knowing and differential is a provisional one, which I would not like to accept as a condition for continued involvement with poetry. If poetry were, in fact, a condition of not knowing, one might reasonably consider discontinuing involvement with it[4] — even as the experience of that disengagement would give positive knowledge of poetry. Hettie Jones's narrative is a recuperation of just such a discontinuity, seen as divided between her experience of LeRoi Jones as the poet who cannot be known and Hettie Jones as the author who gains knowledge of poetry in her account of him. If one were to discontinue involvement with poetry, in other words, the experience of it might be represented in a manner like Hettie Jones's narrative of her marriage to the non–self-identical poet who became Amiri Baraka. The figure of the poet in LeRoi Jones aligns, in this analogy, with the differential, because he is, precisely in terms of Hettie Jones's narration of knowledge, at once outside the book's depicted action even as he is the central figure within it—and because being "outside" has everything to do with Jones/Baraka's work. In his nonidentity as "Jones" (moving toward at least two identities as "Baraka"), he is the catalyst for a profound transformation in Hettie Jones's life, from marital and literary partnership to deep concerns with the coherence of her own identity. As he reaches toward a later politics of identity, a non–self-identical LeRoi Jones emerges as an author precisely as figure in relation to the ground he later construes Hettie Cohen to be—an inadequate identity to whom he was, during a formative period, married.[5]

Poetry and knowledge are here, if not in our best arrangements, polarized along gender lines; knowing the cultural context of the 1950s, with its romance of abstract sublimity measurable in terms of a Gross National Product of broken dishes, should suffice for the suspension of disbelief needed to accept that distinction. In the 1950s, poet as maker meant making it in all senses, in terms both of career and of display behavior directed toward competing males; LeRoi Jones offers an index of the racial marking of that behavior. Male artists in the homosocial milieux of the 1950s often saw themselves as mobile figures for meaning—as allegories, in fact, where the displaced tenor of the soul's unfolding became the vehicle for their careers. Hettie Jones's narrative of bohemian marriage is framed by a form of life that produced allegory in that sense—if not the perpetual one that Olson, following Keats, celebrated—even as her narrative undermines and transforms it. In any case, poetry as defined solely in terms of the production of the poet is an inadequate account of agency, precisely in terms of its shifting and unfolding horizons of allegorical meaning. Hettie Jones's narrative offers an alternate horizon for the partial acts of the poet, which are revised as well by his subsequent shifts of identity and vocation as he moves through the sequence of epochal periods in his career. Race adds a further dimension to these gendered dynamics, so that while change of name is a central concern for both authors, very different cultural logics are inscribed in their names. Hettie Cohen is only Hettie Jones after writing her autobiography (and not simply after marrying Jones); it is a question of resolving authorship and marriage.[6] On the other hand, Jones changes his name from Everett Leroy to LeRoi at the outset of his career through what he calls his "transitional" period; becomes Imamu Amiri Baraka in his Black Nationalist phase (1965–1974); drops "Imamu" in the Third World Marxist phase (from 1974); but keeps "LeRoi Jones" as authorial in both editions of his autobiography and in his selected writings.[7] The names "LeRoi Jones" and "Amiri Baraka" are a matter of cultural politics. Hettie Cohen did not become Hettie Jones in the same way that LeRoi Jones became Amiri Baraka, even as the two transformations are linked.

Hettie Jones's act of self-naming takes place, not in an act of authorial framing outside the text, but in the fact of her narration. *How I Became Hettie Jones* is the most recent of an emerging series of accounts of 1950s masculinist culture by women who had subordinate roles within it, including Carolyn Cassady's *Off the Road* (1990) and Joyce Johnson's *Minor Characters* (1983). Of her identification with Johnson, Hettie writes:

"We shared what was most important to us: common assumptions about our uncommon lives. We lived outside, as if. As if we were men? As if we were newer, freer versions of ourselves? There have always been women like us. Poverty, and self-support is enough dominion" (81). The formula "his wife is a poet too" clearly would not work for her, either during her marriage or after, even as she frequently describes situations where she willingly plays the role of helpmate to further Jones's career. At the same time, she struggles to jumpstart a writing career of her own; one of the

virtues of her narrative is the exactness with which she describes the frus-
trations of not being able to find her vocation as a poet. Baraka reads this
as a claim to martyrdom,[8] but it is more structurally significant than that,
and at the same time more modest: she sees her problem, first, as a lack of
self-confidence; second, as a lack of means; and only lastly in terms of a
specific lack of sympathy or encouragement. In a larger sense, however,
Hettie Jones's knowledge of poetry in terms of her inability to write it is
framed as an alienation of herself that coincides with LeRoi Jones's success
and the impossibility of their marriage. (The irony of becoming a "successful" radical was something Jones himself would come to abhor even as, according to Hettie, he thrived on the attention.) The telos of his career as an
occasion of cultural history contrasts with her narrative of personal dis-
and re-integration in which success heightens the social contradictions
it was meant to address (not exactly news in America). It is here that not
writing poetry becomes a figure for knowledge of it, in several senses:
against the background of the recognition of his career, with its public trajectory and series of rejections of all that had gone before; in the material
history of her at times rewarding but usually unrecognized literary (and
domestic) labor; and in the milieu of writers and writing that inform the
sense of literary style through which she achieves her identity in writing. In
precisely material terms, the lack of poetry becomes literary in the course
of her book.

In this sense, as seldom in critical accounts of either New American
poetry or the Black Arts movement, poetry is identified with lack in her
narrative, configuring a historically important relation of nonidentity to
identity. For Hettie Cohen, this lack is, to begin with, her nonliterariness—
not positioned as a poet, she cannot come to terms with writing poetry—
but it is later described by Baraka in terms of determining social factors
(and indexed to negative contexts for his later politics of identity as well):

> Nellie [Hettie] had something of an inferiority complex. First, she'd
> been out in Long Island under the heavy sun of gentile suburbia, try-
> ing to grow and having to relate to whatever the dominant image and
> peer pressure was for the Jewish middle-class yearning for American
> middle-classdom. . . . The black middle class suffers from the same
> kind of malady, a lack of self-esteem caused by the great nation chau-
> vinism that is so much a part of American life. (1984, 213)

Baraka identifies with Hettie as a figure of lack when he equates "White supremacy [and] anti-Semitism" as both creating the internalized self-hatred that, everywhere in Jones/Baraka's work, is identified with the "middle class." This interpellation is seen as a part of "the cultural aggression of the norm of U.S. life" (213)—but, instead of fitting subject to society, as it does for Louis Althusser, interpellation creates "paradoxical questions in the minds of its young victims. And so the swarms of self-doubts that confused the young Nellie Kohn" (213). The lack of identity and the concomitant lack of poetry, then, are related to a lack of recognition that Jacques Lacan would describe in terms of being the subject of a gaze that cannot see and that thus refuses to confer recognition.[9] At the same time, a moment of social reproduction occurs when Jones identifies Hettie with the cultural aggression that makes her a figure for nonidentity and lack—a moment enacted over the course of their marriage as a process of unequal exchange and one-sided transformation that creates the time line of Hettie's narration.[10] What this ends up being for Hettie is rejection, a lack of recognition concretized as the recognition of her lack—difficult for anyone to go through, even more to become, and even more to write about. This rejection occurs, to begin with, in the withdrawal of the poet in purely personal terms ("Whenever Roi came to take the children he would speak to me from across the room, as if he didn't want to get a good look" [1990, 228]), but it will soon be acted out in more public ways. In her account:

> As if to refute the fact that he'd ever settled elsewhere, his new book, a collection of essays, was titled *Home.* He would neither speak to me nor send money, and wrote instructing me to reach him only through his parents. He did not call the children; they were driven to see him by emissaries. Eventually he changed his name to Imamu Amiri Baraka, and someone told me, though I never saw it, of a newspaper interview in which he denied my existence. (1990, 231)[11]

Baraka describes the transformation as slow to begin ("It was the feeling that Nellie was outside my concerns, that we did not connect up. . . . I had begun to see her as white! Before, even when I thought she was white, I had never felt anything negative" [1984, 287]), but inevitably reinforced by the world at large: "According to many biographies and accounts of my life, it ended, both the living of it and the writing in reflection of it, when I left the 'white world.' They would not honor my life or work" (425). The epistemological status of the last word is important here, insofar as it occupies a central place, if an antagonistic one, in Baraka's narrative. It is, as well, a crucial motivation for Hettie Jones, but one that is distributed through the entirety of her narrative in its concern for a wider context for recognition. In her act of claiming identity, she will rescript her life with LeRoi Jones, as well as Baraka's narrative, in contextual terms—but ones that refuse to position race as antagonistic. Her portrayal of Jones is, in this sense, strategically considerate and low key. In her account, LeRoi Jones makes it as a result of the success of his poetry (arriving with the appearance of *The New American Poetry* [1960] and his first book, *Preface to a Twenty-Volume Suicide Note* [1961]), even as his success is prefigured by the literary networks mutually constructed by Jones and Hettie in the editing and publishing of *Yugen* and Totem Press (as likewise with *The Floating Bear,* which LeRoi Jones co-edited with Diane di Prima).[12] Equally material to the construction of authorship would be the "floating world" of an interracial scene that was intimately a part of their relationship as well as definitive of the emerging counterculture.[13] Hettie Jones describes the horizons of this cultural collaboration, on every level, as at times risky and uncertain ("I realized we might get hurt or killed—and him more likely" [1990, 37]) but always open and progressive. LeRoi Jones's identity as author, readers of her memoir would understand, was established in a world of cross-racial identification.

But particularly with the theatrical success of his plays, beginning with the March 1964 production of *Dutchman* (which won an Obie) and later *The Slave,* the terms of Jones's recognition changed. Moving from poetry to theater meant a conscious shift from a literary horizon to one more directly connected with agency; for Baraka, later, "I can see now that the dramatic form began to interest me because I wanted to go 'beyond' poetry. I wanted some form of action literature." As action, his drama occasioned an immediate response, as a result of which, "the inner-circle hauteur that only the cognoscenti who read *Zazen* . . . could appreciate had now been replaced by a wider circle of public talk" (1984, 275–280). Jones's fame conveyed aesthetic notoriety as much as cultural possibility when his literary reception became a political one, particularly after the death of Malcolm X; there followed his move uptown to Harlem and the founding of the Black Arts Repertory Theater/School in March 1965. Jones's "horizon shift" to Harlem becomes the blind spot of Hettie Jones's book, a gap in narrative continuity that is explainable only as consequences of his celebrity and rejection of her—but not in terms of a consciousness of racial politics as antagonistic. This narrative gap in her account, however, aligns with poetry in his, specifically in his need and desire to go beyond it. Where Baraka's later understanding of LeRoi Jones as an apolitical poet and editor denies the historical moment of his "aesthetic" beginnings, his notion of this period as "transitional" insists on an emergence into a historical role whose politics are in direct conflict with the aesthetic. What results is an allegory of agency, figured initially as a rejection of poetry but then as a poetics of action, that will set the terms for Baraka's *Autobiography*. Poetry in its "impossibility" becomes the negative of action, as in Jones's conflation of self-hatred and literariness, seen from the perspective of "Western culture," in *The Slave:*

> EASLEY: [. . .] You're just filth, boy. Just filth. Can you understand that anything and everything you do is stupid, filthy, or meaningless! Your inept formless poetry. Hah. Poetry? A flashy doggerel for inducing all those unfortunate troops of yours to spill their blood on your behalf. But I guess that's something! Ritual drama, we used to call it at the university. The poetry of ritual drama. (1964, 55–56)

The failure of poetry as symbolic action for the white critic will lead to a politics based on the necessity of that failure as well as the overturning of the perspective that judges it as such—in a series of symbolic positions aligned with Baraka's Black Nationalist and, later, Third World Marxist horizons.

What I see in Hettie Jones's narrative is in part a corrective of the negativity identified with poetry that is constitutive of a symbolic, rather than material, politics of racial and class identity. Jones/Baraka, in his subordination of poetry to symbolic action, arguably risks the form of "ritual drama" the white critic attempts to dismiss his work as being. As a form of textual agency, or literary praxis, poetry in Hettie Jones's account is valued as something other than a placeholder for the blind spot of action, even as its place in a larger political horizon is concretely acknowledged by her. Set against the *grande histoire* of the cold war and the rise of the civil-rights movement, her narrative details a micropolitics of literary culture in material rather than symbolic terms. Moving from metaphors for agency to metonymic details of everyday life, the substance of her *petite histoire* achieves a material density that counters the symbolization of racial or class consciousness with a politics of narrative style. Her involvement with literature is hands on, in real time, but it is not a matter of being seen as the symbol the white critic too easily dismisses in terms of ritual drama. (If there is any specific rejection of the way Hettie Jones is seen as, in her book, it is as the character of Grace in *The Slave*— as a hostage to the black militant Walker's drama.)

Hettie Jones sees herself as literary precisely in relation to a culture of material texts that is accessible in everyday life; she introduces herself as "sitting at an ancient rolltop desk that's stuffed to its top compartments with manuscripts and envelopes and all the related litter of magazine production" (1990, 1). Culture is a fact of the senses, a breeding ground; the physical details of material culture anticipate the horizons of authorship:

> Nearby, running half the length of a cluttered storefront office, is a six-foot-high row of wooden milk crates, housing old 78 rpm jazz records in crumbling paper sleeves. Flakes of this yellow-brown stuff drift down and settle like snow on the dirty linoleum, and the smell of it masks the casual funk from a darker back room, where [the] editor of the *Record Changer,* the magazine published here, sleeps whenever he's not with his girlfriend. (1)

Hettie and LeRoi meet in this milieu, which as a figure for "jazz history"— connected, metonymically, to furtive sex in the back room—will become a matter of style in Hettie's account as much as one of history in LeRoi's. Here, detail is all; the detritus of culture is metonymic in the manuscripts and the paper sleeves of old 78s that form the literary horizons of the *Record Changer,* a chronicle of jazz history for collectors and aficionados:

> These people bought and sold the fragile, tinny history of jazz, all yet to be reissued on unbreakable LPs. Sometimes, concerned as they were with the artifact, they acted as if jazz had already happened, that the real thing was only on wax. . . . Along with lists of collections for sale, the *Changer* featured essays, reviews, and interviews. Folk and jazz music were often interconnected studies. All these collectors and essayists were white. (21)

This breeding ground, either feral or sterile, sets up LeRoi Jones's later diatribes against "that junk pile of admirable objects and data the West knows as culture" (Harris, 184); at the same time, it provided the depth of detail that informed his 1963 masterpiece of jazz history, *Blues People*.[14] For Hettie, the milieu of jazz collectors and critics became a seminar in alternative style. Both went to school in that detritus—a materially embodied knowledge made present by the live history then being played at the Five Spot and elsewhere. The material facts of what I am calling jazz history (perhaps neither *grande* nor *petite histoire* but both) become a metonym for a cultural poetics that articulate a politics as well:

> The new, critical question seemed to be what jazz was, since it tended to change, as from hot to swing to bop to cool, and was all threaded through with the blues, which also would not bow to definition. To call jazz Negro music meant whites couldn't play it and they wanted to; to call it Negro music also put on it what was put on Negroes themselves, and no one wanted that. Part and parcel of every discussion was sociopolitical theory, and the history of racism, and, whatever jazz was, it was on people's minds. (1990, 21–22)

This concern with material culture is the opposite of authorial. The politics of jazz as exemplary—in their seminar, as in the emerging culture at large—were taken up from many perspectives as a form of possibility between subject positions in the hybrid, transformative space of bohemia.[15]

Hettie Jones's revision of authorship thus begins not with a claim to authority in writing her account—presumably after the appearance of the first edition of Baraka's *Autobiography*—but in a differing sense of the cultural meaning of the environment in which shared events took place. Downtown, the Village, the Lower East Side are opposed to Harlem and Newark by Baraka, in a dualistic topography that at the same time isolates the Five Spot—next door to where he and Hettie lived on Cooper Square—in a poetics of original mastery:

> Monk's shit
> Blue Cooper 5 Spot
> was the world busting
> on piano bass drums & tenor

This was Coltrane's College. A ph motherfuckin d
sitting at the feet, elbows
& funny grin
Of Master T Sphere
  (1995, 192)

The Five Spot here as elsewhere provides an analogy to poetic form that coincides with the authority of its master players, revealing the aesthetic underpinnings of such prenational topographies as Harlem and Newark ("New Ark") in a way that anticipates Baraka's nationalism. Within this form, knowledge is conveyed from master to disciple as an unnameable substance possessing culturally marked attributes, many of which are loaded: denigration (to call Monk's genius/work his "shit" for its lack of recognition); convulsive violence ("the world busting" either at the Five Spot or in the Newark riots); aggressivity as a form of legitimation ("A ph motherfuckin d"); and humor ("elbows / & funny grin"). What is not named is the content of the epistemic shift in style from Monk to Coltrane, given here not as a matter of progressive history that may be materially traced but as a shared relation to a sublime experience of "bright moments." This sublimity is precisely the unnameable fact of identity, which becomes identified with its performance, in art, at the Five Spot; in politics, as an articulation of national consciousness (not the final horizon for Baraka). From the material detritus of jazz history, Jones would isolate a cause for historical change; in the performance of jazz, Baraka sees the historical emergence of sublime identity. Context, here, is split, as everywhere in Baraka's work, in a form of projective identification: either aligning with the good identity that survives or insisting on the bad identity that must be overcome. The master/disciple relationship is the form in which good identity is passed on; bad identity becomes the detritus that does not adequately sustain the authority of "love": "The crushed eyes / of dead friends, standin at the bar, eyes focused on actual ugliness. / I don't love you" (1984, 456).

  "'Send a salami to your boy in the army' read the signs" on Katz's delicatessen, in Hettie Jones's account (1990, 9)—a subtle comment on national identity that sees material culture, not authority, as the horizon of performance. Hettie Jones's first cameo portrait of LeRoi Jones emphasizes material attributes, even in humble circumstances, that are the substance of his style:

For his dollar an hour he put in his time. With patience and intelligence, in good humor about the close quarters. He even *typed*. And the way he pronounced his name, with a short *e,* as in elementary, LeRoi, struck me less as pretense than correction—at least it was half the way you said it in French. Anyway, the short *e* emphasized the second half, and that's what he told us to call him—Roi. Roi Jones. (22)

"How You Sound??," of course, is the title of LeRoi Jones's early note on poetics in *The New American Poetry;* here he is caught at a signature moment. In Jones's epistemology, this moment of being named predicts a more encompassing politics of appropriation—simultaneously deracinating, aesthetically inept, and politically degrading. Hettie Jones clearly knows what she is doing when she names, and textualizes, the sound of LeRoi Jones's speech, but she refuses to hear it that way. In an early note on poetics, LeRoi Jones writes, "A saxophonist who continues to 'play like' Charlie Parker cannot understand that Charlie Parker wasn't certain that what had happened had to sound like that"; Parker's sound may be performed, by him, but neither imitated nor named (1973, 380). "The naming, nominalization, of that force is finally a step at making it artificial. The arbitrary assigning of content . . . is the beginning of God as an art object" (381). Hettie Jones's narrative refuses this essential priority in insisting on the material value (not just the index of sublime identity) of sound and its cultural influence; at the Five Spot, "Every night I heard a new sound, or heard sound a new way" (1990, 34). For LeRoi Jones, this newness indicates Monk's expressive genius, while Hettie Jones goes on to describe music as a form of writing: "Music was my first written language—I read notes before words—and it had also come coded." These codes are cultural, a matter of differences inscribed in musical language:

America was the Top 40s, and the Grand Ole Opry on the radio, the *goyische* Mozart and Chopin I played. It wasn't the Latin dance instructor who came with his records to our Laurelton basement—*Ola! La rhumba, cha cha cha, merengue!* And it most certainly wasn't those ancient, non-Western tones I loved to push through my nose: *Boruch atau adonai elohaynu melech haolum.* (35)

As language, jazz provided a lexicon of difference that becomes the site for a negotiation of race. Where these politics of difference are reduced within a liberal politics to appropriation, Hettie Jones sees them as material:

> That summer *Dissent* magazine published Norman Mailer's essay "The White Negro." There I read that jazz was orgasm, which only blacks had figured out, and that white hipsters like me were attracted to the black world's sexy, existential violence. But . . . the young black musicians I met didn't differ from other aspiring artists. And jazz music was complicated, technically the most interesting I'd heard, the hardest to play. All I wanted to do at the Five Spot was listen. (35)

An epistemology of race begins in the knowledge of jazz: while "complicated" and "the hardest to play," it is for her "a music I could trust" (36). Substituting material history for what will become the expressivist genius/appropriation dyad allows her to reject Mailer's specter of the sublime terror of "orgasm" as a figure for race in favor of an embodied difference that, elsewhere in the book, she identifies as "skin."

Hettie Jones offers another account of culture than a singular, authorial one, continually returning to moments of literary collaboration, particularly the editing of *Yugen* and Totem Press. Both projects get notice and credit in Baraka's autobiography, but as detail organized along a time line more concerned with a developing crisis of racial identity. For Hettie, the behind-the-scenes labor of literary editing, publishing, and distribution becomes a central figure for a cultural politics that begins in the dusty archives of jazz history and that ends in poetry. Taking a job as subscription manager at *Partisan Review* again becomes another step toward an "entry into culture," but neither by adopting liberal perspectives nor by buying into a simple notion of opposition: "At *Partisan* I could already see a stir of reaction, a gearing-up of generations. William [Philips] was considering poems by Allen Ginsberg and Gregory Corso" (1990, 49). What resulted was Norman Podhoretz's infamous trashing of the Beats, "The Know-Nothing Bohemians," but also Hettie's mediation in getting LeRoi Jones's rebuttal into print. Her editorial work also brought manuscripts like Frantz Fanon's *The Wretched of the Earth* into the house. Culture—either establishment or oppositional—is a human universe, for once, and she "felt happy to have landed—by remarkable, marvelous chance—in the middle" (49).

Even in this charged environment, her own poetry does not prosper; she transfers her enthusiasm (and distribution contacts), instead, to the publication of *Yugen,* begun in 1958: "Few magazines out of New York, to that date, had promised the new consciousness that everyone downtown agreed was just what the world needed. I know mine was raised by the very act of press-typing each quarter-inch character of that new consciousness in arts and letters" (1990, 53–54). A concern with press type, T-squares, "a rickety IBM with erratic adjustable spacing," and cash accounts become metonymic of "new consciousness," "put together . . . on my old kitchen table." But of what would this "new consciousness" consist? Is the material difference she locates in the details of typography retrospectively determined in the same way that a metaphor of a new consciousness as "spirit" arguably would be? While her literary labor was displaced from expression—"I hadn't yet managed to speak for myself"—it indeed led to a new knowledge of the world: "here at least were these others" (55). Rather than the splitting of identification into detritus and genius, good and bad identity, this real-time labor resulted in "recognition, to which my whole being responded"(55), even if this recognition must be shared with the emerging scene as a whole. Hettie Jones's book is an insistence on such a discursive politics, beginning with the construction of community in the act of editing a little magazine, and later a small press. A deferral of expression in the labor of publishing clearly informs the construction of her narrative; thirty years later, her labor remains unrecognized as the transformative experience it was, overshadowed by the drama of authorship.

Does poetry have any knowledge, and if so, what? In *How I Became Hettie Jones,* poetry occurs not at the site of original genius but as a material fact in a discourse constructed between subjects. As if in support of such a multicentered notion of authorship, we are given, throughout the book, citations from a range of poets, Hettie as well as better-known figures who emerged in the period. These fragments are oddly antiheroic and understated. A poem by Philip Whalen quoted from the first issue of *Yugen,* for instance, says that the speaker will be "Free / a genius, an embarrassment. . . . Like Yellowstone National Park" (1990, 55). Ron Loewinsohn, cited from his Totem Press book, *Watermelons* (1959), ironically interprets William Carlos Williams's "no ideas but in things" as a more comedic claim for a material poetry that is beautiful and absurd "like a White Rhinoceros" (1990, 72). In addition to Hettie and LeRoi, other writers quoted

include Gilbert Sorrentino, Michael McClure, Charles Olson, Robert Creeley, and Ed Dorn—a judicious selection of New Americans. Poetry,
throughout the book, is encountered at the level of everyday life, if intensified and prospective, rather than as a moment of sublime intensity.
Next to this citation of poetry is an insistence on material culture in other
registers—not only jazz at the Five Spot but letters and diaries, cooking,
clothes, movies, and, increasingly, politics. (Olson, for instance, is described not as a sublime author but as a large man; LeRoi Jones's visit with
him is more concerned with social tensions than with "Projective Verse.")
What holds this level of detail together is a literary metonymy of a new consciousness that is realized in immediate terms: "It was this that all my
late-night cutting, pasting, aligning, and retyping finally taught me—what
comes from reading things over and over, taking apart and putting together, the heart of the matter, the way it feels" (75). The culture Hettie
Jones makes of the New American Poetry is understood, through such
labor, as this-worldly, embodied, and coherent. The content of its exemplary form creates, even in everyday life, what Olson would call a "republic
of value."

But what if poetry is differential, rather than referential? If its drive for
recognition equally conveys nonrecognition, or even worse, denial? It is the
advantage of Hettie Jones's book that she presents the world as it appeared
to her then as a possibility, within cultural horizons that are open rather
than retrospectively closed in the teleological narrative of rejection Baraka
tells in his *Autobiography*. Yet even as she chronicles the social changes
reflected in the emergence of a black avant-garde in the mid-1960s, terms
for recognition remain one-sided: "Hey, man," says Ornette Coleman to
Hettie, running into her on the street with plastic horn in hand, "And I'm
redeemed. Despite my doubts—despite this different life—I'm a man
among men" (1990, 189). Even so, the imagination of a culture not divided
by race is the progressive politics of her book, realized in the achievement
of a precise (and hip) cultural style developed out of the mutual recognition of avant-garde poets, artists, and musicians.[16] Overcoming the racial
divide in a cultural poetics that acknowledges the expressive immediacy of
jazz and "projective verse" as material culture rather than as forms of sublime identity is the prospective horizon of her book. At the same time, a
more compelling history is starting to take place—beginning with the loss
of self LeRoi Jones experiences in the death of Malcolm X and ending with

the loss of her marriage that is both a loss of self and the end of a cultural possibility—that can only be partly recuperated even as it is recognized as really having happened:

> Despite the shared name, there were different transformations await-ing us. He would remain, like any man of any race, exactly as he was, augmented. Whereas I, like few women at the time, would first lose my past to share his, and then, with that eventually lost, would be-come the person who speaks to you now. (65)

III

This is only half of the story, but an important half. When LeRoi Jones wrote in *The New American Poetry,* "MY POETRY is whatever I think I am. . . . I CAN BE ANYTHING I CAN" (1960, 424) that was simply not the case for Hettie. In her memoir, she describes this, quite modestly, as a mat-ter of writer's block—an everyday register of writing *as* lack, through a sub-sequent writing *about* lack, that is one of her memoir's accomplishments. While one can argue that Hettie Jones's problem was not lack at all but in-stead the various conditions that constrained her poetic production,[17] it is clear that her memoir explores both senses: she discusses her "lack" of finished writing first of all as a problem experienced in real time and space that takes a real achievement of self to overcome; it would not help this overcoming to see her experience as simply due to the fact that the culture she is in sees feminine authorship as lacking. But this lack proposes a more general figure of anxiety that is part of masculine author construction; oth-erwise put, the formal values of her memoir and of the construction of po-etic agency are constitutively opposed. Being a poet in the culture in which she understood the term came with the privileges of the masculine gender: the drama of recognition, in terms of race and gender, was male. Hettie's memoir claims recognition on other terms than that of poetic agency— namely, in the form of her autobiographical prose, in its poetics of lack. On the other hand, her memoir cannot adequately represent the drama of rec-ognition experienced by LeRoi Jones in becoming Amiri Baraka, precisely at the moment when he abandoned the interracial milieu in which he mar-ried her, along with the entire project of bohemian utopia in the early 1960s. Baraka's recognition is now secure as index of the transformative racial politics of the 1960s, and of the vicissitudes of its interpretation in its later nationalist and Marxist horizons. In his rejection of interracial bohemia and in his representation of real time black politics from Harlem to Newark, Baraka has achieved historical agency.

Recognition for Hettie Jones has also arrived, but in other terms. First, of course, is the recognition she confers on herself in *How I Became Hettie Jones*. Yet there is still a lag in reception indicated by qualifications of what kind of work this is: either as an exemplary autobiography or, in the *New York Times* review quoted on the back of the paperback edition, a "valuable social document" rather than a literary work in its own right. As such, it has taken its place within the effort to restore the contributions of women writers, as well as the presence of women on the scene, in the genealogy of the New American Writing. This act of recovery is not just a historical corrective: it exposes as well the exceptional misogyny of the literary culture of the period, and should not be seen simply as a retextualization of the denied. Consider, for instance, the first figure taken up in the "Muses" section of Brenda Knight's *Women of the Beat Generation:* Joan Burroughs, whose death previously was known as a matter of William S. Burroughs's authorial lore, as "literary" rather than an act of murder for which Burroughs was never called to account (48–53). Literature, as confirmed in Burroughs's reception, in this case is an act of incredible denial—of women, of history, of anything that gets in the way of public fascination with the "oppositional" author. A kind of splitting results that is precisely ethical: very few people live the refusal of consequences that they are willing to accept, without a moment's hesitation, in Burroughs's murder of Joan.

The act of recovery, then, not only is a matter of restoring the literary record but has ethical stakes concerning the nature of authorship in a given historical period. A fundamental shift in understanding the nature of literature should result from these acts of recovery: to begin with, a complete rethinking of the figure of the poet in terms of self-declaration and mastery is one consequence of a revision of the Beat and New American canon. Of course, the Beats themselves saw the exemplarity of their writing in terms both of its vatic stance and its locus of unheroic particulars: what finally identifies the "beat" is a heroic address from an unheroic locus "in back of the Real," to cite the title of Allen Ginsberg's poem. Poetic agency in its most transformative politics, as in Ginsberg's exorcism of the Pentagon, will coexist with the most mundane and personal details—a relation that leads directly to countercultural subject formation in the 1960s, where the personal *is* the political. It is an important consequence of these countercultural politics that Jones/Baraka, in his version of agency, places under erasure the kinds of material culture that are recuperated in Hettie's memoir. "No ideas but in things" is not a basis for black liberationist poetics; its transcendental address must take material circumstances as a negated point of departure.

If I have perhaps overstated the opposition between poetry and prose in Hettie's memoir, it is important to note that, even during a period in which she is preoccupied with her lack of writing, she did write poetry (and includes some of it in her memoir, although none appears in *Yugen*). Another dimension of the becoming of Hettie Jones, then, is the publication of *Drive* (1998), which collects both earlier chapbooks and more recent work. A poetics of transformative particularity, as with the New Americans, is evident in Jones's collection; she writes of everyday details—of cars, lovers, relatives, and kids—but these are framed, as well, in terms of a poetics of identification and solidarity with women in other patriarchal contexts. Any hint of a tone of vatic address, however, is missing; the quirky distancing from the overarching "importance" of poetry makes her writing thought provoking beyond its moments of recognition, its everyday content. Having arrived relatively late to writing poetry, and increasingly sure about her vocation in the last decade, her poetry complements absence, loss, and even lack with an equally heroic refusal of overstatement. While her life is complex, in other words, the deceptively simple terms in which it is recorded are driven, torqued, by emotional density into unique angles of vision and modes of address in which "unlikeness" is a central term. In her avoidance of the vatic modes common to many New Americans, particularly in their political writing, something else is being said in her work. A difference is framed in terms of gender that is at once time valued, site specific, and increasingly clear about its value.

Care for particluars emerges in the material terms of her work. The price paid for this level of attention is, clearly, the gaps and interruptions that make the amount of her poetic output, over four decades, relatively small. Many of the negatives that she transcends so well in her prose memoir seem still at work here, in the elisions and discontinuities of poetic address, to the degree that the poetry may seem adjunct to her achievement of a literary identity in prose. But discontinuity is an acknowledged aspect of Jones's work, to the degree that the refusal or impossibility of an earlier model of the poet is a part of her work's historical register. The question is, What kind of agency does Jones's poetry achieve, once she has written herself beyond the available models of poetic address common to the period that formed her? It is not simply as a tragic witness to the position of women in history that her work makes its ineradicable case. Rather, her poems are simultaneously instances of present negotiation and retrospective clarity, even as the terms of her experience are agonizingly subject to reconsideration:

Over and over the mind returns
to the bent shoulders of the young woman
who types, over and over, the poem

until it is perfectly placed
on the page, the name

of her husband, the name
of her lover
the guilty thrill
of juxtaposition.
  (1998, 73)

In this poem, Hettie returns to the subordinate role she played in the material culture of poetry—typesetting Frank O'Hara's "Personal Poem" (1974, 335), which names both "LeRoi" and "Mike Kanemitsu," with whom she had an affair, for publication in *Yugen*. The handmaid gets her revenge, certainly, but content is not the formal interest of this poem. It is, rather, the way that Jones takes as given an alienated experience—of herself not only as typesetter but as wife and lover—as material for transformative agency. But what sort of transformation is implied? Is it not the knowledge of poetry as differential and alienating, as that which precedes the poet in her act of poetic making? Such that the poem, itself, reconfigures handmaid and adulteress as pre-given terms that have been gone beyond, even if this going beyond bears no relationship to any sort of vatic transcendence?

This form of poetic knowledge is as much a politics as any form of vatic address. It is a poetry of irreducible material circumstances, an ethics of recognition in which poetry's admission of the world is not simply by vir-

tue of its overcoming. This irreducibility of material circumstances is the-
matized throughout the work collected in *Drive*—to begin with, in the
figure of the various cars Hettie has owned over the years: there is nothing
transcendental about these vehicles; they simply get you where you are going or not ("The Woman in the Green Car" [12]). Another figure that argues against transcendence is that of the prison, where she has worked as
a poet/teacher ("The Semipermanent Gate List" [59]). Finally, there is a series of poems that address liberationist politics (such as "A History of War
in Five Acts" [45]), but in such a way that a distance between witness and
victim is always preserved. An ethics of simultaneous identification and
distancing can be seen in the following poem of everyday life addressed to
an Algerian woman who was "persecuted . . . for making Western-style
clothes" ("Dresses: Four of Mine for Naima Belahi"):

> So narrow they seem sewn
> for someone fragile, not a woman like me
> with a lot on her back. And carefully made
> to last, as though I'd believed I'd last
> like that, like the thin-strapped
> plum linen, the bicolor knit, the long
> gray wool, the handkerchief cotton
>   with butterfly sleeves, bordered wings.
> . . . .
> I keep them because I
> couldn't see me, myself enlarged
> unable to wear them, unable to part with them. (95)

To identify the literary strengths of *How I Became Hettie Jones* in this poem
is not hard. There is the same focus on a politics of particulars, the materiality of the dresses—like the banner in the previous poem addressing
"WOMEN OF ALL LANDS" (94)—but here there is also a question of the
differential as much as the referential. Hettie herself is different from the
younger woman who made the dresses; just so, there is a difference between the condition of the Western woman poet, who would take dresses
for granted, and that of the Algerian woman who would be punished for
making them. Materiality and difference, deceptively stated as matters of
content, are brought together in an instance of form: the poem, like the

dresses but composed of different materials, makes a record itself of having been made. With that record of time-valued, site-specific experience, the poet makes her particular claim to knowledge.

Notes

1. Davidson et al. (*Leningrad: American Writers in the Soviet Union,* 42–43, slightly modified).

In the original publication of the present essay, in *Poetics Journal* 10 (1998), the passage is discussed in the context of views on poetic epistemology expressed at the Soviet-American "summer school" of 1989 that is the historical referent of Leningrad.

2. Cited by Charles Olson in "Projective Verse" (1997, 240). The original letter from Creeley to Olson (5 June 1950) is cited in the notes: "Anyhow, form has now become so useless a term / that I blush to use it. I wd imply a little of Stevens' use (the things created *in* a poem and existing there . . . too, go over into: the possible casts or methods for a way into/ a 'subject': to make it clear: that form is never more than an *extension* of content. An enacted or possible 'stasis' for thought" (426).

3. This polemic is taken up in Watten (1997 and forthcoming).

4. This may be compared to what Laura (Riding) Jackson did in renouncing poetry as inadequate in relation to what she called "truth," a different matter than knowledge.

5. Aldon L. Nielsen (1994) discusses the name "LeRoi Jones" itself as a non-referential placeholder, a politically important, "endlessly signifying" site of "radical rupture and absence," that appears obsessively in the work of contemporary non–African American poets. However, he does not treat Hettie Jones's memoir as literary in the same sense.

6. Toward the end of their literary/marital partnership, Jones carries the politics of the name even further, changing her name to "Cohen-Jones" in the last issue of *Yugen* (1990, 168).

7. This periodization is continually referred to by Baraka, and schematized as well in the table of contents of his selected writings, *The LeRoi Jones/Amiri Baraka Reader* (Harris 1991).

8. "She said, as well, that she was a writer, but she had sacrificed her writing, even hidden it from me, because of the crushing weight of my male chauvinism and her selfless desire to forward my career," Baraka (1984, xxi–xxii).

9. To account for Baraka's notion of imperialist interpellation (imagined as coming from outside a social totality), the degree to which Louis Althusser's famous concept is centered in the Lacanian Imaginary needs to be reconfigured in terms of the historically Real, a project inaugurated in Jameson, chapter 1. On interpellation and the Beat generation in 1950s American culture, see Watten (1996).

10. The other side of this transformation, her own, separates two narratological levels, the Russian Formalists' *fabula* (material or event) and *syuzhet* (plot or narration).

11. There is more than enough denial of Hettie Jones in the introduction to the second edition of Baraka's *Autobiography,* written in response to *How I Became Hettie Jones,* as well as in the original version's concluding section.

12. In his version, Baraka appears mildly to dismiss the two periodicals, giving them the pseudonyms *Zazen* and *The Fleeting Bear,* but he also writes about the collaborative aspects of the period in ameliorative terms: "The magazine and Nellie and I were at the vortex of this swirling explosion of new poetry" (1984, 234).

13. In calling for a historical recovery of the origins of the Black Arts movement, Nielsen (1997, 78–82) points out the equal importance of the "New American" literary matrix, configured in the 1950s, and the slightly later appearances of black "coffee-house" bohemia and the avant-garde jazz scene, for its emergence.

14. "Every day I came to the [*Changer*] I had to go through stacks of records looking for the ones ordered in the auction. I studied bands and players from different periods of jazz and began to understand when and how the music changed. Later I would do my own deeper research to find out why it changed" (Baraka 1984, 206).

15. The hybrid space of the avant-garde may be seen as a Eurocentric formation, as Baraka insists, but it can be seen as Afrocentric as well, as in Nathaniel Mackey's novelistic accounts of jazz history in *Bedouin Hornbook* (1986, 1997) and *Djbot Bhaghostus's Run* (1993).

16. See also the style of materialist politics and poetics in her remarks on work with prison writers in Jones 1997. Asked, 'What challenges do inmate writers face?," she responds: "Access to typewriters, let alone computers, is limited and good books are hard to come by. Contact with other writers, critiques, workshops, are rarely part of these writers' lives in prison" (11).

17. For an argument against my use of the concept of lack, see Russo 2000.

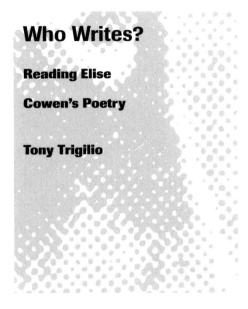

Who Writes?

Reading Elise Cowen's Poetry

Tony Trigilio

What difference does it make who is speaking?

—*Michel Foucault*

I found my name on every page / And every word a lie

—*Elise Cowen*

Elise Cowen and Allen Ginsberg were lovers for a brief time in 1953, during a period when Ginsberg followed an analyst's advice to "try" women as a so-called "cure" for homosexuality.[1] Their romantic relationship broke off by the time Ginsberg moved from New York to San Francisco, right before the composition of "Howl." From that period until 1962, when Cowen committed suicide, the two maintained a friendship that, by many accounts, meant considerably more to Cowen than to Ginsberg. Cowen appears briefly in major critical studies of Ginsberg, but only by virtue of her role in Ginsberg's brief period of bisexuality and her typing of his "Kaddish" draft.

Cowen composed hundreds of poems of her own but few survived. After her suicide, Cowen's parents, angered by the lesbian and bisexual subject matter they found in her work, burned her manuscripts.[2] Not all the poems were lost, however. Cowen's close friend Leo Skir held a copy of eighty-three of her fragments and poems at the time of her death. Skir published some of these poems in various journals from 1964 to 1966; several of these poems have been reprinted in recent anthologies of Beat women writers, Brenda Knight's *Women of the Beat Generation: The Writers, Artists and Muses at the Heart of a Revolution* and Richard Peabody's *A Different Beat: Writings by Women of the Beat Generation*.[3]

A look at Cowen's literary relationship with Ginsberg suggests that her legacy is complex, despite the destruction of so many of her poems. Since Cowen's death, Beat commentators have approached her work and life with seemingly contradictory purposes: on one hand striving to preserve her legacy as a poet through posthumous publishing, while at the same time subsuming her literary contributions into larger narratives of Ginsberg's life and work. In his essay "How 'Kaddish' Happened," Ginsberg himself describes Cowen's typing of his "Kaddish" manuscript as, paradoxically, both uninspiring and influential. As for her typing, Ginsberg characterizes Cowen as an insignificant other, the "girl [he had] known for years and had fitful lovers' relations with" and who simply retyped material from his original typed draft of the poem. Yet he also writes that when Cowen gave him a final typed copy of the manuscript, she critically observed: "You still haven't finished with your mother" (Allen and Tallman, 141).

Histories of the Beat period in American literature characterize Cowen only as Ginsberg's mad girlfriend-poet and typist of "Kaddish." For Ginsberg's major biographers, Barry Miles and Michael Schumacher, Cowen's remark about Ginsberg's mother, Naomi, is a footnote to larger questions of elegy and influence in "Kaddish." Joyce Johnson's memoir, *Minor Characters* (1983), also de-emphasizes Cowen's development as a poet in its discussion of Cowen's relationship with Ginsberg. Skir, an otherwise sympathetic biographer, describes Cowen's response to Ginsberg's 1961 return from Mexico City in terms that echo her portrayals by Miles, Schumacher, and Johnson: "From then until the time she died, her world was Allen. When he was interested in Zen, so was she. When he became interested in Chassidism, so did she. Did he drink mocha coffee? So drank she. When he went down to Peru there was Peter [Orlovsky], left behind downstairs, still there to be with. Peter loved a girl from New Jersey. Elise loved the New Jersey girl. When Allen came back, the New Jersey girl moved in with Elise"

(155). Skir's description of Cowen's patterns of influence reveals the actual burden of such influence. In accounts such as these, Cowen the poet is eclipsed by Ginsberg; she lives in his shadow and her writing is superseded to the extent that her work is mentioned only as a cipher to further understand Ginsberg's. Cowen's relationship, as poet, with Ginsberg required complex movements between authority and transgression, while maintaining the transgressive spirit central to the production and reception of Beat generation literature.

Cowen's poetry itself suggests that her understanding of language and power relations is more complicated than what is described in Beat biographies. As important as biographical response can be, critical studies of the Beat period in American literature too often emphasize biography at the expense of textuality when reading Cowen's work. Of course, reader reception of Beat writing depends on critical understanding of biography; if anything, the neoromantic impulse of most Beat writing demands that readers know something of the sovereign, expressivist self claimed behind each literary work.[4] Thus, it would be a disservice to argue that biography should be displaced entirely in favor of poetry, in the case of Ginsberg, Cowen, or any Beat writer.[5] Beat commentary on Cowen correctly emphasizes her relationship with Ginsberg; yet in doing so, it constructs a figure for Ginsberg that occludes Cowen. Those who write about the Beat generation portray Cowen as if following the lead of Lucien Carr, who called Cowen "Ellipse" and "Eclipse" instead of "Elise," names which seem to reflect with accuracy Cowen's social alienation, but also reify the marginal status bestowed upon her work after her death.[6]

Understanding Cowen as a Beat figure seems to require biographical study to assert her human role in the mutual friendship and influence among major figures in the Beat era. In disentangling Cowen and Ginsberg to examine Cowen's poetry in its own right, one must also reconsider the methods and practice of Beat scholarship. When literary commentary collapses poetry into biography, as it often does with Beat writers, especially Beat women writers, such scholarship is undertaken at considerable expense to the cultural work of the poems themselves. The poems are seen only as illustrations of a biography rather than as texts rich in linguistic and cultural meaning; such an approach generates criticism and commentary that can succumb to the romantic expressivism of its subject matter—given Beat literature's debt to British and American romanticism—and risks a separation of Beat literature from the cultural contexts of period, influence, and postwar identity in which it participated. In what follows, I explore the convergence of Cowen's biography and her poetry, moments where she seeks to move beyond cold war ideals of female subjectivity as she, too, is eclipsed, or occluded, by these same ideals. As this essay will discuss, Cowen's authority as a poet depends upon a revision of consolidated forms of identity that universalize the humanistic impulses of Beat literature as exclusively male impulses. A critical framework for reading Cowen's poems can emerge from this tension between biography and textuality. Her poems engage cold war notions of matronly, muse, distaff women—the lexicon available for critical portrayals of Cowen—and claim a provisional authority largely unexplored by the few who have written about her. Beat commentary has focused on her relationship with Ginsberg and responded insufficiently to the role she played in the literary production of the Beat generation. A close reading of Cowen's approach to subjectivity and sacred language in her poetry demonstrates that Ginsberg's influence inspired her to produce her own distinctive writing as much as it shadowed reception of her work. Cowen's poetry depends upon an authority particularly within, but eventually outside, the function of authorship in "Kaddish."

Who Writes? An Approach to Beat Authorship

Michel Foucault's "What is an Author?" suggests a vocabulary for negotiating the tension between biography and textuality in critical responses to Cowen. Examining literary works with a greater emphasis on what Foucault terms their "author function" in his response to Roland Barthes, while preserving the subjectivity of their authors to some extent, elevates the responsibility of Beat scholarship from the transcription of biographical data (and the chafing of fandom) to the examination of the cultural work of authority and transgression in the shaping of the literature of the Beats' historical moment. In short, such scholarship heightens the difference made when a particular author speaks, and notes indeed what difference her work makes in the broader, disciplinary contexts in which her texts are read and studied.

For Barthes, "the death of the Author" inaugurates a seemingly liberatory "birth of the reader." But in this shift Barthes's negation of critical markers of identity—history, biography, psychology—offers no productive point of convergence with feminist studies, even as his de-centering of authorial mastery might imply such a convergence. Thus, as Nancy K. Miller has argued, "the birth of the reader" overshadows both textual and political representation, generating a critical methodology in which, as Miller argues, "it matters not *who* writes" (104). Foucault claims that studying the "author function," rather than emphasizing the primacy of the author, is necessary to counter the privileging of authorship that, he argues, actually occurred at the moment Barthes seemed to de-privilege authorship. The author function would replace the unity of an author's name as a standard from which critical practice proceeds, substituting a focus on transferences and limitations of power that define the discursive practices of a given era. As promising as Foucault's response to Barthes might seem for reading Cowen, in whose work a tension between authority and anonymity circulates, Foucault's revision presents its own difficulties. At the same time as Foucault asserts that "we must locate the space left empty by the author's disappearance," he claims that the author function itself is bound to disappear into a horizon of textual play (105).

Before Foucault hastens such closure, something specific remains to be said about how the name signified by the author is important in literary studies, and important to reading poets such as Cowen. Perhaps one cannot fully speak of Elise Cowen, for instance, as a female Beat author writing within and against the literary-historical discursive boundaries of her era unless one begins to look at relationships of mutual influence among Cowen and fellow Beats—to see her as a woman working within phallic structures of language, influence, and comradeship that framed Beat literature—and the way that her work itself is imbricated in her cultural moment. Her engagement in the poetry with discourses of desire and religion that often were criminalized in the cold war 1950s and 1960s implies that biography and textuality can be read together as part of a complex, interconnected author function in her poetry.

Foucault closes his essay by projecting modes of future scholarship that eschew authorial individuality and originality in favor of genealogical study of literature. He asks slyly, "What difference does it make who is speaking?" (120). Rather than collapse differences into one originary authority, one which would be localized in the expressivist heritage of British and American romanticism—and, too often, of misogynistic self-reliance—central to the work and comradeship of authoritative Beat founders such as Ginsberg, Jack Kerouac, or William S. Burroughs, readers might instead turn to

a more complicated idea of authority that depends on the exercise of an authority-within-transgression. Foucault's problematic final remark about
what he sees as the eventual disappearance of the author function, his final
question about speech and difference, can open an inquiry into who
writes—a questioning of what intertextual authority is inscribed upon, and
ruptured by, an author as s/he claims the authority of authorship.

Serious critical study of female Beats such as Cowen suffers from a
double bind. If biography and text are linked too closely, as in the commentaries of Miles, Schumacher, Johnson, and Skir, then such a link comes
at the expense of textuality. If biography and text are separated wholesale,
as Foucault concludes is eventually inevitable, then Cowen's relationship of
influence is lost, as are the writing strategies she engages as a woman living
in the early decades of the cold war and writing within a largely male tradition whose own literary outlaw spirit might deny her authority. Reading
the poetry of Elise Cowen requires attention to biographical detail at the
same time that it requires seeing the poems within the cultural context of
Beat generation literature. Writing in an era that sought to exact silence
from those who deviated from social and sexual norms, Cowen sought a
place for herself within a community of Beat writers who spoke loudly and
visibly against postwar conformity.

Yet as a woman within this community, Cowen needed to create a second voice for herself within Beat outsider circles, since her gender destabilized her authority from the outset. This authority-within-transgression can
serve as a guide to Cowen's reconsiderations of subjectivity and selfhood in
her poetry, a poetics of revision significant within the language and context
of Beat generation literature and within feminist reconsiderations of authority and authorship.[7]

Reading Elise Cowen's Poetry

As a Beat author, and the typist of "Kaddish," Cowen produced poetry
that both continues and swerves from the project of "Kaddish" to transform
a dualistic split in Beat literary politics between male and female figures of
divinity and political engagement. Cowen's work shares with "Kaddish" the
tendency to assert the power of redemptive language while simultaneously
distrusting such power enough to want to rewrite it as a reflection of the
fictive nature of redemptive narratives. These paradoxical strategies of assertion and distrust could negate themselves into silence. For Ginsberg,

however, they resulted in an emphasis on the performative elements of prophetic language and a revision of essentialist elements in Western prophecy's authorizing lineage. Cowen's poetry undertakes a similar project; yet, the authoritative discourse she rewrites includes the shadow of Ginsberg's authority itself.

Cowen's poetry is marked by deterritorialized representations of the body, portrayed in poems such as "Dear God of the bent trees of Fifth Avenue" as a body defined by "the uncircumcized [*sic*] sin of my heart."[8] In this lyric meditation on the immanence of spirit, Cowen's speaker commences a symbiotic relationship with a Creator-God who seems to need flesh as much as flesh needs this God. The poem is a negotiation, transforming monotheistic authority through persistent mediation into a language of consensus. Cowen's speaker opens the poem imploring God to merge with her body in order to spread a decidedly fleshly Logos:

> Dear God of the bent trees of Fifth Avenue
> Only pour my willful dust up your veins
> And I'll pound your belly-flat world
> In praise of small agonies
> (Peabody, 27)

This God is a transcendent creator of a world prone and vulnerable, a "belly-flat world" of "small agonies"; the speaker's language might praise these agonies as blissful adorations, yet only insofar as she might unite with the immanent nature of this God of materialist "bent trees of Fifth Avenue." The speaker's unity with her God is represented not in the traditional language of mystics; the poem swerves from standard models of divine madness, in which incarnations of metaphysical power exert themselves one-sidedly upon the poet who would be a subordinated, belly-flat body. Instead, the speaker of "Dear God" represents incarnation in terms of symbiosis, specifically in terms of heroin injection: transforming traditional Christian burial prayer, the speaker reduces herself to "willful dust" that can be "poured up" the veins of a symbiotic God of immanent "bent trees." Desire is an unfettered manifestation of the sacred in this poem; yet, as she states later in the poem, desire is "filtered"—mediated between flesh and Spirit—by the speaker in her relationship with God.

Language that might praise "small agonies" is matched physically by the speaker's heretical insistence that direct experience with the sacred can emerge from sexual intercourse with the sacred:

> . . . I'll pound your belly-flat world
> In praise of small agonies
> Suck sea monsters off Tierra del Fuego
> Fuck your only begotten cobalt dream
> To filter golden pleasure
> through your apple glutted heaven
> Filter the uncircumcized sin of my heart.
>   (Peabody, 27)

Thus, direct experience with God emerges through "filtered" experience, here through desire and sexual intercourse. Sacred experience is expressed through the use of Biblical parallelism. God's productions—his Son, his "only begotten cobalt dream"—become the speaker's *reproductions*: intercourse with Christ adds "golden pleasure" to an "apple glutted heaven" that is already fallen. The traditionally separate spheres of fallen humanity and transcendental Godhood are merged in the poem at the level of material desire.

Syntactic parallelism in the poem balances the competing claims of flesh and spirit and even equates these claims. As Robert Alter writes of Biblical parallelism, such verse suggests that the parallel elements represent "an emphatic, balanced, and elevated kind of discourse, perhaps ultimately rooted in a magical conception of language as a potent performance" (9). In contrast to "referential" language, performative speech enacts the very ideas it represents. As linguist J. L. Austin explains, performative language is speech that is "*doing* something rather than just *saying* something" (235); his famous example is the "I do" pronouncement of the traditional Western marriage ceremony. Spoken within the context of the ceremony, when bride and groom say "I do," they make themselves a married couple through this utterance at the same time that they pronounce their vows through this utterance. Their utterance makes them married at the same time that it says they are married.

Alter's remarks on the performative function of Biblical parallelism can suggest a way of reading Cowen's parallelism. The performative language in her poetry reconceives sacred language and relocates the sacred in the

body. For Cowen, parallelism suggests that matter and spirit circulate between each other rather than subordinate each other; Cowen's parallelism
is a poetic strategy that trusts performativity at the expense of referentiality
in its engagement with the sacred.[9] Her speaker's promises to "filter golden
pleasure through your apple glutted heaven" and "[f]ilter the uncircumcized sin of my heart" are equated through parallel word choice and the absence of grammatical subordination. Cowen's God of "bent trees" possesses
the flesh as this flesh surges through His veins, a representation that equates
metaphysical desire with fleshly desire in this "filter[ed]" exchange.

This tension between Word and flesh is enacted also at the level of language in Cowen's poetry, as in her play on sin as s(k)in in "Dear God"—skin
that evades the knife of orthodox religious ritual and valorizes a transgressive "heart." Her speaker's desires are reified as a "sin" she would rather
evade, a "s[k]in" she prefers to keep "uncircumcized." Cowen engages this
battle between Spirit and flesh, Logos and desire, without surrendering the
tension between these two poles of authority. Desire is transgressive—is
"sin"—and disentangled from institutional orthodoxy, specifically from the
ritual of circumcision. Moreover, as a "sin" freed in the imagination from
circumcision, this is a sin that evades the effects of organized religion's attempt to colonize—to territorialize—the body with the decidedly masculinized shoring of boundaries that results from circumcision. Cowen
adopts a phallic speaking position as she creates a language for desire in
the poem, yet this desire is "uncircumcized," voiced without anxieties of
colonization or castration.

In "Teacher—your body my Kabbalah" Cowen also reinscribes divinity
as direct, embodied experience with God.[10] In this poem, Cowen incorporates the Kabbalist idea that God is manifest in the *sefiroth,* the ten spheres
of being, each known as a *sefirah,* in the Kabbalist tree of life. Through
study and meditation on the *sefiroth,* the seeker directly experiences an otherwise hidden divinity. For Cowen, the *sefiroth* unfolds in the material body
of her speaker's teacher in this poem. As in much of her poetry, she adopts
the body and speech of authority figures, often male bodies and phallic
speech, in order to reinscribe the authority of these figures in language that
destabilizes gender-based hierarchies responsible for naturalizing phallic
control. In her poem "Jehovah," this approach to authority ends abruptly
with a rejection of authority, when she responds to Biblical authority with
only the phrase, "I don't believe a Word" (41). Cowen incorporates the

Kabbalah into "Teacher" to reinscribe her disbelief. Drawing on "Rahamim" and "Tiferete," names for the *sefirah* that she refers to in translation as "Compassion" and "Beauty," she asserts that divinity cannot be experienced conventionally through a separation between self and God, nor—echoing a common Beat complaint—through middle-class values: "God is hidden / And not in picture postcards" (66; emphasis in original).

Cowen's poetry is both attracted to and estranged from traditional sacred language. She embraces images of sacred power so that they may be reconceived, revising the language of prayer in favor of language that is both materialist and incantatory. Her struggle against divine territorialization also is enacted against the backdrop of medical authority, as in her poem "Dream." Drawing from her experiences as a psychiatric patient whose autonomy gradually was turned over to her parents and doctors, Cowen constructs sanity as only a "trick of agreement," borrowing from "Kaddish," that reiterates existing power structures.[11] Cowen's poem recounts a dream in which her parents "are taking [her] to a doctor / as [she is] sick, neurotic." Her parents are "disgusted with [her], tired, throught [*sic*] the dream." Authority is vested entirely in the parents in Cowen's poem, and even the doctor is vulnerable to pathology. He, too, is "sick"; in the closing lines of the poem, the doctor's body, like the speaker's in "Dear God," exposes the "trick of agreement" that must be repressed in order to shore up the boundaries of an institutional authority that pronounces her "sick":

> . . . After talking to the doctor
> who's [*sic*] face I don't remember, he, the
> doctor sits on a bed & strips a
> bandage from his long leg showing
> a drying gash.
>   (Cowen, 8)

Doctor and patient share the same pathological space in the poem. Given the juridic-medical discourse of the era—the emergence of antipsychiatry as a field that sought to correct perceived injustices in psychiatric medicine and equalize power relations between doctors and patients—the doctor's sharing of this wound in the poem is a welcome surprise for Cowen's speaker. Nevertheless, the speaker infantilizes herself in the poem, referring to her parents as "Mommy" and "Daddy"; it is clear to her that her wound is "sick" at the end of the poem, while her male doctor's wound by contrast is "drying," nearly healed. Sharing the wound is an act of agency for the male doctor that his female patient cannot share in this physical and psychic dramatization of phallic power relations. The male doctor exposes his wound—confesses it much as a psychiatric patient would—and this gesture allows a "drying" that becomes the normative standard by which the female patient's sickness is measured.

Cowen's embrace and distrust of sacred language extends to material language. This distrust especially includes representations of desire and is rooted in cold war disciplining of homosexual and bisexual desire. In her poetry, Cowen represents desire in ambisexual terms, at once desiring— and desired by—male and female subjects. In her life, she lived such desire through primary romantic relationships with Ginsberg, Donald Cook (her Barnard philosophy professor),[12] and a woman given the pseudonym Sheila in Skir's and Johnson's autobiographical accounts of the era.[13] Cold war hegemonic discourses of sexual conformity and deviance contextualize the body politics of Cowen's poetry. For Cowen, embodied desire engages the sacred; at the same time, power inequities resulting from culturally constructed sexual norms desecrate the body as they denigrate desire. Representations of lesbian and bisexual desire in Cowen's poetry are framed by cold war ideals of female creativity that limited such desire to criminality, and limited heterosexual desire to procreation. McCarthyism equated transgressive desire with anticapitalist treason; one of the significant consequences of McCarthyism was a criminalization of lesbian and bisexual women.[14] As Lee Edelman and Jeffrey Escoffier have observed, cold war popular culture and popular sociology made homosexuality visible as a mechanism by which it might be erased. Yet the visibility afforded homosexuality by the Beat generation and San Francisco Renaissance also cast homosexuality into a "public eye," in John D'Emilio's words, as a means toward decriminalization. D'Emilio emphasizes that "Ginsberg served as a bridge between a literary avant-garde tolerant of homosexuality and an emerging form of social protest indelibly stamped by the media as deviant" (181). Nevertheless, as Lillian Faderman notes in her study of lesbian pulp novels, lesbian representation was scarce in a literary avant-garde whose "tolerance" of homosexuality paid little attention to lesbian writers and readers. Faderman observes that lesbian subject matter in literature was confined to "cautionary tales" in pulp novels: "'moral' literature that warned females that lesbianism was sick or evil and that if a woman dared to love another woman she would end up lonely and suicidal" (146–147).

Skir's account of Cowen's relationship with her parents reveals much about the cold war impulse to make homosexuality invisible while simultaneously exposing it:

> Elise was in Bellevue. She had gone in with hepatitis . . . then become psychotic.
>
> "Leo," her mother said, "I want you to be truthful with me. Did Elise ever take drugs?"
>
> "Not to my knowledge," I said.
>
> "Her father looked through her writings while she was in the hospital," she said. "He says they're filthy. She seems to have been mixed up with a lot of homosexuals. Did you notice any among her friends?" (156)

While homosexuality was equated with the threat of communism, mainstream U.S. culture specularized homosexuality as part of nationalistic gestures that would, as Edelman states, make citizens even "*better* readers of homosexuality and homosexual signs" (556). The promise of sexual openness that accompanied frank portrayals of homosexuality in Beat literature, as described by D'Emilio, was matched by the desire to drive homosexuality underground. Unsurprisingly, then, Cowen's parents, who would later burn her manuscripts for their sexual themes, here ask Skir (unsure of his own sexuality at the time) to reveal the sexual boundaries of Cowen's friends: at the same time that their comments demand a visible ("truthful") account, these comments also contain a full and open accounting with the disciplinary pronouncement that Cowen's writings were "filthy."

For Cowen, in contrast, the provisional truth of the sexed self is unabashedly visible, as in her poem "Someone I could kiss":

> Someone I could kiss
> Has left his, her
> > tracks
> > A memory
> > Heavy as winter breathing
> > in the snow
> (Cowen, 62)

Cowen's forcefully enjambed lines emphasize a desire for a man/woman who leaves pleasurable memory traces as visible "tracks / . . . in the snow" —or, recalling "Dear God," as revelatory needle tracks on the body. In "Someone I could kiss," the speaker's ambisexual object of desire exists only in a conditional voice—of someone she "*could* kiss" (emphasis mine)—yet the poem closes by asserting the palpable heft and significance of this conditionality, of "his, her" tracks laden "with weight & heat / of human body." As with male Beat writers, Cowen finds spirit and sustenance in drug use and sexual experiences that reach beyond the boundaries of cold war, middle-class norms. Yet for a female Beat writer, this poetic strategy alone is not enough to transform the gender inequities underwritten by these norms. Anticipating the later strategies of feminist poets, such as Adrienne Rich, Cowen's speaker remakes the gender order by diving headlong into its wreck as it unfolds in language. For Cowen, and of course later for Rich, the hierarchy of values presumed by gender distinction finds its matrix in language, and the way out of this wreck is a revisionary language of studied, artful contradiction: in Cowen's poem, "his, her" mark is left behind as both conditional and declarative statement, representing outlaw desire as a combination of both intangible winter breath and the concrete "weight & heat / of human body."

However, for Cowen, any project that would remake the wreck of materialist language would be incomplete without a revisionary language for metaphysical experience. As a poem that reimagines the metaphysical self-certainty of Judeo-Christian mythos, Cowen's "I wanted a cunt of golden pleasure" reads like a continuity of "Dear God." Both are framed by ambisexual speakers rewriting narratives of Spirit and flesh, and both proffer alternatives to Western notions of divinity. Yet this poem more specifically revises the notion of a metaphysical God. "I wanted" reconceives metaphysics in terms of the beginningless philosophy that would have been available to Cowen as a poet who studied Buddhism. Cowen's religious studies are taken seriously in Johnson's memoir, but are subsumed there into larger narratives about Cowen's degenerating love affairs, including one with Cook, and her tendency to follow the intellectual paths laid out by Ginsberg. As discussed earlier in this essay, Skir's treatment of Cowen's religious study and practice also constructs a Cowen who follows Ginsberg uncritically, traversing Zen, Chassidism, mocha coffee, and Peter Orlovsky's "Jersey girl" as if they are of equal significance.

In "I wanted," as in "Dear God" and "Teacher," Cowen continues a Beat insistence on liberating language from institutional religious authority. Yet, like Ginsberg in "Kaddish," she distrusts any language that poses itself as a liberatory, monovocal alternative to metaphysically authorized language. Depending also on parallel syntactic structures, "I wanted" speaks to a lover worthy of "honor," "ease," and "glory"; her vehicles of honor, ease, and glory hearken to a metaphysical "golden pleasure" and an originary authenticity "purer than heroin"—a nostalgia for transcendental verities. However, Cowen's emphasis on a metaphysical frame of reference for her love in this poem is countered by her insistence on the body as a material location for such a frame of reference. The speaker's body is not dramatized in standard metaphysical terms, which characterize the body as the imperfect fallen vessel trying in vain to carry the Spirit. Instead, the body is lifted to the level of soul, a mediation that echoes the embodied symbiosis of "Dear God." The soul in "I wanted" is a "Soul like your face before you / were born," (Peabody, 30), borrowing from a well-known, and decidedly antimetaphysical, Zen Buddhist koan: *What did your face look like before you were born?* The koan challenges any possibility of grasping originary knowledge; to represent what one's face looked like before birth would require an impossibly transcendent language for presubjective, originary experience. Merging the koan with Western metaphysics, Cowen empties *soul,* too, of its transcendental value. If "glory" in "I wanted" can be idealized in the soul, then this soul must be imagined in an absence of metaphysical surety. From such absence, the poem asserts that the materiality of a continuous present, of beginninglessness, might revivify the wisdom of metaphysics:

> I wanted a . . .
> . . . .
> Soul like your face before you
>   were born
> To glory you in
>   breast, hair, fingers,
>   whole city of body
>   In your arms all night
> (Peabody, 30)

In the light of metaphysical certainty—in the "Soul" of such certainty—Cowen draws organic potential instead from absence and shadow. "Body" is as sacred as "soul" in this poem only because the body is localized in a materialist community of flesh, in a "whole city of body"; revelatory possibility lies not in a soul whose originary presence overshadows the body, but in a soul emptied of originary precedence and re-imagined as a materialist body that can be gloried "all night."

Cowen's "I wanted" is a poem of possibility in which desire nevertheless is not fulfilled. Much the same can be said about "Dear God," where sacred desire is imagined as "uncircumcized" yet ultimately is "filtered" rather than unmediated. Both poems hinge on methods similar to Ginsberg's: stylistic parallelism influenced by Biblical language and metaphysical subject matter; a dependence upon language that is performative in the manner of prayer and incantation; a belief that the body becomes a vehicle toward intensified consciousness through sexual expression and drug use, and is a location for revising metaphysical surety as materialist skepticism; and a move from religious verity to variance that depends on a commingling of Western and Eastern practices of the sacred. For Cowen, too, a policing of the body results in the silencing of speech. In her poem "Interview," she describes applying for a position as an elementary school teaching assistant and dramatizes the silence that, for her, results when children's sexual expression is muted. The speaker of the poem encounters a two-year-old boy in the poem who "waggles his tiny cock at me with gleeful eyes" (Cowen, 39). For the speaker, this encounter is uninhibited play, the pure possibility of the imagination, and is also a pragmatic, absurdist pedagogical moment, as suggested by the teaching "interview" at the core of the poem's occasion. At play and as teacher, she takes "revenge / by conning him to / talk" (Cowen, 39). However, when they meet again two weeks later, his first speech—a moment demonstrating the power of the unfettered imagination—is countered by the force and friction of the adult world: "his dreamy / mother says 'Shut up. You talk to [sic] much'" (Cowen, 39). Childhood desire lives on in traces in the adult world, but "dreamy" mothers become agents of silence.

However, Cowen's "I took the skin of corpses" demonstrates a more direct disengagement from Ginsberg's literary style at the levels of authority and identity. The iambic meter of the poem's nine rhyming quatrains bounces like children's verse. Yet in subject matter, the poem is anything but a children's narrative. The speaker ventures into a world that echoes Dr. Frankenstein's. Identifying ambisexually with the Biblical Esther and Solomon, she combines domestic, female-coded sewing with male-coded writing and creativity; by the close of the poem, she is imprisoned by her own efforts, unable to make bail and ready to sell back her own recycled body as a cadaver. With its gruesome landscape of dismembered and dead bodies, the poem is a seething allegory of a woman's search for inspiration in a poetic tradition dominated by men. Cowen engages this question of gender and originality elsewhere, as in the poem "The Lady is a humble thing," which features a quatrain whose traditional rhyme and meter resemble "I took" to the extent that it nearly could function as a prelude to that poem:

The Lady is a humble thing
Made of death and water
The fashion is to dress it plain
And use the mind for border
    (Knight, 164–165)

Cowen's archetypal female image, a "Lady" who is "[m]ade of death and water," assumes identity through practices of humility and through the active efforts of others who dress her plainly. She is never quite a visible subject, though she is the object of others. Her mind enhances this image of her as passive; it is used by others "for border," as an instrument to highlight her plain dress and humility, but not as a means for active, imaginative engagement. Cowen's "Lady" does not seem capable of forging original speech or action. Cowen suggests here and in "I took" that when the body is territorialized the imagination follows suit. For a female Beat writer, commenting on the scarcity of attention afforded women writers in this genre, an apt metaphor for originality in "I took" might be the recycled bodies of others—a continuous tradition excavated for a revisionary future.

But the speaker of "I took" fails: her blue skin privatizes her rather than carries her into the world; she shivers under the protective hair she cuts from corpses; and cutting the ears from corpses does not enable poetic "ear" or rhythm—it only reminds her of blood she has lost. More important, at the level of vision, where Cowen is occluded by Ginsberg, it becomes clear to the speaker that the successes of others—maybe even of Ginsberg—contribute to her own losses:

I robbed the eyes of corpses
So I could face the sun

But all the days had cloudy skies
And I had lost my own.
    (Peabody, 29)

The near-rhyme of "sun" and "own" unravels further in the next stanza, the only unrhymed quatrain in the poem. Here, Cowen's violation of the poem's rhyme scheme underscores the gender differences that separate her thematic and stylistic concerns from male Beats such as Ginsberg:

From the sex of corpses
I sewed a union suit
Esther, Solomon, God himself
Were humbler than my cock.
    (Peabody, 29)

The speaker's skin, hair, ears, and vision have failed, but her "cock" is a vehicle to voice and power: with her cock and empowering "union suit" she humbles the Biblical canon and "God himself." The poem performs an ambisexual speaking voice, violating genre expectation at the unrhymed, dissonant articulation of "cock," a rhetorical strategy Cowen also deploys in her short poem, "Enough." In "Enough," Cowen identifies her speech with male sexual potency—as she does in "Dear God"—yet seems to achieve original speech only by suggesting a simultaneous incorporation and disengagement of the male body: "Enough of this flabby cock in my head / I'll find the cat who's got my tongue / And spit it out" (Cowen, 17). Cowen's poetry engages stereotypes of feminine "lack" in order to rewrite these stereotypes from within. Her incorporation of "cock" and "union suit" in "I took" echoes her poems "Interview" and "Enough," in which the phallus is identified as a "flabby" cultural force that can silence "dreamy" mothers, and one that female poets must "spit . . . out" in order to enable poetic speech.

Cowen's utterance of "cock" destabilizes the gender order in "I took," and in the process continues and revises the authorizing power of her primary Beat influence, Ginsberg. Cowen distrusts the power of language to redeem, yet continually asserts a situational, embodied language that is redemptive. As in "I wanted," Cowen's language distrusts redemption at the same time that it represents redemption in the body. The speaker says to her lover: "I wanted a cunt of golden pleasure purer than heroin / To honor you in." Her strategy of assertion and distrust—desiring a lover who can be "honor[ed]" in a body more powerful and "pur[e]" than heroin—reconceives divinity in performative rather than representational language. Cowen's language stages the sacred each time that it is uttered. In "I wanted," the sacred is enacted when the body is "honor[ed]," emphasizing a situational divinity more apt, to recall Alter, for performative incantation than referential speech. Or, echoing Austin, Cowen's situational language in the poem is "*doing* something rather than just *saying* something" in its relocation of the divine in the body.

Cowen works against fixed gender distinctions in her poetry, as Ginsberg, too, does in "Kaddish," adopting male and female subject positions as Naomi's caretaker and object of her desire. But Cowen's gender representations, of course, carry with them an extra burden of authority to overcome. If male Beats could transgress in order to reinscribe authority, their models nevertheless were in the spirit of romantics such as Blake and Whitman, who had been assimilated into literary history as authoritative masculine-coded figures when the male Beats began their careers. Cowen aligned herself with male Beats against the authority of a Western canon that received them with skepticism; but, as critical response to her poetry demonstrates, her self-positioning paradoxically created the means by which she lived in the shadow of Ginsberg, reinscribing authority as soon as authority is cast off.

Cowen's final moments in "I took" suggest at first glance that the simple, commutative version of Cowen's identity proffered by Beat commentators might be accurate, because in the poem the act of reading produces only falsehood and negated identity. As with Rich, the words are maps, but the language of the fathers leads in misdirection:

> I borrowed heads of corpses
> To do my reading by
> I found my name on every page
> And every word a lie.
>   (Peabody, 29)

Yet Cowen's strategy of distrust and assertion exposes performative qualities of representations of gender and madness, and locates divinity, beatitude, in situations rather than in codified language:

When I become a spirit
(I'll have to wait for life)
I'll sell *my* deadly body
To the student doctor's knife.
  (Peabody, 29; emphasis in original)

Cowen trusts making rather than naming in the poem. Her speaker looks for her name codified on the page but finds "every word a lie." Cowen expresses faith in the linguistic power of naming as a means by which the poem eventually might assert the limitations of such faith. As an alternative to codified language, she crafts a language of situations and relations that might transform her into a subject rather than an object, one who emerges from commerce among spirit, body, and mind. Cowen's figurative language for creativity and criticism, her overdetermined puns on stitching and weaving as writing (given that the Latin for text, *tessere,* derives from the verb that means "to weave"), are even more important because they reconceive the Frankenstein story and thus recall Mary Shelley's role, and her mother Mary Wollstonecraft's, in the shaping of feminist literary history. Her speaker's dead body literally is a "deadly body," made up of dead body parts. But she emphasizes it is hers, suggesting that she has created an identity for herself located in a body that performs many identities—that she is an amalgam of subjectivities rather than one consolidated subject. Unlike Dr. Frankenstein, she returns her amalgamated body to the dead, a gesture of control over her creation that Dr. Frankenstein could not perform in his final moments.

Of course, authorial gestures of control are never enough to forestall vexed critical response. In Cowen's case, critical reception of her work has been limited by the gender politics of Beat literature and scholarship. Focusing on Cowen's relationship to Ginsberg creates the conditions for Ginsberg to eclipse her. At the same time, Cowen's revisionary approach to gender politics itself might be lost without a focus on the biographical context of her work. Biographical focus alone has generated no substantive critical dialogue on Cowen's poems or on her role in the Beat era. Biography and autobiography operate on the periphery of her poems as, in Foucauldian terms, a "system of constraint" that must be both combined with and disentangled from the literary productions of the era (Foucault, 119). Yet Beat scholarship seems prone to biographical overexertions, no doubt caused by the eminent marketability of Beat biography as quest literature, and as literature of self-discovery. For even Ginsberg, this overemphasis on biography comes at the expense of a discussion of his texts, their textuality and historicity. [15] Crucially, for Cowen, a historically specific author function might encourage politically productive expressions of fictive and polysemic qualities—her performative language for an authoritative, transgressive divine madness—that are submerged when her poetry is read in the shadow of Ginsberg's life and work. These qualities enable Cowen to adopt the shadow of masculinized authority as she casts herself into light, part of a process to "find the cat who's got [her] tongue / And spit it out."

Notes

1. See Barry Miles. Chapters 4 ("The Subterraneans") and 5 ("On the Road to California") are especially significant for considering the relation between Ginsberg's early sexual experiences and his analysis at the Columbia Presbyterian Psychiatric Institute (as the result of a theft charge). Miles writes that the doctors at the Psychiatric Institute "convinced" Ginsberg that "his only hope was to return to Paterson, get a job, find a girl, and try to fit into society" (124). According to Miles, Ginsberg "recognized that there was a tremendous gulf" separating himself from others, a gulf that included matters of sexuality, and "after eight months of treatment [Ginsberg] believed the doctors when they said that once he closed this gulf, he would be cured" (124).

2. See Leo Skir, 143–155. Skir offers useful accounts of Cowen's contentious relationship with her parents, including their outrage that Cowen's life and writing did not conform to postwar middle-class cultural standards. As Knight observes, Cowen's parents "had achieved the American Dream with the perfect house in the perfect neighborhood and the perfect job. More than anything, they wanted the perfect daughter to complete the ensemble, and Elise became the focus of their rages" (141).

3. Cowen's poems were published posthumously in *City Lights Journal; Things; Fuck You: A magazine of the arts; The Ladder* ; and *El corno emplumado*. See Knight's bibliography, 344.

4. "Howl" itself, the archetypal Beat epic, alerts its reader in Ginsberg's dedication that the "best minds" under duress in the poem must be named in the process of navigating the poem. The heroic quality of the poem's pilgrimage is intensified by Ginsberg's identification of its particular heroes and its villains as "Howl" moves back and forth between specified American locales and ends in Rockland.

5. Johnson (1983) cites a 1959 journal entry by Ginsberg to confirm this important role played by biography in Cowen's influence on him. Ginsberg wrote, "I've always been attracted to intellectual madwomen"; Johnson calls the phrase a "confession" that "includ[es] Elise in that category" (76).

6. See Johnson (1983,125). She writes that Cowen's name produced "great amusement" for Carr: "Ellipse, he called her. Or Eclipse. 'Well, now, Eclipse, what'll you have?' he'd shout across the room, and his wife Cessa would redden and say, 'Oh, *Lucien!* . . . '"

7. For feminist reconsiderations of authorship that seek to reconcile competing claims of authorial individuality and poststructuralist subjectivity so that female authors can be seen in a continuum that includes both humanism's "dead" author and Foucault's disappearing author function, see Miller and also Susan Stanford Friedman. Friedman, best known for reestablishing the importance of the poet H. D. in the twentieth-century canon, characterizes recent feminist work on authorship as part of a "post/poststructuralist moment" in which female authors can be studied as women writers in history and within the context of poststructuralist theories of subjectivity. Friedman calls for a negotiation between humanist and poststructuralist ideas of authorship that would generate a "deconstruction of the extreme polarization of 'theory' and 'history' and a reconstruction of discourses that combines the two" in a manner mindful of the contradictions of such an exchange (198).

8. Following Peabody's and Knight's titling of Cowen's poetry, I excerpt first lines as titles in discussions of her work.

9. See also Ginsberg's remarks on the composition of "Wichita Vortex Sutra," where performative utterances create a vocabulary for imagining the end of the Vietnam War. According to Ginsberg, the poem emerged from his desire to "make a series of syllables that would be identical with a historical event" (1980, 46). Ginsberg asserts that his desire for a language whose utterance would be "identical" with an "event" finds its religious-historical analogue in Buddhist mantra recitation. "Wichita Vortex Sutra" is Ginsberg's attempt to create a stronger language for pacifism—a stronger pacifist performative utterance—than the language Lyndon Johnson's administration deployed for war: "Where they [the President and the State Department] say, 'I declare—We declare war,' they can say 'I declare war'—their mantras are black mantras, so to speak. They pronounce their words, and then they sign a piece of paper, of other words, and a hundred thousand soldiers go across the ocean. So I pronounce my word, and so the point is, how strong is my word?" (1980, 47).

10. Cowen, undated, 65–66. This poem also appears in Knight, 160–161. However, I refer to the unpublished version here because of what appears to be a typographical error in the final line in its reproduction in Knight's collection. The version in Knight's volume ends with, "God is hidden / And not for picture post-

cards," contrary to the unpublished version, which ends with "And not *in* picture postcards" (emphasis mine).

11. Ginsberg (1984, 212): "By my later burden—vow to illuminate mankind—this is release of particulars—(mad as you [Naomi])—(sanity a trick of agreement)—".

12. In *Minor Characters,* Cook is given the pseudonym Alex Greer. Johnson identifies Greer as Cook in *Door Wide Open* (Johnson and Kerouac).

13. In Johnson's characterization of Cowen's romantic relationship with Sheila, Cowen again is eclipsed by Ginsberg. Johnson writes that, "in loving Sheila, Elise is loving Allen too, reaching him in some place in her mind, living his life—loving Sheila as Allen loves men" (1983, 92).

14. See Lillian Faderman, especially chapter 6, "The Love That Dares Not Speak Its Name: McCarthyism and Its Legacy," where Faderman discusses the cold war and its effect on lesbian and bisexual communities on the East and West coasts.

15. In books and articles on Ginsberg, Paul Portugés's work (1978, 1980) is notable for its attempt to balance appreciation and scholarship. Most recently, Alicia Ostriker (1982, 1997) has balanced personal appreciation and critical commentary in her discussions of Ginsberg's body of work.

Snapshots, Sand Paintings, and Celluloid

Formal Considerations in the Life Writing of Women Writers from the Beat Generation

Nancy M. Grace

Autobiography and its sibling, the memoir, have historically been dominated by and associated with the stories of great men—public stories of public lives, stories deemed worthy of telling because their male subjects have performed noticeably and meritoriously. It is somewhat ironic then that autobiography, the self-writing-its-life, or life writing—the term now in vogue—should be the vehicle that has brought to public attention the presence of women artists in the Beat literary movement. That a telling number of women Beat writers have chosen to communicate through life writing, a form often maligned, trivialized, and marginalized as inferior literature and pseudo history—even denied status as a genre—makes their efforts of self-assertion provocative and our readings of them a challenge.

The first narratives of self by Beat women were published in fairly close proximity to the height of the Beat movement. In 1964, Brenda (Bonnie) Bremser Frazer wrote *Troia: Mexican Memoirs*, the story of her relationship with Beat poet Ray Bremser. The book was published in 1969, the same year as Diane di Prima's *Memoirs of a Beatnik*, a campy self-representational take on Beat mythology. The female voices remained relatively silent until

1983, when Joyce Johnson published *Minor Characters: A Young Woman's Coming of Age in the Beat Generation,* which won the National Book Critics Circle Award that year. Johnson's Beat story was followed in 1990 by *How I Became Hettie Jones,* the memoir of her longtime friend. That same year saw the publication of *Off the Road: My Years with Cassady, Kerouac, and Ginsberg* by Carolyn Cassady, widow of Beat maverick Neal Cassady. More recently, *Nobody's Wife,* the memoir of Jack Kerouac's second wife, Joan Haverty Kerouac, was posthumously published in 2000,[1] and di Prima's *Recollections of My Life as a Woman: The New York Years* came out in 2001. All of these memoirs draw upon the genre's social authority derived from the author's privileged relation to real life. All also benefit from the genre's proximity to culturally dominant discourses of truth telling, particularly history and confession, adhering to Phillipe Lejeune's often-cited definition of life writing as "a retrospective narrative in prose that a real person makes of his own existence when he emphasizes his individual life, especially the story of his personality" (4).

The life writing of Beat women chronicles their intimate relationships with cultural heroes—some of whom have achieved almost iconographic status—the likes of Kerouac, Allen Ginsberg, William S. Burroughs, and LeRoi Jones/Amiri Baraka. Certainly the presence of the women in the Beat movement validates their personal stories as "different" and "unusual," the stuff of which a tantalizing public story is made, and thus constitutes the authority from and with which the women write. And, it was most likely their presence in the Beat community that compelled them to write memoirs rather than full autobiographies. The memoir, focused on a relatively short period in one's life and more open to stories about others than is autobiography (Jelinek, 4), is a fitting form for narratives about Beat women's associations with particular men or participation in the Beat historical moment. The memoir may also serve more effectively to achieve the implicit directive that life writing be introspective and intimate, that life writers explore their inner or emotional life, thus distinguishing the form from mere historical documentation (Jelinek,10). The memoir, focused on a slice of one's life rather than the full sweep, provides a manageable temporal space within which to reflect.

Life writing also takes on political and artistic import for women writers in its connection to self-validation, self-expression, and authority, a conceptual link assuming heightened importance for women writers effectively erased as legitimate artists from the historical Beat record. For instance, when a woman sits down to write her version of her life, claiming the first-person pronoun "I" in conjunction with her given name—thereby identifying hero, narrator, and author with the same signifier—she gestures that her story is one lodged as closely as possible to her lived experiences, directing one toward both a material reality and the author's distinctive perception of self. While the reader may recognize the inevitability of her unreliability, that same reader often suppresses the recognition in a tenacious effort to expect truth of some kind (Smith 1987, 45). Thus, for both the reader and the Beat woman author, life writing may affirm individual female agency and action in ways that fiction, poetry, and other literary forms do not.

While cleaving to some of the general principles embodied in the tradition of life writing, the memoirs of Women Beat writers resist the dominant ethos and form both of autobiography and of the Beat community, both of which stipulate that the "boy gang" allow in women as long as they remain mothers, wives, sisters, lovers, virgins, whores, demons, or angels. Even Carolyn Cassady, who is a painter by vocation and profession, not a writer, and thus falls outside the scope of this discussion, attempted in her memoir to experiment with reconstructed scenes and dialogues, techniques until recently taboo in life writing. Such devices move the narrative beyond the assumptions that autobiography and memoir are historical documents obligated to report life as material and linear fact, that the focus of the text should be what the subject has done or what has happened to the subject. Despite Cassady's efforts, however, she, as have many others, falls back upon the conventional paradigm, creating an "I" that explicitly projects a unified and omniscient truth teller standing far removed from what it reports. Cassady's memoir moves progressively, the reporting "I" structuring reality as a flat continuum, a plane across which she marches to a point of self-resolution. Ultimately, *Off the Road* emerges as history unconscious of itself as art.

It is the Beat women poets and novelists—Frazer, di Prima, Johnson, and Jones—whose engagement with memoir reflects an understanding of life writing propagated by contemporary literary and historical scholarship and feminist studies, which has revealed the complex epistemological realities with which writers of self deal, convincingly challenging the belief in an essentialist self and unveiling the multiple narrative "I's" operating in any text written about the self. Self-representation emerges as self-creation, and the past, plastic and fragmentary, remains beyond the memoirist's grasp, yet always with one as memory. The construction of personal history is both the discovery and the creation of truth, not only for the individual but also for the larger culture in which that self resides. Consequently, life writing, which is the construction of personal and cultural history through the interaction of language and memory, is to some degree a fictional form deserving appreciation on literary terms. The memoirs of the Beat women writers represent two different, yet complementary, approaches to the application of these ideas, each reflecting the movement toward and the embracing of relativist and constructivist methods of textual production. Johnson's and Jones's texts represent a form of life writing that, while firmly and eagerly acknowledging its literary qualities and making obvious the materials with which a self tells/creates its story, identifies more explicitly with history. These memoirs assert that their narrators are to be linked directly with their historical referents, who are motivated to tell a story about Beat, but not necessarily to tell in it Beat style. In contrast, Frazer's memoir and di Prima's *Memoirs of a Beatnik* acknowledge prescriptions of historical veracity, but engage more fully in the imaginative realm and the intentional subversion of reader expectations based on narrative conventions. In this respect, their texts draw more directly upon formal devices associated with Beat writing, such as mischievous narrative solipsism and the conflation/confusion of genres, which effectively disengage the author/referent dyad. Despite this fundamental division, however, both types reveal and reflect modern and postmodern attempts to rupture the boundaries long associated with life writing (lending some credence to the arguments that life writing cannot be considered a distinct genre). [2] In the process, their writing facilitates self-representation through the interdisciplinary play of language with visual art forms including photography, sand painting, and film. Ultimately, the memoirs of Frazer, Johnson, Jones, and di Prima constitute a constellation from which one can identify the range of technical possibilities used to construct an alternative, or corrective, history of Beat culture, Beat art, and Beat female subjectivity. The discussion that follows explores the specific ways in which each author has approached this task, demonstrating that life writing, especially the memoir, is a vehicle by which self is created and by which cultural artifacts embody the shifting of social, philosophic, and artistic values.

1. ANN CHARTERS 1957.
Photograph by Nathan Danberg.
Courtesy of Ann Charters.

2. RUTH WEISS READING AT THE NORTH BEACH GRANT AVENUE STREET FAIR, 1958. *Photograph by C. R. Snyder; © 1958 by C. R. Snyder. Courtesy of ruth weiss.*

3. DENISE LEVERTOV. *Photograph by Allen Ginsberg;*
© *the Allen Ginsberg Trust.*

4. HELEN ADAM AT THE POETRY PROJECT. *Photographer unknown. Courtesy of Anne Waldman.*

5. JOYCE JOHNSON CA. 1962. *Photograph by Robert Henriques; © Robert Henriques 1962. Courtesy of Joyce Johnson.*

6. HETTIE JONES. *Photograph by Bela Ugrin. Courtesy of Hettie Jones.*

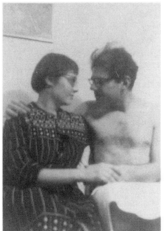

7. ELISE COWEN WITH ALLEN GINSBERG AND PETER ORLOVSKY.
Photograph by Allen Ginsberg; © the Allen Ginsberg Trust.

8. BONNIE [BRENDA FRAZER] AT THE FOUNTAIN. *Photograph by Barney McCaffrey. Courtesy of Brenda Frazer.*

9. JOANNE KYGER IN JAPAN. *Photograph by Allen Ginsberg; © the Allen Ginsberg Trust.*

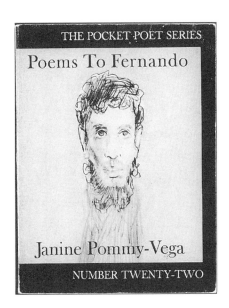

10. FERNANDO VEGA ON THE FRONT COVER OF *POEMS TO FERNANDO*. Self-portrait © 1968 by Janine Pommy Vega; reprinted with permission of City Lights Books.

11. JANINE POMMY VEGA ON THE BACK COVER OF *POEMS TO FERNANDO*. Photographer unknown; © 1968 by Janine Pommy Vega; reprinted with permission of City Lights Books.

12. ANNE WALDMAN CA. 1966. *Photograph by Ann Charters;*
© *1966 by Ann Charters.*

13. DIANE DI PRIMA
CA. 1969. *Courtesy of The
Lilly Library, The University
of Indiana, Bloomington.*

At first glance, Joyce Johnson's *Minor Characters* and Hettie Jones's *How I Became Hettie Jones* seem to be rather conventional memoirs. Each speaks directly to the historic period known as Beat, roughly 1944 to 1964; each was produced several decades after its historical focus, as is typical of life writing; and each is persistently aware of its obligation to report truthfully its subject's life as a nonfiction reality. However, both explicitly reflect a blurring of the lines between fiction and nonfiction and engage in the process of bringing into focus a kind of truth other than documentable facticity. The memoirs of Johnson and Jones, portraits of their lives as Beats and as each other's lifelong friends, conform to writer Patricia Hampl's definition of memoir as

> the intersection of narration and reflection, of storytelling and essay-writing. It can present its history and reflect and consider the meaning of the story. It is a peculiarly open form, inviting broken and incomplete images, half-recollected fragments, all the mass (and mess) of detail. It offers to shape this confusion—and in shaping, of course, it necessarily creates a work of art, not a legal document. (209)

As historians, Johnson and Jones embark on the formidable task of speaking as *gendered* beings, knowing full well that their lives in the Beat avantgarde broke many of the rules for "good girl" behavior promulgated at mid-twentieth century. In this respect, their life writings bear and accept the burden of setting the Beat story straight, of being concrete and verifiable, and therefore believable, history. But *Minor Characters* and *How I Became Hettie Jones* also stand in structural opposition to this very assignment, illustrating that the autobiographical act is an interpretation of past experience and material evidence. The life writer, their stories attest, by sifting and sorting words and stories that suggest, but can never recapture, the past, creatively manipulates facets of remembered experience, be these descriptive, impressionistic, interrogative, analytic, or dramatic. In the process, both Johnson and Jones draw attention to what appears a primary mission of their writing: trying to assert their presence in and account for the Beat historical moment.

For instance, Joyce Johnson's *Minor Characters,* the memoir that first brought national attention to the women of the Beat movement, engages the mercurial natures of self and text, making visible both the evidence with which histories are built and the process by which this is done. Reading the book is not unlike flipping through an album of photographs arranged somewhat haphazardly but nevertheless telling a coherent story, a compilation of linguistic images presenting the self as a fragmented entity existing in fluid time and struggling to inscribe individual identity. In fact, Johnson is keenly aware of photography as central to cultural and personal history and memory, beginning the memoir with the narrator looking at a book with a snapshot of four young men on the Columbia University campus in 1945, the now famous image of Kerouac, Ginsberg, Burroughs, and Hal Chase.[3] The speaker is an older Johnson (née Glassman), meditating on the image of the men themselves, who appear to have grown younger while she, a girl of eleven in 1945, has grown older. The scene and the subsequent fifteen pages introduce the foundational structure of the narrative, a gentle shifting back and forth from past- to present-tense constructions of remembered experiences which conjoin two narratives: the story of her two-year love affair with Kerouac, and, more importantly, her development as a young woman in the fifties. This form, buttressed with explicit discourse on how one's history is built, showcases as a self-reflexive technique imaginative constructions of real people from her Beat past.

Much like the eye scanning the photo album, the alternating of past and present tenses focuses the narratives on the remembered image. The image stands as an experience of the present moment, but simultaneously documenting something ultimately unretrievable, that which lies beyond representation and must be sought in the gaps and fissures of words. In effect, past and present cling to each other, a negative capability, antithetical and distinct, yet harmonious and unified. More than dead artifact, the past becomes something to reflect on, distill, and use to control the temporality of human existence. Johnson's technique effectively problematizes memory and time, illustrating the extent to which what is known as past remains a vivid present through action and what Johnson herself calls "the strangeness" ([1983] 1990, 77) of memory. *Minor Characters* draws upon this strangeness—and the power of imagination—to build a self and a past, rendering both the author's story and her act of creating story. The dual discourse is not immediately discernible; rather it is hidden in a style that aptly suits the static nature of the recorded image. The self who narrates is not confessional, apologetic, didactic, or self-impressed; hints of all these appear but none dominates. What centers the book is a Jamesian consciousness, and true to her literary guide, whom she identifies in the memoir, Johnson's language assumes a tone of detached intimacy, striving methodically to peel back layers of human thought to slow time through the extension of word into images, the fleeting impressions that are experience itself. Like the work of a painter or photographer, she renders, as James said fiction should do, "the look of things, the look that conveys their meaning, to catch the color, the relief, the expression, the surface, the substance of the human spectacle" (12)—all of this holding the reader, paradoxically, sanguine and vulnerable.

The textual self relies upon the novelty of fixed images in and out of time. Johnson, like other memoirists, works through focused visualizing of a particular place to produce a pattern that reveals human experience. The image that Johnson uses to read her own sense of disquiet and disillusion, the stirrings that would eventually lead her to associate with people such as Kerouac and Ginsberg, is a room in her parents' apartment on 116th Street near Barnard College in New York City, which Johnson was to attend when she turned sixteen. The room, dominated by a grand piano, is etched in her memory in colors of red, green, and gold; the furniture wears slipcovers, the Oriental carpet is vacuumed daily, the shade of the Chinese lamp is encased in cellophane, and a portrait of the eight-year-old Joyce Glassman hangs above the piano. It is a sexless, lifeless room: "There's [a] terrible poignancy in this room," a room "of gratifications deferred"; she writes: "It's as if all these objects—the piano, the rug, the portrait—are held in uneasy captivity, hostages to aspirations" ([1983] 1990, 14). The selves that she was, that she has become, that she could have been remain resident in this space which is the text of her story of abandoning her mother's wish that she become a musical composer so as to claim the life of the writer.

While in her memory the Glassman living room remains a museum of lifeless artifacts, still painful for Johnson to contemplate, other spaces when imagined transform into vessels of psychic sustenance for Johnson. She didn't graduate from Barnard because she never completed a required physical education course, but she's still willing to attend a class reunion, and in her present tense rendering of this experience, she meets classmates whose lives have moved quite differently from hers, perhaps more like what her parents had envisioned as her future. When asked what they do, the middle-aged women answer, "I live in Scarsdale" ([1983] 1990, 102). In the hands of a less capable writer, the image of gray-haired, plump women sipping wine and feigning interest in each other might well verge on cruel critique. But Johnson avoids this possibility by using the image as generative form: her memory of the reunion resurrects another Barnard student, her Beat friend Elise Cowen, who committed suicide in 1962. Elise was such an important figure in Johnson's life—her soul mate—that even at the time Johnson wrote *Minor Characters* she was sometimes shocked "to remember Elise is dead and I can't pick up a phone and speak to her" (57). However, through the literary act of fusing memory and language, Johnson linguistically subverts death, bringing Elise back to life, seeing her as if she had lived into her thirties: a feisty presence with short, gray-streaked hair ("but maybe she changed her mind and let it grow long after all"), ready to walk through the Barnard gate to join her friend (104).

Johnson is cognizant of the illusionary nature of these forms. Be they external recordings such as photographs or internal recordings such as memory, they shape-shift depending on who positions them and how they are positioned. Sometimes, a self emerges through the juxtaposing of her own memory with someone else's scripting of memory. Johnson recalls that on the night she first met Kerouac she was "a very young woman in a red coat, round-faced and blonde." Johnson aligns this snapshot with Kerouac's memory of that same person, described in *Desolation Angels* as "a Jewess, elegant middleclass sad . . . looking for something—She looked Polish as hell" (1978, 133). The conjoining of the two images, not totally disparate but not mirror reflections of each other, complicate self-knowledge, suggesting that "reality," the historical construction of Beat no less than other moments in time, lies somewhere within the transactional meeting of subjects and objects, an amorphous and serendipitous meeting and shifting of possibilities.

In the Columbia photograph of the Beat triumvirate, Johnson discovers that when gender is an issue, this meeting frequently obliterates the female. She searches for what's missing from the Beat scene, and it is the women, in particular Edie Parker (Kerouac's first wife) and Joan Vollmer Adams (Burroughs's second wife), whose invisibility strikes her as most telling. Johnson has never seen their pictures, but she constructs her own images based on the tales she has heard and read about them. She imagines Edie full of exuberance and good will, a young woman who worked as a longshoreman, ready to play with the boys, but sensing that Jack would always prefer his friend Lucien Carr to her. Of Joan, she says she might have loved her if she'd known her: witty, well read and beautiful. Joan's intelligence matched William's point by point, but she was unable to defeat her drug addiction, and one night Burroughs shot her to death in a game of William Tell. Was her death "a knowing, prescient act of suicide?" or her final act "a demonstration of her faith and trust. . . . [a] final gift to Bill?" Johnson wonders ([1983] 1990, 5–6), in effect exculpating William but nonetheless imagining Joan as a willful human presence. Edie's and Joan's stories are outlaw stories that reach back to the omphalos of Johnson's own coming-of-age. They are her mentors, her story a more successful variation on the ones they tried to make of their own lives. Creating her life through those of other women is central to Johnson's aesthetics. Forging a kind of solidarity in both lived and imagined experience, she suggests that the self can be known only by knowing/creating others. The individual is the compilation of concentric circles, centers fluctuating, boundaries expanding and contracting with the telling of each new story. Cowen's story, a poignant thread binding the narrative, as well as that of Johnson's friend Hettie Cohen, who defied the ethos of racism by marrying the black poet LeRoi Jones, also function this way. Both complement Joan's and Edie's stories to testify that any woman's emancipation stands upon the ground of all others who have gone before.

The major technique that Johnson uses to construct these stories is ironic, point-counterpoint copula, bringing into significant relationship events heretofore unconnected. This technique underscores both the difficult, sometimes life-threatening, obstacles faced by women in the early fifties and the way in which women associated with Beat struggled to define themselves as human agents and artists. For instance, in Johnson's creative writing class at Barnard in 1953, she learns from a male "Professor X" that if the female students were real writers they wouldn't be sitting in his classroom: "You'd be hopping freight trains, riding through America" ([1983] 1990, 85), he tells them. These words of (dis)encouragement are followed by a description of Ginsberg, who in January of 1954 is in the Yucatan living Professor X's dictate, experiencing poetic visions of his mother and his tragic Beat friends (84–85). Even more disturbing is the way in which Johnson connects her own journey to have an abortion with Kerouac's trip to Desolation Peak, where he would spend the summer as a firewatcher in isolation with God and nature, an event that occurred before Johnson met him and that was fictionalized in *The Dharma Bums*. The juxtaposition highlights the gulf of inequality confronting women like Johnson. Her story reveals a "nature" very different from Kerouac's. Her landscape is void of the lithesome butterfly, comic chipmunk, and joy-filled birds that populate Kerouac's idyllic world. Instead, she must traverse the furtive backroom abortion clinic as well as the subjugated female body itself, lying supine and helpless, its flesh the territory of an impervious social system that denies women reproductive freedom (112–116). In both cases, the alignment of the image of Johnson in a hostile, enclosed environment (i.e., male-dominated classroom and abortion clinic) with that of Kerouac and Ginsberg free to roam the world signifies the desires of the female artist and the bleak realities of actualizing those desires.

Johnson's play with this process is risky—risky, that is, for a life writer who bears the burden of truth telling. But as James wrote, "to represent and illustrate the past, the actions of men [and women] is the task of both the historian and the novelist" (6). With the stories of Joan Vollmer Adams, Edie Parker, and Cowen, for instance, Johnson is concerned with a different kind of truth: not so much the telling of what really happened (she knows that it's impossible to achieve complete representation of the past), but rather the telling of what she and other women associated with the Beat movement felt, which can be communicated more effectively through metaphoric narrative. The making and knowing of herself in the concentric, spiraling stories of others, be they male or female, is not so much a plot, driven by action, but the revelation of character. The narratives blend the truth of historical discourse with the truth of emotive poetics, the former verifiable through the assembling of documentation, the latter through the felt response of author and reader.

Most dramatic are her reconstructions of the life of Kerouac's mother, and through these fictive meditations or imaginative projections Johnson comes as close as humanly possible to claiming the center of Kerouac's life and to proclaiming her own understanding of the maternal moment. Very little is known of Gabrielle "Memere" Kerouac, and what is found in biographies of Kerouac presents her as a domineering woman trapped in working-class domesticity and a dangerous cathexis with her youngest son. But even though Kerouac's mother treated Johnson rudely the one time they met (Johnson and Kerouac,143), Johnson's literary self presents Memere more sympathetically. Empathizing with the older woman, even going so far as to place herself in Memere's body and consciousness, Johnson envi-

sions the heartbreak of a mother who has lost her oldest son and turns to
the younger one for comfort: "I can see how she must have clung to the
younger boy, taking him into her bed night after night . . . breaking all the
Freudian rules. . . . There was her own need, the warmth of her small son's
light little body curled into her own, the dreamy fragrance of his hair"
([1983] 1990, 18). She muses about the old woman's experiences traveling
with Jack across the country, feeling bridal at last: "It's all luxury and gai-
ety, not hardship. With her boy Jackey beside her, she's seeing the world at
last" (164). And finally Johnson confronts the inevitable moment when
death separates them:

> In the room where another child has died, a small boy, Jean Louis
> Kerouac, lies waiting for his Memere. She will kiss him and turn out
> the light, abandoning him to the dark that has taken his brother. One
> day he will go to sleep and never wake up, for all the prayers of the
> nuns at school and the priests in their black suits and his mother's
> weeping . . . She's thinking, I'll never let this one go. I'll protect him
> from everything bad.
> The stone comes down upon him, turns into flesh. (240)

These passages mirror the progression of Johnson's relationship with Kerouac: her maternal needs, her own desire to go on the road, her attachment
to him, the break-up, and his early death. The fictions function as an indirect method of telling another part of Johnson's own story, reifying a set of
complex needs, including the desires to mother and to escape domesticity,
that characterized not only Johnson but many other women who broke out
and into the Beat world.

Throughout *Minor Characters*, Johnson makes evident that the Beat and
the female self are the construction of both the tangible and the intangible,
including the names that we are given and that we give to ourselves:
hers are "Joyce" (a legal label bestowed by her parents), "Rejoyce" (a gift of
Elise), and "Joycey" and "Ecstacy Pie" (endearments from Kerouac). This
ephemeral, linguistic self stands alongside the self built with the traces of
material evidence that testifies to human existence, an understanding that
girds and is most distinct in the conclusion of the memoir. At this point in
her story, Johnson's life as Beat girlfriend has lost its potency, and it is female friendship that sustains her movement from youth into middle age: it

is Elise who joins Johnson to help her complete the Beat woman's story. Separation is the theme as Johnson relives Elise's death by suicide through a pastiche of letters, poems, newspaper clippings, snippets of remembered conversations, and images of one of Johnson's last meetings with her. The form enables Elise to speak for herself, first to Johnson in an upbeat letter dated 1959 from Berkeley and then to readers through her poetry. The mingling of her voice with those of others underscores the extent to which an individual is known through the subjective lens of social and literary conventions. The newspaper presents her as anonymous: "Woman 28 Found Dead" ([1983] 1990, 270); Elise describes herself as "In a black park of bed" (271), and Ginsberg remembers her as "more beautiful than poem" (270). The effect is to emphasize the slim traces upon which knowledge of one's past is based, the disparity between self-perception and the systems of discourse guiding the processes of perception, and the powerlessness of one's own words to convey the truth of what is known about and felt for another human being.

As the narrative closes, Johnson looks again at a snapshot. This time it is a photo of a young girl in black stockings, skirt, and sweater. It is Joyce Glassman, twenty-two, a young Beat woman full of expectancy, happy to sit with a group of men whose voices rise and fall. The forty-seven-year-old woman who views the photo wishes upon the younger one a voice, the giving up of the silence so prevalently linked with Beat "chicks," girlfriends, wives, and mothers. While she has done the best she can, she is left with a sense that one can never tell the past as one would like: "If time were like a passage of music, you could keep going back to it till you got it right" ([1983] 1990, 277). But life is not art, and memoir is not entirely fiction. Time, and ultimately self-representation and Beat history, remain impermanent.

Jones's memoir draws upon some of these same techniques, including scene setting, meditation on memory, and the revelation of a multiplicity of selves situated in the context of linguistic impermanence. However, *How I Became Hettie Jones,* instead of aligning life writing with remembered images or photographs, works more like Navajo sand painting, the ritualistic placement of tiny crystals of sand to form images of magic power. As Jones's story unfolds, we see the traces of her methodical arrangement of textual fragments to construct a self in a magic space where she can heal the wounds caused by her parents' racism, by her belief that she was different from so many other women of her generation, and by the political decision of her husband, the African American poet LeRoi Jones (now Amiri Baraka), to divorce her. The self that emerges through the patient and painful ritual of storytelling is diaphanous and transitory, disappearing and reappearing each time a reader closes and opens her book. But it is a self that is profoundly there each time her story ends, a self intent upon teaching all she knows about the strength of the human heart.

Like Johnson, Jones uses the shifting of past-tense and present-tense narration to signal that the past is a constant present in memory, and it is not insignificant that she begins her story with a brief present-tense image of herself as young Hettie Cohen on the day she first meets Roi, bringing together the two images of herself with whom she has the deepest affinity: the twenty-two-year-old Cohen who has just left her family in Laurelton, New York, for adventure and love in the Beat haven of Greenwich Village, and the fifty-five-year-old Jones who refuses to abandon the passion and expansive spirit of that younger self. It is an effective strategy to set up the narrative, which shifts quickly back to her childhood. This she constructs through a mosaic of remembered images, the careful configuring of fragments of memory like grains of sand for ritualistic purposes. She remembers weaving clouds into a basket when she was a six-year-old at camp, learning to iron with her mother, noting her parents' refusal to speak of their history as Jewish immigrants, and experiencing race for the first time at Mary Washington College in Virginia. All are remnants of her past, hardly a seamless time line, that through her intentional selection and arrangement speak to her deep desire, known since she was a child, to "become—something, anything . . . " (1990, 10). In their placement, the young-woman-to-be living at the center of Beat is cradled within the imagination of the little girl from Laurelton full of hope and potential.

This mosaic effect appears throughout the text. Many of the chapters are composed of subsections of varied length, some just a short paragraph, skipping back and forth in time, creating the illusion of the human self in perpetual generative motion. Indeed, Jones is a skillful manipulator of the temporal and corporeal. Through what Roland Barthes calls the "chronological code," she constructs the copresence of three temporalities: the self of memory, the self of artful creation, and the self of material reality. This feat, more common to painting and film, is extremely difficult to accomplish with words, a medium driven by the impulse to compartmentalize and sequentialize time. Jones, however, manipulates the code with considerable dexterity. In perhaps the most striking example, the weaving of temporal codes reifies the significance of gender differences in her relationship with Roi. At the point when they marry, she reflects on her name being changed from Cohen to Jones, noting that other transformations awaited both herself and Roi. Her narrative self, writing consciously from the present, moves into the past to assume a prophetic stance. Roi she envisions as a static masculine presence: "He would remain, like any man of any race, exactly as he was, augmented." Her own self is more fluid, someone who had to lose her past in order to move into the present to "become the person who speaks to you now," as she tells the reader (1990, 65). But she resists the full loss of that past, and from a point of close narrative proximity to the moment of textual production, collapses the present into the past through the image of the autobiographer looking down from her window at her younger self, stepping along the sidewalk toward the place where her beloved café, the Five Spot, once stood. In only a few words, Jones constructs a discursive interstitial realm in which time and space are captured in static kinesis, her past and present painted together and thus residing as coherent whole.

This focus on place existing as temporal reality is central to her story. Place acts as a metaphor for time and Beat, an epistemological equation that occasionally becomes explicit: "Twentieth Street was a *young time,* a wild, wide-open hot time, full of love and rage and heart and soul and jism" (1990, 71, emphasis mine). The demarcating of a space triggers memory and thus the re-creation of the creation of self. The book is divided into sections named for the places Jones called home in New York: Twentieth Street is preceded by Morton Street and followed by Fourteenth Street and Cooper Square (where she still resides). Community gathering spots, including famous Beat enclaves such as the Cedar Tavern and the Five Spot, receive almost equal attention. These are the symbolic vessels of memory holding the materiality of her story/life, places where she and Roi were happy; where the hip stars of the literary and visual art scenes congregated; where her children were born; where she typed and did layout work on *Yugen,* the literary journal that promoted so many young Beat writers; where she and Roi made love.

Home is depicted in vivid and tender detail—the shape of rooms, the

color of walls, the floor plans, the nearness of her space to the space of others. As one space opens into another, it is always linked by the shadow of
Roi, the presence of their children, the artifacts of domesticity—kitchen
sink, toilets, heaters, and desks that the family carried with them as they
moved. Nothing is wasted; nothing dies. Even an old pair of sneakers that
Jones finds abandoned by the previous tenants of 27 Cooper Square fits her
perfectly and assumes new life. Jones was aware of domesticity as a cliché
when associated with women's autobiographies and memoirs.[4] But in her
claiming and manipulating of the convention, she manages to avoid vacu-
ity, the domestic sphere becomes an analogue for time and an ironic, gendered twist on the Beat belief in home as something from which to escape.
Home then stands as a powerful trope for the rebuilding of her Beat past
and projects the pulse of progression nurtured by remembrance. Memory
evolves as a map of sorts fixing the impulse to live in the becoming by sustaining the palpable past.

   While Jones is ferocious about the need to reconstruct a past, memory
fails her at times, as she knows it must, and cannot reveal all the answers to
her own life or that of other Women Beats, perhaps because these answers
just aren't there. When she encounters the inevitable blank spots of consciousness, she turns to other documentary forms to assemble what might
have been. Writing about the day Roi told her he was leaving her because
she was white, a turning point in his own development through Beat poetics into the Black Power movement, she confesses that all she can see is the
"open door behind his back" (1990, 218). Against that image, she places remembered bits of their conversation and excerpts from Roi's memoir, published in 1984. The scenario she constructs is a plausible rendition of what
likely transpired that day, but the scene is fragmented and contrived, important perhaps not so much because of her attention to veracity but because of its power to express her pain and her need to reconcile that part of
her life with what had preceded it and would follow it.

   Jones is equally committed to pulling herself and the reader back into
the present, frequently reminding one that she is conscious of creation as
an experience of the present, which she signals by demanding reader participation in her storytelling. The first sentence of the book declares as
much. Rather than speaking to herself of herself (the conventional and
clichéd "I was born in a house my father built"), as is typical of life writing,
she opens the narrative with "Meet Hettie Cohen" (1990, 1), a device echo-

ing with gendered irony the epic story of Ishmael in Melville's *Moby-Dick* and situating the reader alongside the narrating subject. We are there with her because the now—Hettie Jones has used a convention of speech discourse, the face-to-face introduction, to join our hands in greeting with her younger self. The tone created is one of acceptance and openness. Her story is contingent upon the reader's presence. Narrative is collaborative.

It is also significant that the introduction assumes the imperative mood. While congenial and open, it is also a directive. The present for Jones becomes a place from which she can exercise her fondness for teaching and preaching. The second-person "you" fuses both of these functions, incorporating the reader into the story and distilling axiomatic thought. She declares, "For those who still don't believe it, race disappears in the house — in the bathroom, under the covers, in the bedbugs in your common mattress, in the morning sleep in your eyes" (1990, 36). Of herself and Roi, she writes: "Look at us there, if you will, in that chilly spring dawn. Two twenty-five-year old kids with a kid, in the middle of a lot of commotion. Do you see race in this? Have you forgotten? It would get worse" (104). At times, her language almost begs the reader to converse with her:

> How do I feel about this, really? It can't be self-hate that's causing my heart to leap at each bound of his legs. It can't be that I've *paid*—what can it be? Why am I happy? Do you call it love as he gathers me up and we push through the door and crash to the bed in a quick, shivery, clothes-on connection? Can you lust for the one you love so domestically? And what, later, was that tender light in his eyes? (166)

Answers to these questions elude her, but the presence of the reader serves as a sounding board for Jones; she uses memoir to reflect upon the difficulties of achieving Beat harmony in a racially divided world—and to give thanks where thanks is due.

Jones also uses the evidence with which language builds the self, splicing the narrative with poems, journal entries, and personal correspondence. Here she shares Johnson's affinity for the contemporary revelation of the skeleton of life writing, but she uses this material more liberally than does Johnson, and thus to a different effect. Many of these collaged texts are authored by artists from the period, including Billie Holiday, Robert Creeley, Charles Olson, Michael McClure, Ron Loewinsohn, and LeRoi Jones. Jones is forthright about the ways in which such texts can speak for her and the culture of the time—their powers of language seem to her greater than her own. These embedded texts present the literary and political culture of Beat history, its intersection with other artistic and social movements. They also enact Jones's sense of self as relational, that is, seeking herself in another, losing herself in another in order to separate from that other. She finds, for instance, comfort in Olson's pronouncement that what remains constant "is the will to change" (1990, 116), company in Creeley's "Let me be my own fool"(148), connection with McClure's "huge reality of touch and love" (77), and sagacity in Kay Boyle's belief that "there's no way even the honest among us can be trusted" (185). In the aggregate, the dialogic blending of voices—some Beat, some Black Mountain—manifests reverence for the individual and choral persona and is akin to the isolation of the individual in the ritual practice of sand painting, where the practitioner gives up personal language to the sacred songs of the ancients to achieve the power to heal.

Most striking is Jones's claim that it is life writing itself, the act of writing and the artifact of that act, that furnishes the opportunity for self-knowledge. An important element of this process is her own emergence as a poet. Unlike Johnson, whose authorial voice suggests that her memoir need not call attention to the author's success as a novelist, Jones uses the memoir to pick at the question of whether she is a writer and, if so, what kind. She claims not to have written, to have failed in some way to engage fully the Beat and bohemian call to dedicate life to art. But the memoir speaks differently, the very material with which she constructs the book implying a hesitant but unavoidable self-reflexivity with regard to literary creation. In the extranarrative literary material that Jones relies upon, she includes four of her own untitled poems and a prose story about Olson. These are powerful reminders to her readers and perhaps herself that, while unconfident about her talents ("Though I admired poets like Denise Levertov and Barbara Guest, I felt I could never write like they did" [1990, 148]), she was writing all along.

The earliest work that she includes is a short, imagistic lyric from the late fifties when she first met Roi, a poem somewhat reminiscent of the poetry of William Carlos Williams, whom she admires. This poem, coupled with the Olson story, a dreamy, fairy tale–like story of a vatic poet who saw in a young woman (Jones herself) promise that others couldn't see, and which was written years later, reflects her persistent turn to canonized male figures of the period for artistic validation. The remaining poems, however,

display through the veneer of life writing itself the development of her poetics. One, written while she lived at Cooper Square with Roi, captures the
tenor of her household life:

> My dearest darling
> will you take out
> the garbage, the fish heads
> the cats
> wouldn't eat
>
> the children are sleeping
> I cannot hear them breathing
>
> Will you be my friend
> and protector from all evil
> . . . .
> (1990, 209)

A fairy-tale motif is evident in the poem: the need to have a husband as pro-
tector. But the lyric voice settles upon distinctly nontraditional poetic material, thereby elevating mundane tasks of the domestic/female sphere into
art. The voice, in Beat fashion, follows the natural breath of the poet, her
plea for assistance becoming a tiny evocation of tranquility and harmony.

However, a poem written earlier, during her Fourteenth Street years
with Roi, questions the myth of domestic bliss:

> I've been alive since thirty-four
> and I've sung every song
>   since before the War
> Will the press of this music
>   warp my soul
> till I'm wrinkled and gnarled
>   and old and small—
> A crone in the marshes
> singing and singing
>
> . . . .
> (1990, 150)

The poem relies too heavily upon a clumsy iambic meter, but it reflects a feminist consciousness unveiling the cultural metamorphosis into hag or "crone" of a young woman who has experienced much of life. The transformation, represented as music, or art itself, is loosely connected to the eighteenth- and nineteenth-century ideal of republican motherhood through the reference to World War II, a configuration pushing the speaker farther and farther outside the boundaries of human community, much as does Jones's association with Beat and bohemia, which ostracized her from the aspirations of her middle-class Jewish family. However, in keeping with Beat poetics, she uses the lyric moment to invest herself with prophetic self-determination: the power to continue to sing, that is, to create art no matter where she is. Out of a Beat ethos conjoined with a protofeminist consciousness, she envisions her older and wiser self who has embraced her independence and her identity as poet.

Ultimately, it is the telling of the story of her relationship with Roi that facilities Jones's conclusions about self-identity and her place in the Beat avant-garde, as she carefully places the pieces of the narrative, like magic crystals of sand in a sand painting, in a configuration that brings both closure and potentiality to her life. The process depends upon not only fragments of memory but also the power of naming based on arbitrary linguistic markers, their socially derived purpose as prescriptions of self. Is she LeRoi Jones's white wife, the former Hettie Cohen, as she is described in literary histories? Is she H. Cohen-Jones, the professional name Roi gave her for the *Yugen* masthead? Is she Mrs. Hettie Jones, the name given her by *The Chicago Manual of Style*? Is she E. L. Jones/care of Mrs. Hettie Jones, the name given her by the telephone company after her divorce? As she ends the book, she surmises that she remains a name, Hettie, the one signifier that has stood constant throughout, elegant in its relative isolation from patrilineal ownership, centering all the others. In this respect, Jones's creation of her own Beat history through that of others serves as part song of confession and part song of praise. Not unlike the sand painter who performs the ritual act of singing a healing chant and creating a magic image, she inhabits a magic space where she can trace the shadowy lines of her past, filling in the gaps, giving color and form to blankness, and daring to ask why she did not write more and why she (and so many other women in the Beat world) remained silent. Answers do not come easily, but by contemplating these stories, she builds a logic to explain her own. The woman who has now become, and has always been, Hettie suggests that in prose and po-etry—both blended in memoir—no one is ever anything less than the great process of becoming, a long sweep of selves held together with imag-ination and faith.

In contrast to Johnson's and Jones's memoirs, Brenda Frazer's *Troia* and Diane di Prima's *Memoirs of a Beatnik* play fast and loose with both the form and the content of life writing, conflating truth/fact distinctions, question-ing the correlation between and nature of figuration and referent, chal-lenging—and often then undermining—a relational act that creates reader identification with the life writer through desires, fears, and other affective bonds (Miller 2000, 423). These memoirs do not make a coherent history of either the female as author or the Beat literary movement. While *Troia* and *Memoirs of a Beatnik* remain partially faithful to the fundamental con-tract between author and reader, delivering on the promise to report the lived experiences of the signatory of the text, that sign is forced to relin-quish considerable space to simulacra, that is, imitations of the authorial presence repeatedly shattered and reconstituted. The result is a hybridity that defies easy categorization. *Troia* and *Memoirs of a Beatnik* slip repeat-edly from history into fiction, from novel into memoir—in effect, per-forming Beat rather than reporting on Beat—and in this respect stand as aesthetically more closely aligned with Beat poetics than do Johnson's and Jones's memoirs, foregrounding an aesthetic that claims a literary tradition while simultaneously subverting it. Both texts have much in common with Kerouac's construction of his ambiguously fictive/autobiographical Duluoz Legend, in which he blurs the distinction between poetry and prose as he remembers his life through the act of "free deviation (association) of mind into limitless blow-on-subject seas of thought" (Charters 1992, 57); with Ginsberg's fusion of poetics and serial life writing in poems such as "Howl," "Kaddish," "Television Was a Baby Crawling Towards That Deathchamber," "Wales Visitation," and "White Shroud"; and with Ginsberg's and Bur-roughs's literary play of fiction and personal correspondence in *The Yage Letters*. Reading *Troia* and *Memoirs of a Beatnik*, then, becomes not unlike viewing a film in which the physical presence of the actor, itself a distinct artifice, subsumes to a great extent the ontological presence of the autho-rial/actor referent and the act of history-making itself.

Memoirs of a Beatnik, for example, is a bawdy narrative, the title of which clearly suggests reflective life writing. And it is to some extent. For instance, di Prima weaves in just enough credible history to sustain her narrator's persona as a concrete referent in a verifiable historical moment, writing quite convincingly of her memories of the fifties bar scene in the Village, the lofts and pads inhabited by painters and writers, the Rule of Cool governing subterranean behavior, and the tempo and tenure of this community which was giving birth to new forms of literature, art, music, and politics. She offers glimpses of what this life must have been like for her as she shaped her identity as a poet: her reading of Greek, her reference to herself as "Lady Writer," her relationship with Ezra Pound, her initial encounter with Ginsberg's "Howl," and the publication in 1958 of her first book of poems, *This Kind of Bird Flies Backwards*. These are but marginal notes, however. The book, originally commissioned by Maurice Grodias at Olympia Press, resists memoir so boldly that the heroine emerges as more of a grainy pornographic film star than a meditative author sitting at her desk writing a Beat history. Di Prima uses tropes of Beat to tell a story, but, unlike Johnson and Jones, she remains fundamentally uninterested in accounting for any particular historical period or social movement and is thus free to be more fictive, inventive, and playful—to depart from the fidelity that is requisite for the author/reader contract implicit in life writing. Di Prima delivers a bifurcated story: one a fictive erotica and the other a nonfictive representation of Beat New York, the former overpowering the latter. Both, however, are told from a female perspective and verge on overt didacticism, establishing a narrative whole that breaks formalist constraints to confound reader expectations of personal history.

The narrative begins in 1953, when di Prima, of Italian descent and a native of Brooklyn, dropped out of Swarthmore College. The text is structured for the most part upon the organic drift of the seasons from 1953 through 1956, but it essentially resists residence in quantifiable temporality, the seasonal motif eventually giving way to chapters focused on disparate concepts, such as "The Pad," "Organs and Orgasms," and "We Set Out." These are linked by a first-person narrator providing an overarching voice of authority and by the cinematic technique of montage, the cutting and splicing of scenes (and thus time) to present a set, or sets, of interconnected ideas. The recombinant form implies an author simply enjoying the process of telling a story, moving from one scene to another much as one's memory floats leisurely through time.

The montage itself is dominated by the concept of identity. Di Prima's most constitutive definition of identity is that of a member of a group—the Beat, the ethos of which, as Susan Mokey argues, "enables both her sexual adventures and the practice of her art" as a poet, di Prima depicting "herself as a representative and an integral part of a community" (165–166). Mokey rightly contends that such self-representation is not analogous to the creation of a self subordinate to another's identity, such as someone's daughter, mother, or "chick." Rather, di Prima's communal self moves comfortably in and out of roles and is aware of her place in an avant-garde. The text, however, as the term *Beatnik* in the title signifies, is unconcerned about constructing a history of its author as female Beat. Rather, di Prima establishes a conception of self and group identity as a dialectical relationship, the construction of the communal identity a process dependent upon one's place in *other* communities. Her story not only reports her own experiences in a subterranean world—the Beat experience with which she did identify—but it also persistently comments on the popular (mis)understanding of this world, the larger cultural mythology of Beatnik life and art. *Beatnik,* a term coined by San Francisco journalist Herb Caen in the late fifties, is a pejorative that through the suffix "-nik" transformed Beat into the evil Soviet "commie" of the cold war decades. Simultaneously, these three small letters diminish and trivialize the demon Beat, converting evil into the childish and comic, effectively nullifying the potential cultural threat posed by those known as Beat. Thus di Prima's story of being a "Beat/nik" reflects the ways in which mainstream American culture, particularly popular media representations, constructed Beat avant-gardism as paradoxically degenerate/dangerous and infantile/inconsequential.

This narrative split effectively undermines the reader assumption that equates author, narrator, and protagonist and leads readers of life writing to associate such writing with concrete historical referents, in other words, the truth. Those who read di Prima's memoir must eventually abandon an all-out search for what we recognize as the historical di Prima, author of the memoir, and instead embrace her creation, something that we understand to be a fantasy di Prima, who soon dominates the text. It is the bifurcated story of these two, that is, the blending of Beat and Beatnik narratives, that subsumes the processes and materials by which the memoir is constructed. For instance, by projecting the popular version of Beatnik onto the story of visiting the family of her college roommate Tomi, a companion in the narrator's Beat life, di Prima performs the Beatnik cliché on her own history. Contrary to what other texts reveal about di Prima's childhood,[5] the narrator of *Memoirs* characterizes her family as illiterate and loving Italians, and as the narrative unfolds, the heritage of loving illiteracy is presented as superior to that of Tomi's Anglo European family, which, while claiming to be idealistically nuclear and upper class, is sexually deviant, self-destructive, and sadomasochistic, and draws di Prima into their perversions. Illiteracy and love then serve as a moral foil to the degeneracy of Tomi's world, explaining the quality of di Prima's real life as she may choose to remember it but also portraying the Beatnik life as cultural critics such as Herb Caen or Norman Podhoretz labeled it—alien, adventurous, dangerous, illicit, and cruel. This reversal codes the image as specious and nonreflexive, just as are Tomi's family and di Prima as narrator. The joke is on those who choose to believe in the Beatnik version of reality and are subtly mocked through di Prima's fictional mirror.

As this example suggests, a great deal of di Prima's fantasy narrative explores sex and sexuality, not surprising in that the cultural myth of the Beatnik life promotes sexual excess as a major theme. The Beat of magazine articles, cartoons, and films is a construction of unrestrained libido. Di Prima experimented widely with sex, and she believed in free love, and while the memoir acknowledges this, it also explores cultural distortions of these realities, beginning with the first chapter, an explicit description of the protagonist's lovemaking in a West Village pad with Ivan, a young man she had just met the night before. As subsequent chapters unfold, a pattern takes shape: di Prima relies on the *illusion* of memory, the setting of a scene in the past and the placing of herself in it, as a flashback or dreamlike technique to introduce sex scenes. This device, characteristic of erotic romance novels and pornographic fiction, enables a dramatic deviation from the truth provision of life writing, and much of the book relies upon these conventions of pornographic literature and films to present a string of characters in a minimal story line frequently interrupted by long scenes of various kinds of sex. Many of these involve heterosexual sex, including group sex, probably the most illustrative being the story of an orgy with Kerouac, Ginsberg, and Peter Orlovsky. Others feature lesbian sex, including sex between di Prima and Tomi, and group sex among di Prima and her college roommates.

For the most part, these are depicted as consensual and sensual sexual experiences, but the memoir also presents rape and incest, and the use of such explicit, violent sex has left di Prima open to the charge that she mimicked the male Beats and pandered to the more popular stereotype of Beats as sex crazed. Instead of developing the story of her life as a Beat writer, the narrator's descriptions of clitorises, cocks, and come subordinate her life as an artist, and thus the story of the Beat movement as an aesthetic movement, to the demands of a sometime publisher of pornography. Indeed, by writing for hire, which she announced in the afterword to the 1988 edition of *Memoirs of a Beatnik,* di Prima figured the female as sex object and male fantasy. The text's lesbian scenes, for example, function much as they do in male-focused pornography, as a salacious trigger of male sexuality; they do little to communicate much about how or why women may enjoy each other sexually. The incestuous relationship between Tomi and her younger brother, fifteen-year-old Sweet William, is presented dispassionately, the narrator admitting that she, di Prima, overcame a "momentary scruple" ([1969] 1998, 39) and observed them through the keyhole of William's bedroom. The scene depicts details of consensual sex missionary style between the brother and sister, culminating in Sweet William forcibly sodomizing Tomi. Di Prima as the narrator calmly watches for a while before wandering off to bed. Here, the narrator mimics the reader of erotica, more so than the reader of memoir, voyeuristically participating in the secret and the taboo. Rape and incest are constructed as the average Beatnik experience, the narrative unconcerned about exposing the cultural forces affirming and sustaining such destructive power relationships. The text, revealing a fundamental indeterminacy, seems to justify or satisfy the Beatnik stereotype while mocking that same construction so vehemently that it slips into an apparent condoning of rape.

The narrator is also the victim of rape in a later scene that can be read as a narrative and cultural device both to excite the sexual passions and to authorize rape. She casts herself as a naive woodland nymph, napping innocently in the sun when suddenly awakened by the weight of Tomi's father, Serge, attempting to rape her. The narrator resists at first, but just as suddenly, however, her fear is transformed: "This was Serge, poor silly Serge, who never got to screw his wife, and if he wanted to throw a fuck into me, why I might as well let him. It wasn't going to hurt me. Not a whole lot. Anyway, it didn't seem that I had much choice" ([1969] 1998, 48–49). In the face of rape, di Prima reconstitutes her initial act of self-defense into a ministration of mercy, the supposedly most expedient way to deal with the situation, and she claims that she enjoys her molestation. The scene, in some respects more shocking than Tomi's rape, is modeled on a particular form of a masculine fantasy: rape, the taking of the female body for male sexual gratification, is accepted as the woman gives herself up not only to the power of the male body but also to the myth of the ministering angel/mother who through the act of sexual intercourse nurtures the male. This is the fantastic fusion of the angel and the whore who restores the male to his full being as lover and father, a recurrent image in male-centered pornography and in many male-authored Beat texts. Again, di Prima's performance of this theme oscillates between meeting the demands of Olympia Press and mocking their formulaic construction, tropes of both Beat and Beatnik becoming the object of di Prima's gaze.

The presence of male-centered erotica, exemplified by these rapes, undermines representations of the historical di Prima's material experiences, the former dominating to such an extent that the latter seem trivial, almost an afterthought. But *Memoirs of a Beatnik* presents a highly complicated process of subverting its own textuality. Di Prima draws upon several narrative strategies to effectively question substance and form throughout the text, so that the text wiggles, waffles, and waves, evading efforts to know it fully. The dirty prose does not overwhelm all other narrative threads and Beatnik mythology fails to win out because di Prima's sex stories, many of which ratify male power, ironically exist as a compilation of stories that also sends a female-centered message, that of a woman's need to shape and assert her sexual identity in ways that defy male power. Through the very indeterminacy of the text, in which both Beatnik and Beat constructions of sexuality are mocked, the masculine genre of pornography is recontrived to convey a woman's coming-of-age from her point of view. Hers is a self who finds joy and liberation in sex, a self nonplussed by menstruation, pregnancy, abortion, and marriage—all institutionalized as taboos which have historically subordinated women to men and which women have internalized. It is interesting that both the Beat and the Beatnik narratives end when the narrator realizes she is pregnant, a scene which di Prima creates as entirely woman- and self-centered: her lover has split for the day, and she serenely begins to pack up her books: "for a whole new adventure was starting, and I had no idea where it would land me"([1969] 1998, 134). In effect, di Prima describes a re-visioning of the male Beat road story; it is now a pregnant woman who on her own willingly and eagerly leaves home to seek adventure. The self that speaks breaks the silence shrouding female sexuality and agency and declares that it is she who can set the rules, that sexual representation, no matter how hard or soft core, need not be an insult to or an assault upon women's rights.

Memoirs of a Beatnik, despite the contradictorily heroic and disturbing qualities of fantasy di Prima, continues to be pulled back into the nonfiction realm to such an extent that all erotic fantasy in the text is eventually, and paradoxically, subverted, the contractual structure of memoir surfacing in the midst of erotic fantasy. *Memoirs of a Beatnik* engages in textual subversion through the persistent undermining of dominant form by the juxtaposition of "other" or antithetical forms, each form collapsing into the space created by the new one to question the existence of the former. Most are nonfiction prose forms, variants on the memoir itself, implying the veracity of the text. Textual subversion begins almost immediately. In the first chapter, di Prima interrupts the erotic story of sex with Ivan by interjecting two paragraphs that shift the narrative perspective and voice slightly to destabilize the suspension of disbelief necessary for fiction. "There are as many kinds of kisses as there are people," the narrator says, assiduously supporting the claim with descriptions of various types. The statement ends with the imperative "List your favorites below" ([1969] 1998, 2–3), followed by a blank space of approximately seven lines intended for readers to use to generate their lists. The interactive form is reminiscent of short nonfiction features which are a staple in popular women's magazines, the kind targeted at an audience of young, single women interested in self-help and romance. Echoing the conventions of the magazine genre, the passage mocks the mass culture form of the memoir, while also subtly suggesting that di Prima's textual subversions are not mere vanity or entertainment but, like many other memoirs, have a nonfictive, didactic purpose.

Midpoint, the text aggressively picks up the pedagogical theme, becoming more like the memoirs of Johnson and Jones by attempting to set the record straight, to teach and correct. Di Prima asks, or expects, to be perceived as "historical" at this point and therefore to be believed. The chapter "Country Spring," for instance, is interrupted with a subsection titled "Fuck the Pill: A Digression" in which di Prima sternly admonishes her late 1960s readers, presumably women, who might think that the birth control pill is the answer to all their sexual problems: "The pill, the pill, the pill! I am so tired of hearing about the pill, hearing the praise of the pill! Let me tell you about the pill. It makes you fat" ([1969] 1998, 75). Describing the negative features of birth control devices and her own seemingly magic ability to have unprotected sex, up to a point, without becoming pregnant, she creates a narrator who has heard science claim to have liberated female sexuality but wants to set the record straight from her own experiences—and thus to assert her own authority. Di Prima's memory of birth control experiences serves as the bearer of truth in a text combining personal confession with deliberative, or political, rhetoric. Even the 1988 revised edition maintains this posture with a note at the bottom of the page warning that the section is not an endorsement of unsafe sex in the era of AIDS (74).

As the book nears its conclusion, didacticism meets textual subversion and the plaited narratives of Beat/Beatnik identity to obliterate vestiges of a unified form or the truthfulness of di Prima's erotic tale. Again interrupting the overarching narrative, di Prima inserts into a chapter on the Beatnik pad two subchapters, which, while not as acerbic as the pill section, face off against a naive reader. "A Night By The Fire: What You Would Like To Hear" makes explicit the relationship between fabula and audience. If it is a Beatnik story that one wants, this device claims "Here it is." On a mid-November evening, the narrator and a group of her friends have an orgy; the sex is explicit and hot, di Prima and friends all in one bed, giving each other pleasure until almost dawn as the fire in their fireplace slowly dies. However, the reality of di Prima's Beat life, and thus the thin membrane of Beatnik myth, is laid bare in the next subchapter, titled "A Night By The Fire: What Actually Happened," in which di Prima shifts her standpoint and retells the story in order to teach a lesson. The group sex portrayed in the previous subchapter is a reader's fantasy; the reality for the Beats on that autumn night in an inner-city pad is indifference, boredom, cold noses, a cheap phonograph playing a Stan Getz record, and di Prima wearing a sweat suit to keep warm. As a result, the concluding chapters, which seem the most memoir-like and informative, become suspect, as does all that precedes them. A reader may even doubt the extent to which the explicit sex scene with Kerouac, Ginsberg, and Orlovsky transpired as di Prima describes it. Life writing, then, as treated by di Prima, is not only a vehicle *and* facade for commercial eroticism but also a form that persistently seeks referential authority outside itself while mocking those very sources. The di Prima who concludes her memoir has puckishly played with a female persona that comfortably wears multiple identities, not the least of which is spoiler of the Beat cultural myth. Her narrative stands as a warped entity of celluloid fragility reflecting lines of naturalism but clearly an artifice for which the Beat detractor bears complicity.

Conversely, performing, or reifying, the Beat myth energizes Brenda Frazer's *Troia: Mexican Memoirs*. To move from di Prima's erotic cinema into Frazer's life as depicted in *Troia* is to enter a Felliniesque world of mutating sense and sensibility, one in which the author remains unconcerned not only about accounting for the Beat historical era and her own subjectivity but also for the artifice of memoir itself. In true Beat fashion, acting out her own movements appears to be Frazer's paramount concern as she constructs the story of her relationship with the Beat poet Ray Bremser, on the run from the New Jersey authorities for bail jumping, with whom she fled to Mexico in 1961 with their infant daughter, Rachel. *Troia* rivals in intensity and grotesque illusion the most surreal literary discourses from the period, generating images of a Mexican landscape upon which an outlaw woman madly makes love with her husband, succumbs to drug addiction, prostitutes herself to support her family, weathers degradation at the hands of U.S. police and Mexican petty bureaucrats, and eventually gives up her daughter for adoption to prolong her own life of unconstrained physical and psychological agency. The Beat self that Frazer constructs is a righteous woman assuming a posture of laudatory antinomianism, a combination of a gritty female Jesse James and a fairy tale princess who dares to defy Mexican and U.S. law as well as obnoxious and violent johns before returning home to an idyllic Greenwich Village scene where true love with Ray blooms again. Confessional and confrontational, *Troia* stands apart as a memoir that in form and content may be the most troubling and provocative of the Beat female life stories.

Frazer's memoir was written much closer to the period it portrays than were the other texts addressed in this essay, and the process by which she composed the narrative also differs markedly. *Troia* was not conceived as a book or as a story of the Beat generation. Rather, it was a collection of highly personal two-page narratives that Frazer, now back in the United States, wrote every day, five days a week, from March to November 1963 and sent weekly to Bremser, who was incarcerated in a New Jersey prison. Claiming that the texts were "literary business," they were able to subvert the prison regulation of only a one-page letter per week (Frazer 2000). The letters, disguised as story, were Frazer's effort to communicate with her husband about the difficulties they had had in Mexico and to establish a platform for mutual forgiveness. They also functioned as a sexual aid for the couple, denied conjugal rights by the New Jersey penal system. Frazer quit her job as a clerk/typist and went into virtual isolation during this period in order to concentrate on communicating with her husband. Often using music as a stimulant, she would sit at her typewriter each morning and spontaneously compose the text, which she had mapped out the day before, "reconstructing in [her] mind, going over things, and feeling things evolve about what [she] would write" (Grace 1999a). The letters, unrevised, were then sent to Bremser. The process, requiring strict authorial discipline, produced a collection of microstories, a selection of which were later, at Ray Bremser's prodding, arranged in a four-part book by her editor, Michael Perkins. Frazer herself was not involved in the construction of the narrative, which was published by Croton Press as *Troia: Mexican Memoirs* and then in 1971 in England as *For Love of Ray* (Grace 1999a). The storytelling process, unusual in that Frazer's motivations were radically different from those of most life writers and that the narrative whole was assembled by someone other than the author, much the way Burroughs constructed *Naked Lunch* and other texts, challenges analysis of her formal techniques.

The narrative voice of *Troia* immediately sets Frazer's memoir apart from the others in this study, violating expectations of the normative function of life writing to persuade the world of the importance of the self called "I." Unlike Johnson's and Jones's narrators, who appear more stable and reliable because the authors are fundamentally interested in correcting history, Frazer's narrator is a textual self created in correspondence with her husband in their own private world for their own private purposes—she has no need for, and little tolerance of, other readers. Even Bremser, her intended reader, is repudiated, and the text's other readers bear the brunt of this rejection as well. The preface to the book stridently defies anyone to understand or care about the "I." Calling the reader a "thrill seeker," an "other" who tries to use worthless philosophy to shelter Frazer from herself, this textual self screams on paper: "I intend to clear the atmosphere at least for my own breathing. That's how much I care for your morals—clear enough? Get off my back—I will moan and groan in misery no more"

(1969, 5). This self is openly confrontational and confessional, apparently unconcerned about anyone, even her partner in this epistolary marriage. It is through this disregard for conventional readers that Frazer nullifies the author-reader contract grounding life writing in veracity. In fact, in the preface to *Troia,* Frazer repudiates a writer's obligation to meet reader expectations, stating that a writer must concentrate only upon "those few minutes when you overcome the frustration, bridge the gap, and hold something incredibly beautiful to you; the point where you don't see yourself anymore but you are there" (1969, 1). Later, she speaks directly about the self she has created; writing, she has discovered, is a transformative process: "I can hardly believe that what I write is me. So it's all confusing if you stop to think about it seriously—better to make it a game, maybe even revel in it" (1969, 138–139). In this respect, her solipsistic immersion suggests that literary categories are inadequate to describe both the self and the process of creating and that adhering to any particularly prescribed arrangement of the text, especially the kind of factual obligations expected of historical textuality, will actually distance one from the truth. Frazer, then, as a neo-Platonist or expressivist, simply renders experience in its condition as a reality of the present, unconnected by links of logic :

> Usually I start out thinking of the general beauty of the things we undertake, . . . reworking conversations we have had with friends, or interesting conversations I have had with johns . . . and then from that I start considering, though briefly, what the other participants feel. But I usually prefer to have faith in what we personally have done, said and felt, and if the opposite reaction was not good, then it is they who have missed out, somehow. (1969, 139)

The "they" who have missed out are the others who have shared Frazer and Bremser's Beat adventures on the road, and the passage makes clear that these individuals are secondary at best to Frazer's creative processes. She's interested only in her own linguistic journey, the "me" about which she writes and marvels because it allows her to transcend herself. Thus by eschewing all form or design, she paradoxically generates a textual self freed to open itself to another—that is, freed to create confession, a genre with which life writing and Beat literary production have long been associated.

The confessional voice appears in Book One, the confrontational tone of the preface giving way to a voice intent upon disclosing as a sign of trust in her confessor the darkest recesses of Frazer's life. To this end, the self that Frazer creates speaks as a reporter and confidant for Bremser, her audience of one. "I was trying to get at the truth," she has explained. "I had this huge burden of guilt because I'd told him that. . . I couldn't live the desperate life anymore . . . I'd asked him to turn himself in. . . . and so then he was in jail. I was just sort of weepingly trying to make things okay between us" (Grace 1999a). Akin to *The 1001 Tales of Arabian Nights,* the text sustains the couple by using narrative to ward off death. Here, death would be the end of their relationship, which for Frazer would mean the potential loss of Bremser, initiator of the self she most valued. Consequently, she is reluctant to move ahead too quickly, to conclude too fast. Rather she elects to confound death as long as possible through a narrator that Frazer perceives will most inter-est her husband. For the most part, this self is a hooker and a sexual rene-gade. Much of the story reveals her experiences as a prostitute, a brutal life that she entered at Bremser's insistence that she support them. He also sometimes served as her pimp or watched as she sex had with other men. Detailed descriptions of these liaisons (although not focused as explicitly on the body as those in di Prima's *Memoirs*), some perhaps embellished as Frazer draws on memory and imagination (1969, 139), depict a woman who resisted and embraced sex for hire, as the following passage illustrates:

> The young man asks to sit down and I allow him to join me. His youth is a motivation for me to set the price as soon as I can. I am nervous, he tells me how impressed he was by my entire profile in silhouette, like a queen, a young queen. . . . We somehow achieve a good enough fuck and unity through conversation. . . . He wants me to sleep there and give him more. . . The second was an aftermath and reluctant for me, for I never want to do twice what I am getting paid for once. (1969, 100)

Following the masculine pattern of denying violation of the female, Frazer was often repulsed by the men who paid her but often overcame her dis-gust by allowing her body to respond to physical pleasure, much like the response of fantasy di Prima when raped by Serge. This kind of confession may have appealed to both Bremser and Frazer, who could have been aroused by the idea of his wife/herself finding sexual pleasure and pain simultaneously. This hypothesis is supported by the fact that while in Mexico they were both reading, and were much impressed by, the Marquis de Sade's *Juliette*.

However, the influence of de Sadean sadomasochism makes it difficult to accept Frazer's claim of female liberation: de Sade, who took such pleasure in torturing women, hardly seems a role model for female empowerment. Frazer, by embedding her philosophy of sexual freedom and pleasure in the conflicting discourse of prostitution grounded not in female liberation but in male exploitation of the female, ultimately thwarts liberation for the woman. The truth that she confesses is the contradictory discovery that as she becomes more self-assertive and independent as a prostitute—that is, more fully "woman"—her Beat effort to free herself from middle-class sexual mores leads to costly drug addiction, life-threatening abortions, humiliating beatings at the hands of johns and Bremser, and the devastating loss of her daughter. In other words, her attempt to shake off the guilt associated with sex for hire destroys the very woman she seeks to create.

The confessional role is eventually abandoned, and the memoir evolves into personal reflection and fiction. Mixed with the titillating sex stories are several threads suggesting that the letters-as-story allowed Frazer to confront Bremser with the pain he had caused her, and to address herself, to contemplate who she was: a young woman who had left a middle-class life in Washington, D.C., and become a street hustler. At times, Frazer as narrator reflects on how weary she is and how conflicted she feels, how the myths of romance and Beat freedom have been shattered by Bremser's behavior, how salvation may still be possible for her, and how the couple has deluded themselves into believing that rebel life on the margins can effect real cultural change. It is the story of her daughter, Rachel, however, that best expresses the shifting nature of the memoir as it moves from reflective history into redemptive fiction. Rachel is a ghostly presence, always "the baby Rach" whom Frazer seems to speak to throughout the letters, almost as if her tiny weight is still nestled against her mother's breast. Unafraid, uncorrupted, open to natural wonderment, this construction of Rachel is an innocent version of her mother, an elegiac shadow of Frazer herself, symbolic of Frazer's deep love for and desire to create the more laudable mother that the account implies she wishes she had been. Rachel's story also condemns Bremser for convincing Frazer to give up their daughter (an act that

Frazer can never fully forgive) and at the same time acknowledges that Frazer too carries the burden of participatory guilt: "Ray is in control I discover later, and I am just a useless wife who was so tired out that I did not dare to enjoy anything any more. . . The baby Rach sleeps next to us on the seat and I am unable to take care of her anymore. Say this is the end" (1969, 112). It is this heady weight of condemnation bound to guilt that anchors the memoir through the absence of the child.

These are gut-wrenching stories told with little conventional narrative structure and context from within which to discern their verisimilitude. So the story projects only minimal awareness of a self in a historical setting or the background detail requisite for an uninformed reader trying to find context and perspective for the story. The text carries vestiges of linearity, the adventure story contrived through Perkins's construction of the letters, but it relies most fully upon the free movement of mind through memory and feeling, the original form of Frazer's letters. The result is fragmentation and surrealism. Chapters and paragraphs, for example, begin in medias res. Time shifts suddenly within paragraphs and sentences, just as memory moves from moment to moment, and the narrative voice frequently repositions itself, breaking the illusion of narrative consistency and character development. Bremser himself becomes a mercurial presence sliding between polarities of concrete and shadow, the present-tense, second-person "you," whom Frazer addresses, a wispy other alongside the more potent remembered past. Other figures are treated similarly, often floating in and out of the text without explanatory apparatus; her sister, mother, father, and numerous people identified only by an initial or a first name (a convention of life writing to protect the referent and the author) are as ephemeral as wood smoke. Frazer depicts brief interactions with them and then they vanish, ironically legitimized as historical referents through the coded initial but given almost no narrative attention as representations grounded in temporal and corporeal veracity.

The effect of these narrative devices used to manipulate time is to dehistoricize *Troia,* which becomes a dreamlike, disembodied reality in which temporality and corporality are obliterated. This condition is, of course, an ironic and subversive configuration of memoir, which by definition claims serving history as its function. Indeed, time, space, and the body are contorted in *Troia,* spiraling away, toward, and around the events it records. Long, snaking, bebop sentences with distorted syntax capture a sense of speed and time travel, and Frazer's language, effecting the immediacy of memory, creates large cosmic movements across vast expanses of the New World, as in the following example:

> A road which grows out of the solid surety of modern highway dot-
> ting in weak secrecy into the plain to Abasolo where another almost
> not to be seen road, goes nowhere, but goes—we want to see where
> all the roads go, since then, but this first trip just get us there and
> quick, get us there where we are going, and we don't know yet that
> nothing waits but the bottom waiting to be scraped in our own whim-
> sical and full-of-love fashion—got to get there and quick—damn the
> crying and wet diapers and laps full of Gerbers on the bus, of leg
> cramps and numb to view—Padilla, Guemez, Ciudad Victoria,
> chicken salad sandwiches and the unknown feeling of a waterfall. . . .
> I look out and God drops from his hand the myriad stars and con-
> stellations I have never seen before, plumb to the horizon flat landed
> out beneath the giant horoscopic screen of Mexican heaven. (1969,
> 11–12)

Like a great, prescient, female eye sweeping the terrain, Frazer's textual self is empowered to unite the elements in a grand, metaphysical swirl. So great is her power that she can condemn the daily drudgery and dirtiness of motherhood while integrating it into her vision of the cosmos. Paradoxi-cally, visionary power appears to come to her through the ability of the self to focus on the extreme detail of the material world, including the mun-dane, to resist hierarchy and to zoom in toward thing-ness itself. In this re-spect, Frazer was intentionally following, but using for expression of female experience, Kerouac's method of sketching, setting an object before the mind and drawing it with words through concentration and visualization. "It was copying," she has explained,

> but it's different from sitting down and copy book copying. It's more
> like what you hear changes the way you think and the way you speak.
> The way he, Kerouac, fits words together—the sweetness of it, the
> way things expand when you look at it. I tried to keep those things in
> mind, to keep the transcendent quality in mind. . . . If I sound like
> Kerouac, it's because I tried to. I read him while I was writing, just like

I listened to Bessie Smith. I think it is in *Dr. Sax* that he talks about looking at the grain of the wood in the stairway of the porch of the house where he grew up. A way of concentrating, visualizing . . . I obeyed him. (Grace 1999a)

Like Kerouac's prose, Frazer's language moves toward the sublime and epiphanic by exulting in the surreal, a world apart, where odd images—chicken sandwiches and waterfalls, wet diapers and baby food—symbolically link the existential and the eternal. In this world, Frazer achieves an apotheosis of sorts, in which life writing is the vehicle by which she initially records and reflects on her experiences but moves beyond historical encoding to a state of sublime removal from time.

By the same token, surrealism, for both Kerouac and Frazer, effects the grotesque, horrific, and nightmarish. In Fazer's memoir, the surrealism of nightmare proves a useful tool to confront those events and emotions that so often elude the memoirist, especially the Beat woman trying to illustrate how she must put her body on the line to effect self-liberation. One of the most disturbing scenes in *Troia* is Frazer's account of an abortion, the surrealism achieved in part by the placement of the scene in the midst of a series of blasé descriptions of sex for hire. The procedure is a success, but while under the anesthetic Frazer has frightening dreams and feels herself about to vomit; after the surgery, she watches a nurse pull "ten yards of bloody gauze out of her womb"; then she runs screaming from the room as the doctor shoves a piece of vertebra in her face to demonstrate that the fetus was two months developed (1969, 167–168). The surrealistic play of images, portraying Frazer's experience as the object of gender terrorism, effectively communicates the intimate, emotional, and interior world of the memoirist, which is often difficult to do.

The nightmare of life in Mexico eventually devours its transcendental qualities, driving Frazer to separate from Bremser and eventually to return alone to the United States. This does not mean, however, that *Troia* concludes by assuming the mantle of realism. Normalcy, signaled by Frazer's return to her father's house and then to New York City, means taking on a more conventional female role, in this case, the fairy tale ending of romance. Frazer, walking alone in the Village, sees Bremser magically appear before her; they go back to his pad, have sex, and the romance begins anew, a classic subordination of the female to the sexual prowess of the male and the promise of love eternal. Perhaps this the only way her editors, Perkins and Bremser, could envision it. Perhaps it is the only way Frazer could envision it as well. The narrative self who concludes by finding the perfect "fuck" — the physical manifestation of the "Holy Grail" for which the Beats quested — has quashed the voice of anger that had so compellingly promised revolution, that is, movement out of Beat and into the counterculture of the sixties and early seventies. But in so doing, the memoir offers a different kind of revolution: a textual coup d'etat, the intentional collapsing of genre boundaries into a form that stands in aporic tension—neither fact nor fiction, but always both.

Conclusion

It is not so easy then to say that women from the Beat generation have written their memoirs and leave it at that, assuming a stability and purpose in the genre. Life writing, especially as claimed by the women writers, proves flexible enough to facilitate its own reshaping. The four female Beat memoirists have crafted their art so that memoir, a genre that first validated their subjectivity through their relationships with famous men and one commonly believed to depict truth rather than fiction, becomes the vehicle by which they escape the shadow of the famous Beat man's persona and participate in the creation of their own history and subjectivity. For Johnson and Jones, this meant reflecting years later on their early lives in the vortex of an exhilarating historical moment and on the form of memoir itself. For di Prima and Frazer, it meant scoffing at, and sometimes blatantly ignoring, that very form and those who dare to read it. Such acts constitute resistance to textual prescription, and, while not void of tension, ambiguity, and contradiction, illustrate the extent to which the women took responsibility for asserting their place in a pivotal period in American history. Beat women writers refused to wait for others to do this for them. Because they were there, carving out for themselves niches of resistance, they were able to create life stories that both alter and sustain cultural memory. By writing their own history, becoming both subject and creator and presenting themselves for public inspection through memoir, women writers of the Beat movement have joined their male compatriots as fellow travelers—and as innovative artists whose life writing questions the critical mechanisms that have long upheld the artifice of literary hierarchy.

Notes

1. The Haverty Kerouac memoir, engaging and artfully written, can contribute to the historical understanding of the emerging sense of the female self in the early years following the Second World War. As life writing, however, *Nobody's Wife* is problematic since Joan Haverty Kerouac never finished it, and the published text was heavily edited, perhaps rewritten, by John Bowers, the brother-in-law of Haverty Kerouac's son, David (vi). The text may well convey the voice of Kerouac's second wife, as her daughter Jan attests, but as either a valid history of women in the Beat era or an exemplar of Haverty's work as a writer, the book remains suspect. It may be more accurate to categorize the book as a novel that uses the names of real people rather than as a work of historical research and remembrance.

2. Paul de Man's essay "Autobiography as De-facement" is often cited in critical discussion of the validity of claiming that autobiographical writing is a distinct genre. De Man distinguishes between autobiography and memoir, grouping the latter with "mere reportage" and "chronicle" (919). With respect to Frazer's and di Prima's texts, de Man's analysis has some merit, especially his conclusion that "the works themselves always seem to shade off into neighboring or competing genres"(920) and that "the distinction between fiction and autobiography is not an either/or polarity but that it is undecidable" (921). It is important to note, though, that de Man uses these characteristics to argue that autobiography is inferior to fiction, a position with which I do not agree.

3. This photo appears in the Dennis McNally biography *Desolate Angel: Jack Kerouac, the Beat Generation, and America.*

4. Jones was at first hesitant to use home as the structural focus of the memoir: "I thought, oh god, people are going to think this is corny! You know, women always talk about their homes." However, she found the concept appropriate for several reasons: "I wanted this to be a woman's book. I thought men would not focus on their homes. But here I mean 'home' not just in terms of where we lived, but 'home' as the art scene. So it seemed like the likely place to locate not only my life but the literary life. And also because of the business of race, where things come together in terms of race. So it seemed very logical" (Grace 1999b, 124).

5. See, for instance, draft chapters of di Prima's autobiography, owned by the University of Louisville, and her recently published memoir *Recollections of My Life as a Woman: The New York Years* (2001). In both, she details how one of her grandfathers read Dante to her and listened to opera with her; she also describes the anger and hostility expressed by family members toward her and her own anger in response, especially toward her father.

To Deal with Parts and Particulars

Joanne Kyger's

Early Epic Poetics

Linda Russo

> . . none of these
> came into the story,
>
> it was epic, heroic and it was far
> from a basket a child upset
> and the spools that rolled to the floor . . .
>
> —H.D., *Helen in Egypt*

> I weave my own wiles.
>
> —Penelope in Homer's *The Odyssey*

Penelope marks time at her loom, weaving and unweaving. When her tapestry is done, the story told in *The Odyssey* will end. The inevitable is deferred by the making of that enduring present. Her repetitions maintain possibility, keep the narrative open, and history marks that only in passing. The generic origins of epic, the grand poetic form of history, heroics and culture, lie in the exclusion of her experiences and her actions—except where these might reflect on a hero's renown. If mythic figures like Helen of Troy and Penelope do not resemble women and only men are like them, it is perhaps because they are invented by men, pieces of a male mind, as Alice Notley writes in "Homer's Art" (1992, 491). Joanne Kyger's first book of poems, *The Tapestry and the Web* (1965), stands beside H.D.'s (Hilda Doolittle's) *Helen in Egypt* (1961) and Notley's *The Descent of Alette* (1996).[1] All are acts of imaginative intervention into epic invention, animating female presence, remaking the gender ideologies and histories transmitted from generation to generation in epic form. Their work is barbarous to the epic lexicon and makes the heroic narrative, the epic's raison d' être, a linguistic field in which the particularities of women's stories—in the revision of female epic figures—are given play.

Kyger has authored over fifteen books of poetry since *The Tapestry and the Web* was published. Many of these, such as *The Wonderful Focus of You* (1979), *Phenomenological* (1989), and more recently *Some Sketches from the Life of Helena Petrovna Blavatsky* (1996) and *Patzcuaro* (1999), dwell in and question received realities textual, social, and historical, often by taking up myths and mythic lives and altering structures of experience through the innovative structure of the poem. But it is *The Tapestry and the Web* that, by intervening upon the structure of the epic, constructs a new poetic space in which to explore and challenge received notions of gender and poetic authority, particularly those notions of the feminine fostered by cold war culture and reinforced in poetry by the masculinist rhetoric of the New American poetry—exhibited, for example, in Charles Olson's "Projective Verse" and Gary Snyder's *Myths and Texts*. As if in a direct line from Sappho, *The Tapestry and the Web* appears to be a collection of fragments. The poems are for the most part untitled; though summoned together in the table of contents by their first lines, they resist being woven into a categorical whole. As a web of various aberrant threads, these poems assert a new mode of poetic authority that diverges markedly from masculinist conceptions of the role of poet as maker. As she wrote in the third "Tapestry" poem, Kyger chose to work "with the detail / on the fragment" and to search "for bigger & better things" (1965, 40).

The heart of *The Tapestry and the Web* radically revises the story of the artful and long-patient Penelope, who while waiting for the return of her adventuring husband, Odysseus, delays by deceit 108 eager suitors, weaving a tapestry by day and unraveling it by night. Her story, rendered together with apocrypha, is reworked in two serial poems: a thematically united, six-page group, therein untitled but elsewhere referred to as the "Penelope poems" (1981, 86), and a nine-page sequence of seven numbered and two unnumbered poems titled "The Odyssey Poems."[2] The Penelope poems are indistinguishable as a series separate from surrounding poems except for their focused treatment of Penelope. Further distinction is blurred in the thematic interactions with poems scattered throughout the book, especially three poems titled "Tapestry," so that references to Penelope appear sporadically in *The Tapestry and the Web,* creating an evasive figure whose identity is diffused in a mode that can hardly be called a narrative. This tactic ensures that Penelope—and the untitled Penelope poems—will not be completely subsumed under their companion piece, "The Odyssey Poems." In their obscurity they shift about as apocrypha against which "The Odyssey Poems" appear more contained and defined.

   "The Odyssey Poems," for their part, continue to deform the figure of Penelope while incorporating the figure of Odysseus and the story of his return to Ithaca into a new narrative complex, one that collages references to contemporary contexts and details, as in the first poem, which appears to place Odysseus outside of San Francisco, where "the long paths and eucalyptus / are another country" (1965, 53). While the Penelope poems and "The Odyssey Poems" were not conceived of as purposefully disruptive— Kyger later described *The Tapestry and the Web* as "just the poems that I thought the strongest work I had done" (Ellingham 1982b, 109)—together they evince a large-scale renovation of *The Odyssey* as poetic and cultural authority, and the making of a female self through assembled and reassembled particulars. The figure of Penelope is opened to a radical recomposition, after which *The Odyssey* itself must be read anew.

   The totemic image of Snyder reading from *Myths and Texts* "sitting crosslegged on a table, with Jack Spicer sitting cross-legged *under* the table, like a troll under a bridge" (Kyger 1992, 191) serves as a figure for Kyger's hybrid poetic lineage and the divergent forms of poetic authority she encountered. During her early years in San Francisco, she developed mentor relationships with poets Robert Duncan and Jack Spicer and then traveled for four years (1960–1964) in Japan and India with her then-husband, Gary Snyder, during which time she wrote, alongside *The Tapestry and the*

Web, the provocative and illuminating *Japan and India Journals* (1981).[3] Thus *The Tapestry and the Web* grew out of Kyger's immersion in and subsequent absence from a persuasively male context, where writers were the dons of antiestablishment culture. Kyger had left the establishment—in this case, the University of California, Santa Barbara—one credit short of a bachelor's degree, and arrived in San Francisco in 1957, a year marked by the censorship trials about "Howl" and the overnight success of Jack Kerouac's *On the Road,* whose attention in the national press set the tone for the Beat Generation. As Michael Davidson shows in *The San Francisco Renaissance,* while "the Beats provided the most public demonstration that some sort of literary ferment was occurring in the Bay Area," the Beat movement was "only one strand in a much more diverse and eclectic movement" (60). That same year San Francisco felt the aftershock of the closing of Black Mountain College—where Charles Olson, whose "Projective Verse" would become a persuasive document, had been rector—as many young male poets arrived in search of community. A few found it in the Sunday Meetings held under the aegis of Duncan and Spicer.

Amidst these poetic upheavals, a young poet like Kyger was exposed to various poetic options, and she chose her influences as much as they seemed to have chosen her. In The Place, a popular North Beach bar, Kyger met recent Black Mountain émigré Joe Dunn, who invited her to the Sunday Meetings, where she found Duncan and Spicer informal teachers to several younger, predominantly gay poets, who were her classmates, the Sunday Meetings her first poetic school.

She was drawn to the mythic consciousness of Duncan and the exactitude of Spicer rather than the jazzy street vernacular of the Beat poets, such as Allen Ginsberg, Kerouac, or Bob Kaufman[4]—a situation which may be attributed to Kyger's marginal presence in the histories (though not in the fact) of the San Francisco Renaissance, largely histories of social and poetic exchange.[5] The poem is for Kyger not an occasion for lofty proclamation and protestation, as in Snyder's essay "North Beach," which declares "the spiritual and political loneliness of America" to be an occasion to "hitch a thousand miles to meet a friend" (1977, 45), or as in the opening line of Ginsberg's "America," "America I've given you all and now I'm nothing." As she comments dryly in her journal, "what woman ever writes a poem 'America I Love You'" (1981, 234). Kyger could develop an alternative to a poetics that, though tremendously popular, she felt to be ill fitting. Both

Duncan and Spicer, to different degrees, preferred a poetic authority invested in the making of poems rather than in political self-expression, and her desire to forgo a lofty masculinism was no doubt welcomed at the Sunday Meetings. There she encountered a rhetoric that focused on a poetic authority emergent in the process of composition rather than prior to the poem: the authority of the poet who is called into action by poems. This process of composition enabled someone with little traditional poetic authority to create her or his own. And because what lay behind this authority was not the muse and remained ungendered, it usefully counterbalanced otherwise popular prohibitions on female poetic genius, such as those Kyger encountered in Robert Graves's *The White Goddess,* which, in her words, inveighed: "if you happened to be a woman you had no access to the muse herself since you WERE female and couldn't take a (same sex) female, or a male, as your muse, therefore you could never be a great poet" (Kyger, undated, n.p.). Within this tight-knit poetic community that fostered her desire to develop her voice, poetry presented her the opportunity to fit herself to the role of a universalized poetic subject, not at the expense of gender, but in bringing the female self into closer view, identifying as "a human self, with all attendant identity anxieties" (Kyger, undated, n.p.).

The introductory poem of *The Tapestry and the Web,* "The Maze," written in 1958, was composed for the Sunday Meetings and can be read as a point of connection between Kyger and both her teachers—and a point of divergence from them. It met with much approval and was received as proof that she had achieved the much-valued voice espoused by Duncan and Spicer. "The Maze" contains an allusion to the figure of Penelope, who would emerge in the coming years as a significant guiding figure, "singing high melodies," a co-conspirator at the center of "their design" (1965, 12). The poem opens with an image in which the present and the past are fused: "I saw the / dead bird on the sidewalk / his neck uncovered / and prehistoric." The bird one encounters in a routine way, on the sidewalk, reveals its ancient source, proposes the existence of another, mythic, knowledge. The poem presents a willful, solitary adventurer "shrugging off hands / in treacherous places." Juxtaposed to the bird's selfless revelation, a literal maze in "the dead / governor's garden" is a form of patriarchal knowledge pointed out by an uncle. It embodies layers of both personal and mythic history; it is a pathway back and into history and her self:

the sky disappeared
and I
could hear
the sound of water
rushing

I knew each corner
without pausing

Held captive in a cave
Ulysses
sobbed for his wife
who was singing high

melodies
from the center of a
cobweb shawl
of their design
   (12)

The maze is easily navigable once it is revealed; "she knew each corner" because, the next stanza suggests, of her knowledge, in myth, of the captivity
of Ulysses and his wife. The "I" is "amazed"—confused, mixed together,
held together—by the poem that presents a defining architecture in which
memory and will are aligned with myth as guides.

The maze is a "made place" like that referred to in Duncan's poem "Often I am Permitted to Return to a Meadow," a place where new imaginations
are created, what Duncan calls a "place of first permission" (1960, 8). It is
where Kyger enters into the maze of mythic forms and figures to confront
that which is and is not hers—and to find or make her own. The imaginative and actively critical reweaving that Kyger undertakes in the Penelope
poems and "The Odyssey Poems" contrasts sharply with the disturbing
closing image of "The Maze":

                She

tortures

             the curtains of the window
                 shreds them
                 like some
                         insane insect

     creates a
                 demented web
             from the thin folds
             her possessed fingers
             clawing . . .
             (1965, 13)

She is helpless and can but claw the curtain into a "demented web" that
is, nonetheless, of her own design. The demented web maker recalls the
female creative genius domesticated and entrapped, as in the unnamed
female protagonist in Charlotte Perkins Gilman's *The Yellow Wallpaper,*
whose husband administers a putative cure that drives her insane. The web
maker at the window symbolizes the consequences of a failure to step into
the maze. She must act or be prohibited to act, proceed sanely or go insane.
The limitation that the image of the window proposes—that her adventures are another's, witnessed, or are purely imaginary —contrasts with the
image of a worker amidst a maze of texts the later poems reveal. In this light
"The Maze" anticipates working a way out of the maze over the six years
in which the rest of *The Tapestry and the Web* was written. It is a text that speaks
of its encounters with other texts punctuated with acceptances and rejections
of instruction; later, these serve as points where the text swerves out in a singular, unpredictable direction, a direction unanticipated by the precepts of the
tradition from which, like Athena from the head of Zeus, it sprang.
    No poet's education in the 1960s would have been complete without the
instruction of Olson, particularly that conveyed in his much-circulated essay, "Projective Verse," which appeared as a pamphlet from Totem Press in
1959.[6] There, prominent scrutiny is paid to the poetic line. In Olson's anat-
omized theory of the connection between head, ear, and syllable, and heart,
breath, and line, the line served as a measure of "the man who breathes as
well as his listenings." Although his focus on the breath privileged masculine force, it offered specific enough directives: "one perception must im-

mediately and directly lead to another" (1997, 239–240). Apropos of "Projective Verse," Kyger wrote that it hit her "like a whallop" (1981, 60). The poems in *The Tapestry and the Web,* chronologically ordered, mark the influence of Olson's blow; those written in late 1959 radically reconceptualize space in the vein of Olson's "graphic intervention in the field of the regularized page" (Fraser 2000, 178).[7] While in earlier poems, like "The Maze," the poetic line departs with regularity at the left margin, diverging only occasionally and then at quite regular tab stops; in later poems the left margin is dispersed by lines commencing in a scattered fashion down the page, a style that is crafted to achieve a visual balance. For Kyger, understanding the page as field translated into a consideration of how one "could move the line around very carefully" in relation to other lines on the page to dictate "how the poem was going to move, how the voice was going to move in a certain way, and how your physical speech moved thru the line" (1977, 63). "Physical speech" is both corporeal and conceptual. On the one hand, the line materializes the physical body, going "through your hand, and . . . out on the page" (64) and this spatialization reflected her imaginative complexity; the page space would reflect her "head space" (64). This realization, Kyger said, came from working with galleys set on a Linotype machine, where spacing was vastly different from that of her typewritten manuscript, the spacing of both technologies contrasting with where her "head space was" (64).

Kyger's engagement with Olson foregrounds a concern for a formally encoded conceptualization of her interiority and corresponds to a poetic epistemology where the poem, by piecing various materials together, enables a particular knowledge of the world. "Stories," as she wrote in the poem "vision of heaven & hell," are "spun out, *connected* / and put together" to become "our knowledge [and] expectancy" and it is "this creation that remains" (1965, 36, emphasis in original). Thus "put together," the structure of the poem was a frame upon which her self-knowledge could be enacted as history, given a precedent, and confirmed. Here Duncan's influence is perceptible, particularly his sense that the poem defines a world arising from a conscious retrieval of "first things that might define a world" (1960, 79). In "Those things we see are images of the past," Kyger drew upon the notion that things are also relics, "images of the past" out of which one constructs an understanding, an "interpretation," of the world:

From now, always, on the turning point, viewing back
                    and that delicious interpretation
    is the world, HOW CLEVER OF US

            An entirely new thing each time
        blind or not about it, always inventive—seeing
            stones,
        persimmons,
    moving a stone in dirt, oh where does it go
            she's fleet footed
        to be a tree, to be Jack Spicer in a dream
            to carry this around all day.   and every night
        the waves chuck full of things to happen

                    As clear as you can See
        it's done, isn't it, isn't that a *fact.*
        (1965, 49 emphasis in original)

Here the present is temporally complex; locating oneself in the present entails an interpretation of the past, a "viewing back" on "images of the past" that are not lapidary but shift and change, become decontextualized and foreign, thus new. Real things (stones, persimmons) are connected with the imaginary (being a tree, being Spicer in a dream) by a mythic version of the self. The line "She's fleet footed" recalls Hermes, Zeus's herald with winged golden sandals, and positions the "she" of the poem as a messenger; the metonymy around her recalls not the past but another temporal plane, ever present, which surfaces in the poem as possibility, "waves chuck full of things to happen." Things stay in the present, as the poem is present, as words are present in the poem, pulsating with potentiality, more real than the things/images they represent. It is this radical clash of words as representing things real and imaginary and the poem as a site of the slippage the adept poet/messenger might make between the two that makes Kyger's treatment of myth not simply a revision, but a re-envisioning. Thus, Kyger enacts what Duncan describes as "the poetic imagination [that] faces the challenge of finding a structure that will be the complex story of all the stories felt to be true, a myth in which something like the variety of man's experience of what is real may be contained" (1985, 6). That structure, for

Kyger, would emerge from finding the self, the "fleet footed" she, at a crucial nexus; the poem, finally, is what "you can see" clearly, what's "done" and emerges as "a fact."

Spicer's poetic instruction extended beyond the text into the field of poetic production that played out during Kyger's years in the Bay Area. He arranged her first public reading, at the Beer and Wine Mission on March 7, 1959, one of the most important events that preceded her trip to Japan. His magazine *J*, of which eight issues were published from 1959 to 1961, was her first print forum. Undoubtedly *J*'s permissive and accessible submission policy encouraged her to submit "Tapestry #3" (the second "Tapestry" poem in *The Tapestry and the Web*, beginning "The eye / is drawn / to the Bold / DESIGN"), which came out in the fourth issue. It was Kyger's first published poem and a defining occasion: "The world changed. I thought people on the street looked at me differently" (1992, 191). She was on her way to constructing, as the first line of the poem suggests, a new "bold design" in her poetry.

From Spicer's poetics she gained an eye for "the Real," a nonsubjective reception of poetic voice enabled through what he called "Dictation," drawing an analogy that illustrated a "difference between you and the Outside of you which is writing poetry" and the imperative "to keep as much of [one's] self as possible out of the poem" (1998, 7–8). In *The Tapestry and the Web*, Kyger's use of myth serves at once as a surface that makes that difference between the poet and "the Outside" perceptible. Her inclination toward myth was also encouraged by Duncan, who accorded it mystic powers: "The mythic content comes to us, commanding the design of the poem; it calls the poet into action, and with whatever lore and craft he has prepared himself for that call, he must answer to give body in the poem to the formative will" (1985, 13). Kyger synthesized these. Through the figure of Penelope, Kyger's own life could be seen and worked upon a mythic frame. She could keep herself "Outside" while dwelling "inside" myth, using poems as a structure in which to observe her situation as an American poet/wife abroad at a distance that provided some perspective on the difficulties and dissatisfactions associated with her roles.

Kyger discusses her interest in Homer in such situational terms. The Homeric landscape provided her with a conceptual "home," a web of images and associations that she called the "Homer Dome." This was a narrative that she could "get inside of," one that invited her, such that she "could fall in and out of that story for some time." She could find in the Homeric search for home a home for herself, while also connecting to poetry as a tradition. By thus connecting, she "learned that there was a big Story" in which being a woman entailed certain constraints (1983, 110). In the Penelope poems, Kyger explored a detail of the "big Story" that remains undeveloped in (or excised from) the Homeric texts she encountered while working in San Francisco's Brentano's bookstore, where she would jot off letters to Duncan and sneak into the overstock area to read. Kyger addressed what has long been a point of difficulty for Homeric scholars: the question of Penelope's intentions and character. As feminist critics have noted, all that could be heard in *The Odyssey* is not; Penelope's *kleos*, or "renown," literally all of which is heard, is characteristically "identical with her capacity for endurance and her faithfulness to Odysseus" (Katz, 5–6). In a more radical reading, Kyger included what is not heard in *The Odyssey* to formulate an interpretation. She inscribed another Penelope, scandalous, promiscuous (or simply unfaithful), a Penelope written over by canonical myth, to whom she found an apocryphal reference, possibly in Robert Graves's *The Greek Myths*. It explains: "Some deny that Penelope remained faithful to Odysseus. They accuse her of companying with Amphinomus of Dulichium, or with all the suitors in turn, and say that the fruit of this union was the monster god Pan" (373). The role of Pan, downplayed in *The Odyssey*, would figure significantly in Kyger's retelling.

In this sense, *The Tapestry and the Web* anticipates the revisionary project that characterizes a feminist poetics shaped by the second-wave women's movement. Yet, writing in the late 1950s and early 1960s, prior to the second-wave women's movement and in the absence of any supportive community of women writers, Kyger wrote singly, not to demystify "woman" or to understand her own writing as specifically feminine. In fact, for Kyger the question of poetic identity was not at base a question of "male or female" (undated, n.p.); rather she saw it as her task to be "the instigator" and "propagator" of her own definition of female—one that could encompass the contraries of being herself the muse to her circle of male poets and her life the medium of her own poetry (1974, 150). Neither was she occupied by the multifarious surfaces of a deep-rooted misogyny that were to galvanize the next generation of women—except in that she "hate[d] the word 'female'" when it implied "a traditional role in which the woman is supportive to the idea" (150). She was highly critical of the dynamics she witnessed in other American couples whom she observed when she lived in Japan, especially those occasions upon which men gave too many orders and women "[fell] all over and [talked] baby talk" when they came into a room (1981, 232). The critique she was to render in her treatment of *The Odyssey* was a protofeminist consequence of her own sense of American women's culturally instituted subservience, which had been made starkly apparent to her outside of its naturalizing context. In a feminist critique of patriarchy, Kyger confronts both the representations of women and the structures in which these occur. And though it precedes the sexual revolution, *The Tapestry and the Web* lays bare this nexus of concerns in order to move through them, aiming for a revolution in consciousness nonetheless.

Life in Japan was estranging and, though often lonely, it proved to be productive; in Japan Kyger would reconcile with gender-biased conceptual restraints that tended to masculinize poetic production. Her anxieties took an alarming turn when she realized that being a woman and a writer was at the heart of much of her discontent—"I wish I had never known writing and then I'd be more content with what I am doing now instead of wishing I was proving myself by writing" (1981, 36). Though the marital frame immediately defined her in a most concrete way, she continued to see herself in relation to her North Beach friends, with whom she corresponded, and continued to identify strongly as the one woman among her male peers. So involved was this identification that news from home could invoke antagonism, and on one occasion she singles out another woman as a figure of dissimilitude: "I get nervous. Everyone seems to be writing and publishing but me. Thea says in a letter she sent all her things to Evergreen—but that they sent them all back—I should think so" (1981, 40).[8] Though she felt strongly that her perceived conceptual restraints did not affect her practice of writing (undated, n.p.), she felt at the same time pressured to measure up to her male—and not her female—peers. The "everyone" to whom she refers, more likely than not, are specific men; whether Kyger is implying that the fact that Thea was a woman lay behind her rejection is not clear. Nevertheless, her "I should think so" places a disdainful distance between herself and Thea.

While literally outside the concerns that in San Francisco were made evident on a daily basis, Kyger, as Snyder's wife, was sensitized to other sex-based limitations. On the boat to Japan, she decided to stay only a short time and not to marry, but soon after arriving, she and Snyder wed—as expected by the Zen Institute, where Snyder was a student. She felt at times "trapped," "overpowered," wished she had not married, and was reticent toward his matrimonial prerogative: "He seems to have plans for me, although he claims no—and I will not fit into them" (1981, 10). Her feelings toward Snyder typically fluctuated from love and acceptance to unease and a seemingly externally prompted self-criticism: "indeed I am bad tempered/foulmo[u]thed etc." (13). Struggle was laid out in gendered terms: "Is his own masculinity threatened that he must fight so hard to assert himself & show no regard for my desires or identity. As far as I can recall he has always treated women this way, at least that is what I have been told" (30). Out of the tension between wanting to write and being called upon to fulfill the role of wife came an imagined alternative, "a room all my own to decorate with pictures and plants just the way I wanted with no one to intrude, high ceilinged light & airy" and she hoped "someday to be able to make it alone writing in such a room" (31). But her own desire conflicted with Snyder's highly conventional expectations and her sense of obligation to them. While she felt that she would have to leave, she worried about what would become of his plans: "I want him to be happy & have what he wants, a family etc. But I must live too, I see no solution" (31). Seeing no way to achieve her solitude, she was beset by self-doubt: "I wish I could just pack up and get out for a day or so, then perhaps I could see things clearer, perhaps the faults are all mine—he leads me to think so" (31). The wish to be alone was inseparable from the need to write; in writing, in being alone, came the possibility that her identity was not overdetermined. This hinged on the question of how to act that also occupied her (249). Solitude proposed a space in which to act freely. In anticipation of this she asked Snyder "what if I was involved in doing something & didn't want to do the dishes for say a few days—I want to feel the freedom of acting that way should the possibility arise." But her husband was inflexible: "He would not grant me that, he said" (33).

Kyger attempted to become a more serious student of Zen—not at the institute, which prohibited female students, but in her home, though there she always felt inadequate in light of Snyder's strict discipline. She moved her Zen practice from a context in which she felt pressured to "do more and more Zazen to get anywhere at all" (1981, 2), bringing it to bear on her writing practice. Zen-inspired questions of self mark her personal writing from the early part of this period: "For my fractured consciousness, Zen

Buddhism seems to me the only path out of the nothingness of Western philosophy. I need to find that discipline, that art form" (3). Toward the end of her journals, her writing becomes the focus of inquiry. Striving for Zen-like clarity, she reminded herself to "[a]im for a whole new way of using language. There should be no artificial abbreviations (of sentences etc.) in poetry. Closer to the mind it comes out how? Or the mind close to the poem, comes out with its own good poetry" (242). Zen informed her poetic sensibility, a meditative noticing of the movement of the mind that is evident in the fifth of "The Odyssey Poems," "Meeting May 20":

> 'for by day my one relief is to weep and sigh
> Am I to stay
> winding and coming back, goes out and sees, dreams
> are awkward things
> a cigarette falls behind the bed
> I *can't* get out of bed
> she pushes
> where where are the walls,
> out the window the poetry, dishes broken, things torn up, please
> please don't weep anymore.
> the suitors are sickened w/ blood, look
> how they decay, kill them all
> an eagle takes a terrified dove
> and she places a good chair to hear what goes on
> (1965, 57)

But the usefulness of Zen was limited. It was, after all, what her husband's Japan could offer her; he was its privileged subject. Its nonintrusive approach would not accomplish the work of negotiating the dueling expectations that constituted, in part, their marriage. Oblique questions of consciousness such as "How can i be something specific/yet undefined?" (1981, 61) offer a weak accompaniment to her specifically gendered struggles for self-definition, and in the imported figure of Penelope she discovered more powerful poetic tools. On July 26, 1960, she wrote: "To penetrate (Penelope) the depth found within, the actual feeling, go into. Not idealistically, not ideas of psychological sort" (43). Mythic themes forge multiple relations to the biographical; rewriting Penelope's role in *The*

Odyssey, Kyger managed to mingle her own willful vision and pursue the Zen-like "[q]uestions of identity & how to act" that urged her on (249). Penelope enabled her to address poetically the sexual and intellectual anxieties and apparently immutable dictates which together bolstered the muse/poet binary—one that was at the heart of her husband's marital presumptions—and then break with them. Penelope's story prompted her to explore the "big Story." It offered a model of resistance in the wake of a series of decisions that she had wavered over, of others' desires acquiesced to.

Further, Kyger chose to follow an aberrant thread—the apocryphal story that challenges the Penelope valued in *The Odyssey.* Thus in *The Tapestry and the Web,* Kyger's rather standard poetic treatment of *The Odyssey* challenges its premises in subtle ways. Kyger's desire to write through *The Odyssey,* coupled with her refusal to occupy the place designated feminine in the process, overturned an epic mode of production that imagines text to be communicated to the male poet by the disembodied female muse. This significantly complicates conceptions of the epic text—and casts doubt on Kyger's fitness as an epic poet. With this different view and her desire to entertain different mythic aspects, Kyger swerved away from contemporary poetic concerns into her own feminist space. Her conceptual swerve mirrors the apocryphal "swerve," the aberrant narrative line, that it was her project to follow. This departure, however, presented a formal concern: how she could ever be a great poet, ever "write an epic the way [Pound biographer Charles Norman] says a great poet must," that is, ever "have the command of a world/universal view" (1981, 225).

One answer to this question would be articulated years later, in the wake of the Vietnam War, by Alice Notley, who struggled to write an epic about her experience of the war that did not champion heroism. Notley suggested that there are two choices for the aspiring female epic poet: she might make her heroine manlike in action, knowledge, and/or experience, or try to suit epic to what a woman is like, to "make something lofty and grand in another way than a man's" (1994, 103). Kyger's revision of *The Odyssey* follows this second tack. Through disassembling parts of the epic and expanding on certain particulars, *The Tapestry and the Web* risks the question of how as a woman Kyger might assemble her part in relation to the heroic, the larger whole. Like "the Homeric rhapsode who sew[ed] together songs" (Nagy, 21) recomposing parts that had been dispersed,[9] Kyger returns the epic story to recomposition, as it had been in the oral tradition, where the text remained open to potential reweaving with the unwritten and the unperformed. Her retellings produce another set of truths and potentialities. Thus Penelope is a potent figure not only because *The Odyssey* tells so little of her story and leaves her in relative obscurity (*penelope* means, literally, "with a web over her face"), or because it provides her with a web of appearances beneath which she carries out her true design, but also because Penelope's craft, her complicated tapestry making, resembles Kyger's own.

Kyger's aberration is her introduction to an augmentation of this apocryphal tale. As she points out in an untitled poem that serves as an introduction to the Penelope poems,

> Somewhere you can find reference to the fact that PAN was the
> son of PENELOPE
> > Either as the result of a *god*
> or as a result of ALL the suitors
> > who hung around while Odysseus was abroad.
> (1965, 29 emphasis in original)

In the Homeric version of the myth, home is the site of those repetitive activities —like tapestry making—that limit female experience and preserve the place of women and men in relation to it. The duplicity at the heart of Penelope's tapestry-making ruse is gestured toward in Kyger's book title by two trails of reference leading out—the enduring tapestry and the provisional and remade web. Enduring and provisional, Penelope's tactic, by delaying remarriage, ensures Odysseus's return to a place unchanged in his absence while at the same time creating the time for that to happen, the time in which Odysseus's story unfolds. What occupies *her* time is not of importance; what matters is what must not happen: his home must not fall into dissolution; only then is his heroic homecoming assured. Penelope's "circumspection," her craftiness, ensures this.

But in Kyger's version, home opens onto non-traditional narrative, generative rather than preservative: spawning Pan not only represents her sexual adventures, it introduces into the mythic genealogy the unpredictable, a "monster" (half goat, half man) who runs about generating his own undisciplined and prolific narrative in "12.29 & 30 (Pan as the son of Penelope)":

And where did she hide her impudent monster?
He was acres away by then I suppose in the sunlight leching
                    at some round breasted sheep
girl.
    the cock crowing at dawn never had bigger thoughts than he did
about waking up the world.
(1965, 31)

The apocryphal reveals a schism between the mythic and the real. Against its borders both sides are rewritten. Revelation shifts focus, consigns new significance despite the tightness of the authoritative whole. Pan is "Bred of the weaver," "bold" and "the result of impatience" (30). His appearance and characteristics bear witness to his lineage in an attempt to wake up the world to a sexualized image of Penelope. Because this Penelope is otherwise covered over and encoded, Pan's promiscuity becomes an acceptable symbol of her sexuality which remains, even in Kyger's radical version, displaced, "acres away". Her sexual power is related to narrative determinacy. In Kyger's revision Penelope has the power to thwart the return of Odysseus; she is concocting his adventures rather than weeping for his return:

    I choose to think of her waiting for him
                    concocting his adventures   bringing
            the misfortunes to him
    —she must have had her hands full.
        (31 emphasis in original)

Kyger delegates to Penelope—not Calypso or Circe, Athena or Zeus—the power to control Odysseus's fate; it is she who, by inhibiting his return, controls the epic trajectory and, in doing so, prolongs the length of their marital caesura. This is reinforced by the fact that Penelope shows no enthusiasm for his return: "She did not run up and embrace him as I recall. / He came upon her at the house & killed the suitors" (31). Doubt is further propagated by Kyger's jesting tone. Unhinged from the gravity of Penelope's situation as *The Odyssey* retells it, "12.29 & 30 (Pan as the son of Penelope)," the fourth poem in the Penelope sequence, works in the mode of question and assertion to sardonically cast doubt on the canonical interpretation. It is a corrective that is decidedly playful but that also renders a serious protofeminist critique of the romanticized tinge upon what Adrienne Rich would, in the next decade, call the institution of motherhood. A tone of gossipy levity runs throughout in comments such as "What a birth / THAT must have been. Did she turn away & sigh and I believe she dreamed too much" (31). Thus Penelope is brought into a contemporary context resonating with accusative clarity on current expectations and mores:

> Refresh my thoughts of Penelope again.
> Just HOW
>   solitary was her wait?
> I notice Someone got to her that
>   barrel chested he-goat prancing
>   around w/ his reed pipes
>
>
> is no fantasy of small talk.
> More the result of BIG talk
>   and the absence of her husband.
>   (31)

Though "Someone got to her," Penelope "knew what she was doing" (31). Penelope, in other words, is not a victim in a schema that renders women powerless in narratives of pursuit and conquest or constraint — of which, in myth, there are many. Instead she is an agent in the construction of her own domestication, one that is deviant and empowering. Kyger imagines not the chastity represented by Penelope's weaving and unweaving, but rather the sexual activity her tapestry making and unmaking is supposed to have replaced.

Penelope's life is left relatively untreated in *The Odyssey.* She makes a few appearances in the epic, always in relation to her task. Though it represents her passivity and chasteness, when those characteristics are overlooked, as in Kyger's creation of a more dynamic Penelope, her life emerges as a yet-to-be-textualized imaginative space. As rhapsode, Kyger steps in to rectify the paucity of details regarding Penelope, the substantive loss of her in the canonical retelling. She suggests that the tapestry making is an act of self-creation, much like her own poetry: "I believe she dreamed too much. Falling into her weaving / creating herself as a fold in her tapestry" (1965, 31). This craft, Kyger's rendering suggests, is like that of the poet who breaks from the tightly woven web of authoritative voices and follows up new strands, a process that begins by refuting the so-called facts: "We are in a tighter web than I had imagined. / that story / about him capturing a girl in the woods was a lie!" (30). "Linear space," Kyger has said, "was not a space that I really thought or experienced in. Although it's a good space for your head to follow at times . . . but that space is really, like chunks of things" (1974, 155). When the facts are suspect, when accusations of lying are tossed about, narrative begins to dissolve. Kyger's lack of interest in preserving linear narrative as a structure freed the poem as a space for invention in which she could see "chunks of things" and explore between them possible, unrealized connections. The web of half-truths and accusations characterizing Penelope's story is collaged with chunks of story from Kyger's own lineage, which reveals a compassion for a tragic figure, who is, like Pan, "of another sort":

> My mother always remembered the
> crippled boy in her grade school class who teased her.
> he was ugly.
> of another sort.
>
> But then are You one
> or many.   Could I meet you, drive away the
> children who beat you with sticks.
> (1965, 30)

In a reference to both Penelope and Kyger as craftswomen, the crippled boy is shown to be a product of imaginative interminglings: "But then I forget you / have been made by the excellent craftsman, she / is lovely" (30). The poem stands as a record of her mother's memories and a testament to Penelope's procreative craftsmanship—details otherwise lost.

Kyger seemed to have felt *The Tapestry and the Web* coming together— or failing to—as early as April 1962, during her travels in India with Snyder, Ginsberg, and Peter Orlovsky. This trip recalls her struggles with self-definition and her inheritance of their poetic lineage. Significantly, questions regarding her own project in developing *The Tapestry and the Web* emerge at the same time. After a particularly trying evening during which an "overwhelming reaction against Ginsberg choked and suffocated" her and she felt "if I give up, I'll walk into the ocean and swallow it into myself," she wrote in her journal: "The words are not precise, not muse. The tapestry book here. Not a key to lead me on, not a passageway that begins to turn. Nothing to send me on, it always stops" (1981, 97). "Muse" becomes inadequate as a descriptor for her work. Perhaps the male poet, represented by Ginsberg, cannot be relied upon to mediate her voice, which, rather, he suffocates. The loss of voice, what she calls "giving up," is equivalent to a loss of self, to drowning.

In 1963, her last year in Japan and the final year of her marriage, her anxieties waned and her journal writing moved into a more productive poetic space. Textual encounters were occasion to reflect on the significance of her patrilineage and shaped a path that *The Tapestry and the Web,* and "The Odyssey Poems" in particular, would follow. In one journal entry, she copied these lines from Charles Norman's 1960 biography of Ezra Pound, which reflect Olson's central image in "Projective Verse": "The poet's line reveals not only his manner of expression, hence the way he thinks, it reveals his identity almost, it might be said, his way of breathing. And this individual structure is all that can be called different in the poets" (1981, 227). On this occasion to rethink Olson's influence her own aesthetic choices regarding the line were confirmed. She also copied "thus no matter where the discussion starts, it is always necessary to return to the line and its structure" (227). This justification of the line as primary, a detail through which one might, in part, address the daunting epic whole, could have been reassuring. It meant that what Kyger perceived as a woman's craft, dealing with "parts" and "particulars"—like Penelope the tapestry maker who focuses on the fragment—though it seemed contradictory to epic's episodic historical movement, might instead constitute a component of that movement. Still, according to Olson, writing large was a measure of poetic greatness; through the practice of projective verse, he writes, "the problem of large content and larger forms may be solved" (1997, 248). Next to what she had read of the celebrated achievements and comprehension of Pound, Kyger's own achievements appeared to shrink to inadequacy: "What can I know without reading & observing all of mankind," she wrote, "[m]y own mind but a risky & perhaps lopsided direction" (1981, 225–226). For her part, Kyger was reading Emily Dickinson's poetry, Gertrude Stein's lectures, and Edna St. Vincent Millay's letters—the work of three women poets who, in various ways, approached large content without the "larger forms" that

Olson deemed necessary. Though daunted by Pound's purview, Kyger nevertheless undertook a poetic treatment of history: her own history and the fact of epic as a part of her historical, poetic inheritance.

"The Odyssey Poems" witness Kyger's homecoming made strange by the myths and mutations she had brought along with her from her sojourn in Japan. After four years abroad, she returned to San Francisco on January 20, 1964, the deadline for the first issue of *Open Space*. Edited by Stan Persky throughout 1964, *Open Space* was to be a working space to help make young poets visible. Kyger was one of these young poets. Poems from "The Odyssey Poems," written between April and December 1964, appeared in four of its thirteen issues. Parts of "The Odyssey Poems" appear in her Japan journal alongside an emerging sense of independence and discussions with Snyder over the possibility of divorce. Her textual experience provided a way to navigate the changing nature of her marriage. The figures of Odysseus and Penelope are equally disrupted; the gender identities of this mythic pair, which had been replicated in her own marriage, are distorted. Though "The Odyssey Poems," for the most part, leave out any reference to Pan, the symbolic weight of his generative swerve continues to propel Penelope away from her prescribed role in *The Odyssey*. Kyger further contemporizes and develops Penelope's character, and, coincidentally, the primacy of Odysseus's story degenerates into an oddity—a collage of details mythic, fictional, and contemporary.

The epic and its ideologies examined in "The Odyssey Poems" are thus brought into the present to bear the scrutiny of Kyger's own experience, through which an understanding of the myth and her commentary on it would emerge. Forging this temporal link, Kyger titled the first of "The Odyssey Poems" "April 8. The Plan," and like many of her poems it evokes the present, and presence, by creating an intersubjective space, beginning "Where ever you go I am with you./ and bring you back" (1965, 53). The poem returns received words, "Where ever you go I am with you," a profession of faith and companionship despite distance. The source of the quote is unrevealed; it could be Athena addressing Odysseus in *The Odyssey*. It could also, in a characteristic twist, be an address to Penelope, since in Kyger's poetic imagination Penelope, unbound from her tapestry-making task, does "go" and Kyger is "with" her and does, in her poetic sequence, "bring" her "back"—back, that is, into a plausible reality, back "to life" and away from restrictive fictions. The unattributed quote achieves mythic status and suggests a perpetual rereading of this familiar assurance, a rereading that continually occurs in the present: it is brought back into contemporaneity and localized. Thus retelling history does not reproduce it, but rather produces another history, a history that incorporates the telling self as both an agent of history—a history maker—and an historical object—an element to be incorporated in future iterations. Perhaps written in anticipation of her homecoming, this poem, in reweaving and altering Odysseus's homecoming, accommodates her own.

> The morning venus
>   sailing into the bay,
>   lifting him asleep onto the land
>   he has returned to
>   and doesn't know where he is.
>   outside of San Francisco
>   the long paths and eucalyptus
>   are another country
> (53)

Juxtaposed to an account of Odysseus's arrival home to Ithaca is a description of Kyger's personal geography, her San Francisco. It witnesses her homecoming at the same time that it is made strange by Odysseus's and Kyger's presences. Typical in these lines is Kyger's ambiguous use of subjects and verbs, so that meaning shifts: the verb phrase "doesn't know" can be read as the complement of either "he" or "land," so that Odysseus is lost to himself and also a foreigner to the land in which Kyger is a native. The Ithaca to which Odysseus returns and the San Francisco to which Kyger is returning become one and the same.

    This web of gender identity (Kyger/Penelope becomes Kyger/Penelope/Odysseus) is indicative of the intricate weaving of narratives and details that characterize "The Odyssey Poems." Whereas in the Penelope poems Kyger stood relatively distinct from Penelope, as an "I" thinking of "her," in "The Odyssey Poems" their identities blend. Penelope's narrative bears details current to Kyger's life in her/their expression of dismay, as the following passage from "April 23. Possibilities" illustrates:

> She comes and rages
> quit eating the coffee cake and cottage cheese
> put the lid on the peanut butter jar
>   sandwiches made of cucumber, stop eating the *food*!
> (1965, 56 emphasis in original)

In the collaging of memories, myths, other's stories, and the present narrative of the "I" who is writing them, the poems are a series of tapestries and webs, distinct vignettes juxtaposed like a blending of threads where language play and image play reorient the mythic and the contemporary. This weaving is extended across gender as well. For example, the first three poems ("April 8. The Plan," "Whether he is dead or not . . . ," and "Land at the first point you meet") seem to be the descriptions of an "I" who is Penelope and a "he," Odysseus. But in the fourth poem this switches to a "she" addressing a "you," commenting first on Penelope ("Still after fifteen years or more she doesn't know") and then addressing an unspecified "he" and a different "you":

>   climbing over the rough ravine
> and up an impossible cliff, naked, you mark how high you can go
>   coming back to his opinion of her and hers of him
>   listening sometimes
> to *him* raging, you leave me alone. you dream of me.
>   and there, she withdrew
>
>   and wept for odysseus
> (56, emphasis in original)

Now it is Odysseus who is the figure of obscurity, Penelope-like, with a web over *his* face. The instability of his identity allows Kyger to negotiate his symbolic weight. With Odysseus no longer the mythic hero-adventurer, a more heroic Penelope (and Kyger) emerges. An altercation ensues after the male figure descends from his great height, "coming back to his opinion of her and hers of him." This suggests a demystifying of the heroic figure— who is then wept for—but also an exchange across the gap between *The Odyssey* and "The Odyssey Poems" in which it is *his* raging that is heard. The effect, however, is complicated by the obscurity of some of the referents. Who is the "you"? Is it an imperative to her to leave him alone, dream

of him? Or is it her appeal to be left alone and dreamed about? The confu-
sion is central to the confounding of myths, and that confounding an occasion for the weeping that overcomes Penelope and with her the implied "I"
of the poem. Withdrawing from the mythic world, Penelope/ "she" weeps
for the loss of that world, but also for the loss of contemporary men as
heroic figures. Descending from the "impossible cliff," he remains, after all,
just as he went up it—a man.

The break between "she withdrew" and "and wept . . . " also signals a removal from both the world of contemporaneity (the story of the "she") and
the world of myth (Penelope's story). She is in a space between, an inter-
stice in which she can escape her own life but also realize the distance from,
and relationship to, that other, mythic place. Within the frame of the great
epic of Western tradition, Penelope weeps for the loss of a presence desired.
But in the frame of Kyger's epic revisioning, "she" weeps perhaps for the
loss of the heroic as a narrative she can live inside and turn to for a sense of
stability and definition. In mourning this, Kyger risks a betrayal of her
mentor Duncan and turns onto a path unmarked by his dictates. That loss,
these lines imply, while liberating for the female figure, can only be remade,
reenacted in the lost object or image, but never restored. This is reflected in
her journal entry on New Year's Eve 1963, in which Kyger decided to forgo
mythic sources. She planned for herself a newly disciplined course:

> Resolutions: In order to rise as a poet, the craft of poetry must be
> studied and known. Painful as it may be, hours each day should be
> spent scanning poetry sheets and volumes of the past. New conscious
> ground expansion for poems and ordinary proficiency both executed
> daily. The craft should fit like a glove. Exactly: from my own life, not
> sources from myth. (1981, 269)

There is tension here in what appears to be a satire of Poundian didacticism
and the imperative in the last line—to take one's life as a source, rather
than "sources from myth"—in which Pound serves as but another mythic
presence in the "volumes of the past" that Kyger urges herself to scan "hours
each day." Or this last sentence might signal such a breaking away, a realization that a glove-like fit of craft can't be achieved through another's discipline, especially when that discipline, like Snyder's Zen studies, are
exacted at the cost of one such as herself, expected to accommodate his

demanding study schedule through her domestic labor. Indeed, the under-tone of sarcasm in this resolution suggests that these closing pages of *The Japan and India Journals* are tinged with an ironic self-awareness: the "reso-lution" may follow Snyder's model, but the resolve is finally her own, "from my own life, not sources from myth." Kyger, about to part from Snyder and return to San Francisco, faces the opportunity to live out this self-directed resolution. Kyger's own life was, as *The Tapestry and the Web* shows, always a source for "conscious ground expansion." Through a contrivance of mythic images and innovative structures, through hybridizing them with her own—the whole of her identity-consciousness, from practicing Zen to writing poetry—would serve to (re)define the role she was, according to contemporary mores at least, given to play.

The last of "The Odyssey Poems," "From our soundest sleep, it ends VII," includes the comment "It has been difficult to write this." This poem de-scribes Odysseus as "that great fighter / having a guide, a female presence who pulls her own self into battle also" (1965, 61). Kyger, too, is that fe-male presence, pulling herself into battle with difficulties, both practical and intellectual, enacted in the pages of her journals and poems. Penelope's alternative narrative, vitalized in adjoined apocrypha unearthing Pan's gen-esis, is openly played against *The Odyssey,* confounding and confusing canonical mythos and rendering the figure of Penelope more complex and far more ambiguous than tradition allows. Her retelling of epic history does not reproduce it, but rather produces another history. Kyger includes what is not heard in *The Odyssey* to create an intricate, structured poetics, a reimagination of poetry and of her identity as a poet. The poems that com-prise *The Tapestry and the Web* uncouple and rework concepts of gender and poetic authority she inherited from a poetic tradition sustained through Homer, Olson, Duncan, and Spicer and ultimately swerved away from. Her work is charged by what Kathleen Fraser has called "an innovative neces-sity," the need to improvise "one's relation to language as often as is neces-sary," a strategy especially pertinent for a woman poet who situates herself in a tradition whose imperatives grant her a limited range of options for self-creation, few role models, and fewer publishing opportunities (207). *The Tapestry and the Web* broaches the question of how poetic knowledge is formed despite this paucity and, cleaving the possibility for a postmod-ernist feminist epistemology from epic structures and ideology, anticipates questions of gender and genius that feminist scholarship would pursue.

Notes

1. Kyger's work also compares to poems in Barbara Guest's first collection (1962), "Dido to Aeneas" and "The Hero Leaves His Ship," the opening lines of which declare "I wonder if this new reality is going to destroy me" (20). While such foreboding does not characterize Kyger's approach, she realizes hers as an encounter with a potentially destructive "new reality" nonetheless.

2. "The Odyssey Poems" begin with "Tapestry," the second of three poems thus titled, and include "Note: 'Somewhere you can find reference'," "We are in a tighter web," "12.19 & 30 (Pan as the son of Penelope)," "A song in the rope," and "waiting again."

3. These journals have recently been republished as *Strange Big Moon: The Japan and India Journals 1960–1964* ([1981] 2000).

4. It is important in understanding these familiar involutions to recall the schism that existed between the Spicer-Duncan circles and the Beat writers. Michael Davidson writes, "the San Francisco Renaissance was by no means unified, nor did it necessarily revolve around the figures who read at the Six Gallery [Ginsberg, Michael McClure, Snyder, Philip Whalen, and Philip Lanantia, Oct. 7, 1955]. . . . Two major poets of the period—Robert Duncan and Jack Spicer, both of whom were intimately associated with the formation of the Six Gallery— were not part of the reading, nor did they identify the Beat movement as 'their' renaissance" (3).

5. The appearance of *The Tapestry and the Web,* published by Donald Allen's Four Seasons Foundation in 1965, as well as Kyger's inclusion in the re-edited British edition of *The New American Poetry,* published two years later, *New Writing in the U.S.A.,* edited by Donald Allen and Robert Creeley, seems to signal that she had gained some ground lost by having arrived on the scene too late to be included in Allen's *New American Poetry,* an anthology published in 1960. Something might be made of her exclusion—whether it was to blame for her status as a missing female poet of the Beat generation—but relatively little has been made of Kyger in the anthologies and literary histories that seek to recapture and contextualize the San Francisco of the Beat Generation and the San Francisco Renaissance, with the exception of the hasty geneaologies of anthologies specific to women writers that inadvertently misplace Kyger as a female beatnik. The recent biography of Jack Spicer by Lewis Ellingham and Kevin Killian is an exception. Alan Golding's *"The New American Poetry* Revisited, Again" also illuminates.

6. Though the oft-republished "Projective Verse" originally appeared in the literary magazine *Poetry New York* in 1950, its publication by LeRoi Jones's Totem Press sealed its cult status. It was reprinted the next year as the leading essay in the "Poetics" section of Donald Allen's *New American Poetry,* thus appearing as the most significant articulation of the breakaway, anti-establishment aesthetic that the anthology sought to portray.

7. For an elaboration of a later generation of women poets influenced, in part, by Olson's field, see Kathleen Fraser's "Translating the Unspeakable: Visual Poetics, as Projected through Olson's Field into Current Female Writing Practice" (2000, 174–200).

8. It is unclear who Thea is; she is referred to in the journals by this name only.

9. In Pindar, Gregory Nagy finds reference to the fact that Homeric poetry had been scattered about, that it was the rhapsode who joined the pieces together, so that the master poet Homer is the ultimate joiner retrojected as the original genius of epic (21).

Revelations of Companionate Love; or, The Hurts of Women

Janine Pommy Vega's "Poems to Fernando"

Maria Damon

> Let her who is capable of the greatest suffering suffer most for Him
> and she will have the most perfect freedom.
>
> —*Saint Teresa of Avila*

Janine Pommy Vega's delicate lyrics of absence and the transfiguring power of spiritual belief in the continuity of life have received no critical attention. This itself should come as no surprise, as her work shares this fate of neglect with that of most other women writers associated with the Beat generation. But it is nonetheless an absence that needs redressing; this essay can only begin to tease out of the shadows work and lives that could bear far more intense and sustained investigation. Pommy Vega is still active as a poet, as a teacher of poetry (especially in schools and in the prison system), as a performance poet in the post-Beat tradition, and as a spiritual seeker who travels globally and climbs mountains as part of her spiritual practice. Her obscurity has in some measure helped her to survive and to craft her own poetics of service. Because her image was not ossified early on by her having to conduct a literary career in the limelight, as Allen Gins-

berg, Jack Kerouac and William S. Burroughs did, and because she has not
been burdened with the task of child rearing, as have other women of her
era who had literary aspirations, she has remained, in some sense, truer to
a "process" of experimental life than to either a stereotyped picture thereof
or a role primarily supportive of others' revolution. In what follows, I examine one set of poems, "Poems to Fernando," which appeared in Pommy
Vega's eponymous first volume (1968). A close look at the poems and the
book as literary and cultural objects enables us to understand more fully
the Beat phenomenon as it addressed the particulars of its female participants' experiences, especially expectations about and experiences of
romantic love, reproductive technologies, and the sacred/devotional. These
closely interrelated issues were, to be sure, centrally important to many
women of that generation, but they were worked out by Beat women, and
by Pommy Vega in particular, in ways that both partook of and departed
from consensus-driven norms governing such matters, deemed near and
dear to the female psyche.

Pommy Vega, like a number of her cohort—white women from working-class or modest middle-class backgrounds in the postwar, cold war
years (Pommy Vega's father was a milkman in Union City, New Jersey, and
she had her early visionary experiences accompanying him on his rounds
at dawn)—could not abide the stultifying life that lay ahead of her as a
good girl in the suburban mold, and ran off to a putatively more fulfilling
life in the bohemia of Greenwich Village (1997, 1–2). One difference between Pommy Vega and some of the other women in this volume—Joyce
Johnson, Hettie Jones, Helen Adam—was her relative youth. She was sixteen when she met Peter Orlovsky and Allen Ginsberg in Greenwich Village
in 1958 and became Peter's lover. The day after her high school graduation,
at which she was valedictorian, she left home for good to move in with her
much older demi-monde friends. It is her precocity that marks her (like
Anne Waldman, though she moved much more intimately in the social
circles of Beat, and much earlier, than Waldman did), and that makes her
early work especially poignant. Her biography embodies the aspirations
and fantasies so well described by Wini Breines's chapter on Beat women in
Young, White, and Miserable: Growing Up Female in the Fifties: smart and spir-
ited women with creative aspirations were, in that era, all dressed up with
no place to go. College was, to be sure, an option and often even de rigueur
for those who could afford it—not for the purposes of achieving one's own

creative or professional potential, however, but to find a suitable mate whose children one could raise with the proper values. Saying no to that model in favor of the kinds of affective attachments that promised more leeway for one's own development took a great deal of courage.

This is especially so for a woman as young as Pommy Vega at the time when she made the commitment to live a nomadic, bohemian life of the spirit—a commitment manifested in her abrupt and highly performative decision to leave home forever immediately after the high-school gradua- tion party arranged for her by her mother (1997, 3). This life of the spirit was one where—it was hoped—eros, creativity, and the sacred would be permitted to be intertwined mysteries worthy of exploration, rather than diluted into a bland formula for a sterile and predictable family life. Nonetheless, what fascinates about Pommy Vega's life story and early work is precisely the primacy she gives romantic love in its most idealized, and, some would argue from a contemporary feminist perspective, uncritical form. Far from rejecting an ethos of romantic love, she embraces it; far from rejecting heterosexual monogamy, she makes it the source of her crea- tive inspiration. However, she does so, as I shall argue, with a difference. Heterosexual monogamy is no end in itself; it is just the jumping-off point for a spiritual path that has brought Pommy Vega far from that original model of love; thirty years later she is an ardently independent seeker of the "goddess" in herself and in many times and places. Her recent book, a trav- elogue called *Tracking the Serpent: Journeys to Four Continents* (1997), docu- ments her visits to sites of goddess worship in the ancient world. Moreover, even in her earliest work, her concerns are explicitly spiritual in nature, and her imaginative writing moves effortlessly from rapturous descriptions of her lover to equally rapturous invocations of God as the prime mover and ultimate source of creativity and love itself.

Her first book of poems, *Poems to Fernando* (1968), dedicated to her hus- band, the Peruvian painter Fernando Vega ("shining in eternity") after his sudden and unexpected death in Spain in November 1965, is characterized by an articulation of the nexus of memory, creativity, suffering, and tran- scendence typical of much Beat poetry, and of much mystically inflected poetry of the postwar era in general, such as that of the San Francisco Renaissance poets (Jack Spicer, Robert Duncan, Helen Adam, Robin Blaser, et al.) and the East Coast "magic workshop" poets (Stephen Jonas, Gerritt Lansing, Robert Kelly, et al.) (1968, 3). However, while Pommy Vega shares this nexus of concerns with many Beat writers (most famously Allen Ginsberg in "Howl" and "Kaddish"), the delicacy and fragility of her verse has more in common, I would argue, with other experimental women poets such as H.D., Joanne Kyger, Lorine Niedecker, even Edna St. Vincent Millay in its refusal to separate female sexuality, sensibility, and experience from the realms of either the sacred or the aesthetic. In distinction from the male poets who take on such subjects, the work is not polemical or pronouncedly oratorical. It is, by contrast, delicately articulated and attentive to detail, acutely intimate—one might say, as in the cases of Niedecker and Kyger, understated and rooted in the mundane, and, as in the case of H.D., intense in its compactness. Thus Pommy Vega's particular poetics takes a familiar Beat project—to effect a marriage of Heaven and Hell by sacralizing the profane and making it intimate, a matter of private domestic life rather than a public celebration of the lower depths as in "Howl" or *On the Road*.[1] Her scale is smaller and more nuanced than that of her male counterparts, and perhaps less ambitious or grandiose in not taking on all of society. Nonetheless, she shares with Ginsberg and Kerouac a desire to turn the Hell of loss or abjection to spiritual grist and seeing the "will" (20) of the "Lord" (5)—or a cosmic pattern—both in the minutiae of observed natural detail (inherited from the William Carlos Williams branch of American poetry's genealogy) and in the personal catastrophe of complete abandonment. Both the everyday and the catastrophic become vibrantly charged with spiritual possibilities.

Moreover, using romantic companionate love—even marriage, in this instance—as spiritual vehicle is something the male Beats simply did not do, as they tended to see that kind of love as symptomatic of the straitjacketing society they repudiated. (The famous exception to this observation, of course, is Allen Ginsberg's long "marriage" with Peter Orlovsky, so perhaps, because of the celebrated nature of this exception, I should specify heterosexual companionate love.) For them, the rosy colors of romantic fantasy were fine grist for contemplation, but if given too much importance, turned out to be merely camouflage for marriage which they viewed as a trap. Jack Kerouac, for instance, describes many sweet and fleeting liaisons in his work, some in great detail, but they are neutralized by being described as hopelessly doomed from the start and sometimes also by being fictionalized; this gives the writer a distance from which he can work through his recent passions from an elegiac present in which he is either staunchly a bachelor or fleetingly married to someone else (who never makes it into a novel). The title of this essay, in fact, intends a reference to Barbara Ehrenreich's landmark work on Beat masculinity in *The Hearts of Men,* which analyzed this apparent misogyny as an attempt to resist the conformity of the paradigmatic company man or the "man in the gray flannel suit," the ideally normative and responsible American male. This essay will explore, not the hearts of (Beat) women in the plural, as its focus is only one part of one book by one woman writer, but rather the heart of this particular woman poet; her verse as to some degree representative of the kinds of pain women in the Beat era suffered; and how that pain becomes aestheticized—in other words, how it becomes poetic.

Unlike, then, Kerouac's novelistic explorations of failed romantic love revisited from a narcissistic distance in which the writer focuses on himself, "Poems to Fernando" is written for—not about—the painter, over a series of months during the last year of his life. Though published some years later, the poems are immediate and fresh, many taking the form of personal address complete with second person pronouns; and this effect makes the emotion almost unbearably intimate for the reader. Their elegiac power comes partially from the innocence with which the poet, not knowing of the impending death of her husband in the first several poems, nonetheless revels in his almost otherworldly significance to her—a significance that makes it possible for her to survive his loss, as she has already endowed him and their relationship with supernatural powers that transcend time and space. Before his death, she writes:

in-here is gone forth to meet in-there, &
we ARE bound below a sound or gesture;
beneath distance, before time, at the foot of the
silent forest, meet me here, I love you.
  (12)

and after his death, she writes:

For my love with you is deep as the space between stars
& that my song is sung before does not lessen its validity;
I speak to *you*, always as I would speak before or write letters
to the space between clouds, that patch of sky—

or the sky deserting me, to that place invisible beyond me
I cannot see and do not let go,
O you know this!
. . . .
you know all this . . .
. . . .
    ::the heart is faithful, listening
still to the language between us.
  (15—16, emphasis in original)

and, in a poem with the note *"on train to holland/ 12-29-65,"*

Dawn on the flooded marshline
reflected in the ponds &
bluish shadows
   hang on the trees,
pale blue horizon twilight.
This also is thine and the work of thy hand,
frost covering the bushes in the field.
Blackbirds over the mauve fields
frosted and pale green
Good-morning Fernando!
    the sun rise red
    & the winter trees.
  (18)

Among the technical devices used here to heighten the effect of closeness
and brokenness in the latter poem is a kind of allusion to—if not strict
adherence to—synesthesia and the rhetorical trope of *apo koinu*, in which
the latter part of a phrase is both a logical syntactic extension of the previous words and also fits the phrase following it in a different syntactic rendering (e.g. "I went to the store was open"). Is "bluish shadow," for instance,
one of the elements reflecting the "flooded marshline," are these shadows
hanging on the trees, or both? In the second stanza, are the blackbirds
frosted and pale green? Are the mauve fields pale green, too, as well as
being frosted? Or is the pale green a synecdochical reference to trees surrounding the mauve fields, or the shrubbery punctuating them, so that the

word echoes back to the previous stanza's "frost covering the bushes in the field"? Within such a minimalist poem, these slippages and indeterminacies, far from indicating a lack of writerly control, layer the spare winter scene with intricate texture; it provides the objective correlative for the poet's grief. Moreover, this hypersensitive attention to physical details of the landscape also indicates a degree of dissociation commonly experienced by mourners in early stages of shock—physical reality appears to be both extra vivid and simultaneously flattened out, as if the world were an illusion being performed for the benefit of the mourner. The relationship between trauma, dissociation, and modernist poetics in such devices as the objective correlative, syntactic slippages, and the like could bear much further discussion; here, however, such a chain of resonances shows how elaborate a poem this is, and how acute an expression of shattered consciousness that achieves, in survivalist mode, a vision of higher wholeness mediated through "the natural." See in this vein another modern woman poet's "nature poem" that also invokes the utterly vertiginous disorientation of modern life, H.D.'s classic "Oread":

> Whirl up, sea—
> Whirl your pointed pines,
> Splash your great pines
> On our rocks,
> Hurl your green pine over us,
> Cover us with your pools of fir.
>   (1914, 54–55)

While this is most often taught as a "perfect" imagist poem because it is seamlessly "whole" in its union of elements, it also seems obvious that one of the poem's effects is that of chaos, of a world turned upside down by turbulence, of an acutely destabilized subjectivity unable to find a clear center of gravity. It is also, though, a magnificent vision. For both H.D. and Pommy Vega, visionary proclivities helped to mediate the uprooting experiences of modernity; Pommy Vega's, moreover, stood her in good stead during the early months of widowhood.

Poems to Fernando differs markedly from other Beat women's work in how Pommy Vega uses the romantic relationship as thematic material. For the most part, Beat women have either used a long-bygone primary relationship with a better-known man as a vehicle for revisionary memoir—Joyce Johnson's *Minor Characters* and Hettie Jones's *How I Became Hettie Jones* are exemplary here—or attempted to depict, for the voyeuristic enjoyment of nonparticipants, imagined sexual excesses of the Beats —Diane di Prima's *Memoirs of a Beatnik* serves in this capacity. The celebrations of women's quotidian and paradigmatically feminized activities and roles—as mother, caretaker, housekeeper, and in other "helping" capacities—abound in poetry by the period's women, but these are often uncoupled from the fierceness of erotic attachment itself and seen as worthy in and of themselves, whether or not the man is around, and often he's not. Even the joyous eroticism of Lenore Kandel's *The Love Book* celebrates eros but keeps the male figure unspecified. *Poems to Fernando,* on the other hand, is emphatically for Fernando and to him, across the boundaries that separate life from death; the painter is the poet's muse. The poet is infatuated with her husband (rather than with either her own pleasure or her role as wife/mother) before and after his death; she moves into widowhood buoyed by the conviction that they are still connected and that he receives her daily communications, sees what she sees, and shares her experience with her. In this sense, the girlishness of the book is completely winsome and poignant; it is a work of ingenuous genius like Rimbaud's earlier verse. It is particularly the first half of the book, the eponymous section "Poems to Fernando," which is divided into poems written before and after the painter's death, that is of interest in this regard—the wholeheartedness of the emotions first of love and then of shock is more compelling here than in the remainder of the book, which represents the life the poet resumed in the United States, where she plunged headlong into drug use in an attempt to manage the suicidal despair she experienced after she was widowed.[2]

The literary style of "Poems to Fernando" also has a nuanced relationship to Beat (which of course has a nuanced relationship to itself). Its lapidary, broken qualities and its unusual punctuations, such as the Charles Olson–derived caesura, slightly distorted syntax, occasional archaisms, and so forth, link it with the Black Mountain school or even the imagists as much as if not more than with the loud, long-line oratorical Beat poem epitomized by Ginsberg's verse and some of Gregory Corso's, notably "Marriage" and "Bomb." In its defamiliarizing tendency, the language announces itself as literary—a tendency the Beats tried to avoid in their somewhat reified view of and quest for the "natural" language of everyday speech.

(These, again, are broad generalizations: who could deny, for example, that "Kaddish" reaches into the highly stylized language of the King James Bible at times? Or that Beat use of hipster jive is just as stylized as any gesture toward lyrical archaisms?) Pommy Vega's yearning is formalized in fragments and a direct address that breaks through a description of landscape: "Spring! / & I not with you?" (11), and invocation of proper names: "I Love You Fernando" (22). One of the most complete and piercing lyrics, written a month after Fernando Vega's death, is striking for its use of archaic, balladic imagery, which recalls some of the Black Mountain poets' (especially Robert Duncan's) use of the tropes of high chivalry, but this poem is decidedly from a young woman's point of view:

> early in my life a root was
> grafted with a wild branch
> White roses grew, & this is my love with you.
>
> now if you take the branch away
> the root will come away also:
> for they are of one piece
>   & the bush is blooming.
>   (17)

The simultaneity of loss and indivisibility, of rending and continuity, of growth and love in the face and fact of death draws on several literary histories, processing the *rosa mystica* of Catholic symbolic repertoire and Dante's erotic/religious poetry through an almost Dickinsonian system of perception.

Moreover, syntax is broken as emotion and/or perception exceeds the possibility of expression ("Sitting alone on a somewhere high roof of tiles / you come to me / and here we make love" [7]) in both ecstatic and traumatic moments of utterance. These techniques call to mind John Wieners, Jack Spicer, and Robert Duncan, gay fellow travelers of the Beat movement who also at times distinguished themselves sharply from it, and who wrote in both highly elevated archaic language and spare, twisted lines that move easily between high and familiar registers of diction, and between intimate address and mediumistic conduction. The fractured and slightly distorted syntax of "Poems to Fernando" also resonates with the verse of Emily Dickinson, H.D., Joanne Kyger, and the early work of Denise Levertov.

It is worth noting that Robert Duncan, according to Richard Cándida Smith, pointed to his long and deep-rooted domestic situation with the collage artist Jess as something that marked him as non-Beat. To be a domestic poet, he claimed, was to be something other than what Beat meant—nomadic, transient, unattached (265–268). In Pommy Vega's case, a restless bohemian nomadism has kept travel as a primary feature of a free and inspired life:

> with love in my
> pocket I'm on my way
> home / a train
>   after this How
> no one knows
> —but I'll get there:
> your eye, who has seen
> you love, with my
> pockets full, that you're home?
>   (9)

But in "Poems to Fernando," as this poem indicates, that travel is only free and inspired insofar as it is tethered in a spiritualized love relationship between a couple. Thus the domestic is not equated with domicile as it is in Duncan's case (a stable home as well as a monogamous relationship) but with intimacy, romantic eroticism, a promise of eternity.

All of these, moreover, are nurtured by imagination—one might say projection. Throughout the first portion of "Poems to Fernando" the poet is traveling to meet her husband; the second portion is written in the first shock after his death. Thus Fernando Vega himself is the sacred absence, desire for whom calls language into being in all its delicate, tenacious beauty. He is the written-about and also the prime mover, the point of origin of all longing and all langue-ing: speech, writing, and other forms of union and contact. He is what Kenneth Burke would refer to as the "God-term" in this epistemological system, and he's not present—at least not physically. In the poem written after Fernando Vega's death on the train to "Holland," there is even a slippage,which occurs elsewhere as well, from an address to "thee"—presumably God—to "you," Fernando ("this also is thine and the work of thy hand. . . . Good-morning Fernando!" [18]). Thus, later, this slippage suggests that when "His will is done" (20), Fernando Vega is implicated as willing his own death, Christ-like, and further, that this self-sacrifice on the painter's part enables the writing subject, his widow, to clarify her relation to the sacred. Penniless, rootless, and now un-attached to a male (such attachment being the sine qua non of American 1950s to 1960s female condition), her challenge is to turn this Hell—of marginal social location and its attendant emotional and material instabil-ity—into heavenly meaning, a marriage of Heaven and Hell resonating with, but inflected with gender difference from, Ginsberg's tasks in "Howl" and "Kaddish" to find "holy" and "blessed" the detritus of social organiza-tion: his mother, himself, and all denizens of mental asylums, back alleys, and transient hotels.

In spite of Vega's dramatic absence as an active member of the couple (an absence reminiscent, despite my earlier disclaimer, of the typical Beat do-mestic arrangement), he is present for the reader in the form of a self-por-trait illustrating the front cover of the book, number twenty-two in the famous Pocket Poet series from City Lights, which could be considered the showcase series for Beats and their fellow travelers (e.g., Frank O'Hara, Anselm Hollo). Centered in the middle of the visual field, heavy-lidded, full-mouthed, bearded, and dark-curly-haired, Vega functions well as dark ethnic Other to the author's fresh blondeness (pictured on the back cover), as representative bohemian artist, and as iconic Christ figure. Foreground-ing this latter role is not recherché: in a recent memoir, the poet says bluntly, "In fact, [Fernando Vega] looked like Christ" (1997, 4). Because he had decided to grow earlocks as a sign of a return to Judaism, and because from the beard down the portrait fades into a pillar of light, mildly cross-hatched lines resembling falling liquid, the painter's head also looks like that of a decapitated goat, eerily disembodied and sacrificial. The poet's back-cover photograph highlights her youth, her blonde beauty, and her bohemianism (she seems to be wearing a dark-colored man's cap, which heightens her ingenue-gamine appeal, and of course the requisite black turtleneck)—but it also partially obscures her. In this back-cover design, the figure of the author occupies about half of the space. She looks as if she's being pushed off the page into darkness, while the other half is given over to jacket copy against a light background:

Hard love poems
sounding through
a fine voice of
extreme sensitivity . . .
Fernando Vega was
a young Peruvian
painter who died
suddenly in Spain in
November 1965.
This is the author's
first book.

This paratextual juxtaposition of him and her works on multiple levels. One can't help but think, "What an ideal fantasy couple!" on the order of Mick and Bianca Jagger (except that in that case, the looks of the two members of the couple mirror rather than contrast with each other), Bob Dylan and Joan Baez, or other sixties-era countercultural romantic dyads—or even Mimi and Rodolfo of another bohème. One is also fleetingly reminded of Picasso's drawings of satyrs and nymphs; ethnic lines (and by suggestion species lines) are being crossed by this daring young renegade couple.

At the same time, as the author is a woman, it is touchingly significant that Fernando Vega claims pride of place as the honoree, dedicatee, and central subject of the volume, while Pommy Vega appears to be melting into the shadows. Like the brilliant female mystics who exhorted their readers to pay more attention to God than to His humble instruments (themselves) who were but spokespersons and inadequate ones at that, everything in the volume—from the front and back covers to the dedication to the poems that function as quickly-sketched notes and observations to a beloved— points toward the centrality of the male love object/subject and away from a self-regarding authorial ego. Moreover, as painting and drawing are valued over photography because of the relative immanence of the latter and the ability of the former to idealize, so Fernando Vega is spiritualized (as well as bestialized) through his drawing of himself while Janine Pommy Vega is materialized in a photograph; although the picture is idealized through her extreme youth and beauty, the medium suggests that he is the proper subject on whom our attention should be trained. His drawing is a trace of him, and thus emblematic of his talent; her photo serves a more humbly documentary purpose. Even in this glamorously low-rent portrait of a lifestyle as well as a life, devotion triumphs over narcissism in a rather remarkable way; the author is consistent in her desire to place him first, although in another sense, like Christ, he has been sacrificed for her own growth as an artist in that his death becomes the occasion for her first published volume.

In fact, looking at this drawing of Vega one might sense that he is being offered eucharistically—to be consumed as holy. One might say that there is a great deal of projection going on, that the painter in his absence becomes the repository for all of the poet's idealized aspirations and that this is a typical and politically retrograde position for white middle-class women of that era; it was standard, and encouraged, that one live through one's man's accomplishments and qualities, and one's job was to nurture public awareness of his greatness (by laying out his clothing for him in the morning, feeding him well, raising his children to reflect well upon him, telling one's friends of his wonderfulness). Even though we are in deep bohemia rather than the suburbs here in this entire volume, one could argue that the paradigm is identical, as indeed it was for many Beat women, like Hettie Jones, Joanne Kyger, and Diane di Prima, who did typically gendered—and hence less highly regarded—work of support (editing, cooking, raising families) for their poet-consorts who occupied the alternative limelight as creative geniuses.

In entering the subjective world of *Poems to Fernando,* one might use the diminishing term "infatuation" to describe its emotional landscape, and see the abdication of self-centeredness as problematic for an oppressed caste (women). However, if one reads the poetry with nonpresentist generosity, one might instead concede that abject experience here (certain forms of devotion deemed "inappropriate" or excessive, infatuation with an Other, voluntary poverty, drug addiction, a sudden death that leaves one completely alone in a foreign land) is dignified through love, and through a faith in the sacred nature of human experience subtended by a transfiguring intention. After her husband's death, the poet writes:

> this life for its miracle of unity, I don't always
> see/ and you show me;
> Love reaches out beyond death/ & *is met*
> in the universe.
> /He holds me up and trips me when I must fall.
>   (15, emphasis in original)

(Abject experience is also, as will be elaborated below, dignified through considerable writing talent.) The lowest depths can, and must, become grist for the spiritual journey—and for the beautiful narrative.

To contextualize the work still further, perhaps the prime modern referent here is Jean Genet, whose writing has been acclaimed as "feminine" (for the subject position one can infer from both his style and his thematics) by second-wave feminist literary theorists Hélène Cixous and Kate Millett. A classic outsider, Genet writes, in a similarly compelling blend of modern urban sensibility and somewhat archaic diction and imagery, of saintliness as "turning pain to good account" (205) in the yarns he spins of the criminal and homosexual underworld of France through which he vagabonded and in whose grimmest prisons he served time in the mid-twentieth century. If we use his dictum as a guideline, we can also include as precedents to Pommy Vega's verse texts from the Western female mystical tradition, especially such early modern texts as Teresa of Avila's *Interior Castle* and Dame Julian of Norwich's *Revelations of Divine Love.* (Of the aforementioned modern women poets, Kyger, Levertov and H.D. all fairly consistently placed spiritual/mystical experience near the center of their poetics; di Prima has come to it in her later work such as *Loba,* after decades of fierce political and hetero-domestic engagement.) In these medieval texts, suffering for an explicitly spiritual purpose is a prerequisite for spiritual insight and salvation: Dame Julian prays to have all the sensations and experiences one would have of dying, without actually dying, in order to be able to identify with Christ's passion and then to love him the more fully afterwards (84); the epigraph I have used for this essay speaks directly to Teresa's claims for suffering as intrinsic to the spiritual path.

The importance of suffering in the Christian tradition (and Pommy Vega identifies herself as a "renegade Christian who didn't go to church but believed in Christ and the existence of angels" [1997, 4]) is well documented and in fact widely caricatured, but the relation between a Beat/bohemian aesthetic and these values has not been adequately explored in what little Beat criticism there is. Since many members of the Beat world came from immigrant groups that practiced Catholicism, the Beat valuation of mysticism or nonrational spiritual experience instinctively if ambivalently drew from this tradition even as it explored other spiritual paths, notably Eastern ones like Buddhism, whose first Noble Truth is "There is suffering." The foregrounding of deep suffering as an inevitable but also potentially ennobling part of life was key to the Beat project, aimed, at the public level, at undermining the facade of the consensus-driven 1950s as happy, prosperous, and expansive, and at the private level, at validating the intuition that there was more to life than personal accumulation of wealth, social conformity, and the suffocating model of the nuclear family as contented work -cum-consumer-unit. The texts used as referents in the foregoing passage, *The Thief's Journal, Revelations of Divine Love,* and *Interior Castle,* each has its own spin on suffering which is relevant here: in Genet's case, the aestheticization of one's own pain in the interest of creative survival; in Julian's case, the conscious experience of all kinds of life-threatening pain— psychic and physical—in the interest of expanding one's capacity for compassion; in Teresa's case, personal and communal salvation through the demonstration of self-sacrifice and service (Teresa was writing guidance books for the community of nuns for which she was responsible, and so her writing is to be seen also as an instrument of community formation). All of these are relevant to considerations of Beat work and of Pommy Vega's creative career.

A future in-depth study of Pommy Vega's work and possibly that of other Women Beat writers (especially, in the context of spirituality and infatuated devotion, Elise Cowen, Pommy Vega's roommate before her involvement with Fernando Vega, whose life for a period revolved around the unattainable Ginsberg) could usefully undertake a comparison of this work with the early modern texts and writers mentioned here with an eye toward understanding the connections between abjection (masochism, suffering), spiritual devotion, mysticism, and sexuality. (The work of the medieval spiritualist Margery Kempe would also be of interest in such a study.) What is interesting about Pommy Vega's text in relation to the other women's is that, like Genet's although it is firmly set in the twentieth century, the sensibility it articulates is somewhat anachronistic, touched by medievalism and at times baroque style. This juxtaposition is part of why it is, again like Genet's novels, an "outsider" text.

As in the texts by the aforementioned women (and Genet), the spirituality of "Poems to Fernando" is not implicit but thoroughly explicit; it even uses the standard diction and imagery of the Judeo-Christian tradition. The opening poem, "The Last Watch," is the only one in the cycle that is titled, and it seems to predate the romantic narrative that comprises the yearlong poem sequence, functioning therefore as an invocation/opening—but also, because of its subject, an aubade, a saying-good-bye before the story is even told, thus placing it firmly in the elegiac mode. Written in Jerusalem, where the couple lived in 1963 and 1964 as Vega reconnected with his Jewishness, its first stanza thematizes religious activity as a way of indicating the natural cycles of day and night:

> The monks' prayer sung bowed down in the dome
> comes round ascending sound
> calling far as the land reaches
> Wakefulness now in the last watch—
> Lord near us!
> & churchbells toll no hour thrice . . . .
> (5)

The poet places herself in the position of both anchoress (female religious recluse) and romantic lyric poet, in distinction from the monks' communal ritual:

> dogs barking endlessly nightlong, a sign
> of the ending of days, are lain down in stillness;
> From my threshold of silence candlelighted I listen
> alone, the flourish of wind through the trees—
>
> dawn of grey rose, expansion of morning.
> (5)

The poem goes on to invoke specifically the appearance of the dove to Noah (the poet as prophet) and the annunciation (the poet as ingenue):[3]

> Awake! lone bird at my window exulting
> each morning just now pure voice of clear water
> over scales sings his varying plainchant,
> (5)

and then rushes into a romantic (both Blakean and Wordsworthean) celebration of nature in highly charged biblical language:

: Delight of the First Day sings Origin's creature
Joy blessed with creation, and the Reigning of light!
A shower of thistlefall tongue could not tell
of this river I listen to, silver and lilting
and Swiftly Gone; merged beneath morning
he returns to his home unseen among the fountains.
. . . .
I come into *clarity,* deep blue beginning
. . .

    (5–6, emphasis in original)

The religious tone is sustained throughout the poet's explicit addresses to
Fernando, and after his death she addresses God thus:

you have taken him from me & the pain
runs/ deep as my life
/ & I bless you.
   (16)

In other words, the poet's spirituality is not initiated by the death of her
husband; she already has a well-cultivated yearning for transcendence and
an intuition that solitude, nature, and erotic longing are all inextricably
linked in the visionary life. Rather, one could say that the poet's strong spiritual orientation helps her survive the devastating trauma of loss by enabling her to see it as part of an overall beneficent plan that involves her
own spiritual maturation and expansion.

One might well ask why a young woman writing in the bohemian world
of the late 1950s and early 1960s would seem to fit so strikingly into a tradition of Christian mysticism whose strongest expression is to be found in
medieval and early modern texts. Feminist scholars of history and religion,
most notably Ann Braude in *Radical Spirits,* have pointed out the strong tradition in American religion of female antinomianism (Anne Hutchinson
et al.) and later, in the nineteenth century, the rise in female spiritualists
claiming authority from sources outside the established religious channels
of the day. Braude connects this rise of spiritualism and the large representation of women in these popular practices with a rise in political activism
on their own behalf—women's suffrage—and on behalf of other progres-

sive causes such as abolition, temperance, and Native American rights—a
link that Henry James satirized in *The Bostonians*. It is intriguing to think
about Pommy Vega's work, and other Beat women's inclination toward
alternative religious practice, in this light, especially as the Beat era precedes so closely the rise of second-wave feminism, and as many Beat
women can be studied as protofeminists. However, while there are aspects
of this historical model that I do think resonate with a broad picture of Beat
women's writing and experience, there is in it something that does not altogether fit the case of "Poems to Fernando." Pommy Vega's particular lyri-
cism, one that blends erotic and spiritual intimacy with observed details
from both the natural world and her own psychic condition at any given
moment, relies heavily on her cultivation of nomadic solitude and points
her away from the role of public artist. If anything, she seems to eschew
roles of overt leadership, spiritual, literary or otherwise, in favor of the
space and autonomy to track her own experience minutely. Does this make
her more like one of the male Beats than like her female counterparts who
were raising families and editing journals? It is hard to draw absolute conclusions when we keep in mind Kerouac's dependence on his mother, Ginsberg's long-term relationship with Orlovsky as a source of (admittedly
questionable) stability, LeRoi Jones/Amiri Baraka's high-profile commitment to grassroots community activism.

In nuancing the interpretation of modern female spiritual experience to
more accurately resonate with Pommy Vega's, one can speculate that what
mystical experience has to offer is strong, seemingly unmediated access
to one's own experience—not filtered through received authoritarian texts
or authority figures and experienced in privacy. The upwardly mobile,
intelligent young woman of the 1950s United States was, as many Beat
women remind us in their memoirs, supposed to live through the accomplishments of the man who chose her as a suitable wife and as the mother
of his children. This vicarious life was to be the sum total of a woman's
pleasure, meaning, and fulfillment. This was ultimate joy, achievement,
accomplishment.

Ironically, though, not only were women's experiences of worldly accomplishment to be achieved through their husbands' exploits, but they
themselves were to be desensitized, literally anesthetized, for the crowning
moment of their own life purpose. As Ehrenreich, Adrienne Rich, and
others have amply and angrily chronicled in memoirs, medical histories,

and feminist social science treatises, the medicalization of childbirth reached an all-time high during this baby-boom period, and the process of giving birth was conducted in the woman's complete absence of consciousness. In other words, the event most important to her and deemed most important by her society—the one which made her an important person, which gave her whatever identity she was allowed to have—was one of which she herself was to have no memory, in fact no experience. She was to be inert matter for the doctor's ministrations, and these ministrations were in turn mediated by instruments largely unnecessary to the process, the most ubiquitous of which was the forceps. The putatively most important moment of a woman's life, that is, was one in which she was rendered first unconscious and then useless—but in which her body was displayed for professionals and functionaries as a public experimental province.

In contrast to this paradoxical situation in which, at the height of their earthly careers, women were dramatically objectified, knocked out, and instrumentalized, mystical experience seemed to provide a nonphysical, private, and putatively direct consciousness of one's own experience. It is noteworthy that one of Dame Julian's stipulations when she prayed to have her sickness-unto-death experience was that she remain fully conscious during her suffering, so that she would suffer all the mental terrors and doubts and feel the physical agonies one (Jesus) might feel as one (Jesus) approached death. This thirst for consciousness and the cleaving to one's own sensory and mental experience differs sharply from some of the spiritualist practices of the American nineteenth century and of the present, in which mediums go into trances and sometimes even claim to lose consciousness while they are channeling otherworldly visions, advice, and messages.

As it was for Julian in the fourteenth century, being conscious was clearly a precious and embattled condition for intelligent women of Pommy Vega's generation, and if one cultivated one's inner life, one had to guard it strenuously and guarantee it some kind of privacy. In another of the paradoxes that riddle this postwar era and its promises to upwardly mobile women, one was both to be the guardian of one's husband's privacy—and as such one was often isolated in the new suburbs and condemned to the private sphere traditionally associated with the feminine—but one was not allowed privacy because women were presumed to have no interiority beyond reproductive cavities and spaces.

On the other hand, the liberal dictates of rights discourse (after all, women had been granted the vote only some thirty years earlier) meant that theoretically, women might aspire to have the same needs, rights, and privileges as "their" menfolk, including the right to their own cerebral, emotional, and intellectual processes—that they might have a private realm within as well as being the protective spirits of others' privacy. What would, a decade or so later, with the advent of second-wave feminism, become a celebration of (coded-feminine) "subjectivity" over (coded-masculine) "objectivity"—a reversal of gender-typed hierarchies of discourse—had its roots in a liberal-progressive myth that women could achieve what men already had—the right to subjective experience. To bring mystical experience from the middle ages into twentieth-century rights discourse, then: if someone thought she heard God talking to her, if she saw her crucifix start to bleed and was filled with a sensation of love beyond understanding, she could at least be master of her own narrative. And if she was savvy about it, no one could take that away from her. Of course, this is not to deny the heavy penalties for those who did transgress the rules of experiential decorum; the high rates of shock treatment, heavy pharmaceutical subjection, incarceration in psychiatric facilities, and so forth, especially but not exclusively for women, have been noted as characteristic of life in the 1950s and 1960s, leading to a whole genre of literature, the antipsychiatric novel, which includes such well-known works as Sylvia Plath's *The Bell Jar* and Ken Kesey's *One Flew Over the Cuckoo's Nest*.

Excess of feeling, unmanageably aesthetic experience (in the sense of the root word feeling), rather than submission to social and medical anesthesia, was the hallmark of mystical experience. In an overly regulated society, as in Genet's prison experience and his lifelong surveillance by French systems of welfare, child protection, juvenile and adult prisons, and the legal and juridical state apparatus, visionary freedom as inner freedom is the realm left for the individual subject to cultivate, as Pommy Vega's deliciously clandestine image of returning home "with love in my / pocket" suggests. Moreover, the signal experience of mysticism is, paradoxically, that of union. So the most private, unregulated experience of inner freedom is also one of a dissolution of boundaries and of merging with an Other/higher being. One gets to have one's cake and eat it too. Under such conditions, one could say that Pommy Vega's continued childlessness, which has lasted to the present writing, if not entirely intentionally, is an implicit protest against the system into which she was to be inducted. The right to experience one's own pain—the impossible tearing of the root from the branch, be it the physical suffering of childbirth or the emotional trauma of loss—is one of the rights Pommy Vega's poetry and poetics claims.

In fact, Pommy Vega's suffering, as it turns out, was not over. On returning to New York, she embraced drug addiction as the alternative to suicide, then moved to Peru to live for a number of years in complete (drug-free) seclusion; one of her titles is *Journal of a Hermit &,* resonating again with the image of Julian of Norwich, the recluse who nonetheless had access (through a window in her cell that looked onto the church's interior, and through the pilgrims who sought her out) to the company of others. Since her return to the United States (punctuated by long periods of travel in the interest of mountain climbing and spiritual pilgrimage/tourism), Pommy Vega has lived in rural upstate New York. She has continued her devotional practice by teaching writing workshops in the prison system. While her work and life no longer manifest a belief in the redemptive possibilities of romantically loving one man, but rather in being of service to incarcerated people generally (a project she shares with Hettie Jones, with whom she has coauthored the PEN pamphlet *Words Over Walls: Starting a Writing Workshop in a Prison* [1999]), she practices a "poetics of service" through a continued contact with the abject, the outcast, and the poetic—a practice that would possibly be compromised by too much allegiance to a stable domestic situation. Moreover, in 1980 she suffered a near-fatal car accident; she has recovered but it was another close brush with death and as such has challenged her to expand herself as a vessel ever further, to accommodate the kind of experience she wants to be worthy of.[4]

"Poems to Fernando" offers a lens through which to understand some of the tensions that faced women who fled conventional success (that is, marriage into the white upwardly mobile, middle, or upper classes) for a countercultural United States during a time that was particularly disempowering for such women. It is unusual because it remains an out-of-the-way text, still out of print and hard to come by, and has not attracted the attention accorded to some of the more recent memoirs by Beat women about their relations with prominent Beat men. Nonetheless, it shares with those memoirs some of the poignant and pointed contradictions experienced by smart girls who wanted some higher plane of aspiration than "death in the suburbs" (as Hettie Jones has eloquently put it) and did not see that alternative as precluding either the ecstasies of *amour fou* on the one hand or the degradation of traditional and quotidian gender roles on the other. For more daring or unfamiliar visions of the forms companionate love can take, we may have to wait for more texts to surface from lesbian Beats and Beat women of color—or even confirmed ascetic celibates who nonetheless embraced a Beat life. And in fact, how fair is it to criticize "Poems to Fernando" because its author, at the risk of apparent self-contradiction, wanted to have it all? Who wouldn't?

Notes

1. For a fuller explanation of the Beat project's consisting of marrying Heaven and Hell, see my "Victors of Catastrophe: Beat Occlusions."

2. Janine Pommy Vega, personal communication with author, November 1999.

3. The combination of these two tropes—poet as prophet/poet as ingenue—works as a traditionally (eighteenth- and nineteenth-century) feminized view of eloquence or female genius: she is inspired (prophet); she doesn't know what she's saying (ingenue); she's possessed (prophet +ingenue = genius.) The bird also, with whom the poet identifies in the passage, is a figure for unselfconscious (nonrational, naturalistic, i.e., feminized) inspiration.

4. Janine Pommy Vega, personal communication with author, June 2000.

From Revolution to Creation

Beat Desire and Body Poetics in Anne Waldman's Poetry

Peter Puchek

The poetry of Anne Waldman, a protégé and long-time colleague of Allen Ginsberg, presents a telling instance of what may be termed Beat desire. If desire as expressed by Ginsberg, Jack Kerouac, William S. Burroughs, Gregory Corso, and other Beats involves the impulse to break free of T. S. Eliot's classicism and the New Critics' hermeticism, to make a poetics of body and soul organically fused to each other and to the underside of America's mid-century prosperity and geopolitical ascendancy, then Waldman's variant of Beat desire reflects visceral needs to write in accordance with the aesthetic models of Beat progenitors and to live by their outrider philosophy. In her poetry the personal and political frequently intersect, a linkage apparent throughout postmodernity and detectable earlier in the two key cultural movements that have shaped her poetics and informed her life: the Beat rebellion of the fifties and the more politically subversive second-wave feminism of the late sixties and seventies. In Waldman's case, these two influences have contributed to passionate, though sometimes ambivalent, convictions.

More specifically, Waldman's Beat desire draws on the stylistic innovations of Ginsberg's breath line and Burroughs's cut-ups, the countercultural subjects that she extends into feminist and multicultural concerns, and the Buddhist practice of surprising the mind through attention to the body and karma rather than to ego. This last aspect, Buddhism, plays a critical role in Waldman's recent poetry, particularly the two-volume epic *Iovis: All Is Full of Jove* (1993, 1997), just as the movement against the war in Vietnam and the sixties counterculture were central to a fascinating early volume, *Baby Break-down* (1970). As this essay will argue, Waldman's early poetry implicates her in the politics she opposed, even as her emerging Beat sensibility expressed most dynamically in *Fast Speaking Woman* (1975) eventually overcame a pre-occupation with the divisive issues of the sixties that, by variously eliciting her desire and frustration, once suggested an ideological fetish. Consciously constructing her poetry as Beat writing from the mid-seventies on, Waldman left behind the conflicted politics of revolution to formulate a poetics of cre-ation grounded in Beat desire and a corresponding urge to develop and enact a Beat feminism.

In the mid-sixties, before falling under the spell of the Beats and lending a young woman's voice to their no-longer-young male mythos, a then-twenty-year-old Waldman met Frank O'Hara and attended Charles Olson's noted reading at the Berkeley Poetry Conference.[1] Inspired by major poets on both coasts, she began writing the poems that culminated in 1970 as two substantial but substantially different volumes, *Giant Night* and *Baby Breakdown*. While *Giant Night* celebrates the New York Waldman settled in, its almost exclusive focus on the Lower East Side poetry circle (with which she had become heavily involved) obscures the sociocultural and political upheaval of the sixties. However, *Baby Breakdown* tells a very different story, a narrative at once more national in scope and more period specific. The volume includes seemingly requisite descriptions of drug taking and allu-sions to astrology, Bob Dylan, the Beatles, and the Rolling Stones. Most of the poems in *Baby Breakdown* express a lighthearted sensuality and indulge in offbeat wordplay, but at times the speaker identifies unambiguously with the movement against the war in Vietnam. In part through juxtaposition with these overtly political poems, the poems that simply highlight an al-ternative youth lifestyle begin to work politically as well. This linkage be-came so clear that by the late sixties much of the nation, not only its young people, conflated antiwar politics with the counterculture's indulgence in sex, drugs, and rock 'n' roll. As shelter from the storm of draft fears and police aprowl on the streets (the latter image a recurrent one in *Baby Break-down*), sensual counterculture desire assumed an ideological dimension. To many it came to represent a lifestyle the legitimization of which on a mass scale was every bit as important, or more so, as stopping the war.

For example, in "Young People and Life" from *Baby Breakdown*, young Americans "take a lot of dope & take over," a blend of fact and prophecy often repeated in the collection in essentially the same terms (1970, 47). The sublimity here, however, attaches itself more to taking over than to taking dope. Ultimately, it is in the antiwar movement alone that Waldman will position the fever pitch of desire, ecstasy that runs real risks, courting despair, as she described in "Altogether Another World":

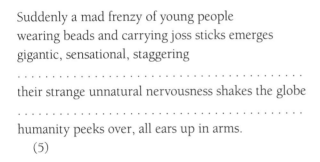

Suddenly a mad frenzy of young people
wearing beads and carrying joss sticks emerges
gigantic, sensational, staggering
. . . .
their strange unnatural nervousness shakes the globe
. . . .
humanity peeks over, all ears up in arms.
    (5)

These visionary lines from "Altogether Another World" indicate that political revolution is *Baby Breakdown*'s chief object of desire. Successful revolution, though, remains unrepresented, an absence that Lacan helps explain with his theory of the Real, all-the-more sought after because unattainable, sublime yet articulable only as an empty sign. In turn, sex, drugs, and rock 'n' roll fill the void, but, having lost sublimity, they actually cement the state's hold on these same political dissenters.[2] The sixties counterculture, from its self-deceptive position figured here in Waldman, would claim that life can't be reduced to cold war politics, for vibrant, self-expressive sensuality supposedly exists beyond the reach of state hegemony. Yet the very perception of distance between private sensuality and public opposition is ideology.

In *Baby Breakdown*, however, the government, its war, and its law enforcement agents prove to be omnipresent, with the politics of the day constantly blaring from the television in Waldman's apartment or happening live in protests right outside her street. Beginning to doubt the antiwar movement, the poem "How the Sestina (Yawn) Works" moves away from the apocalyptic romanticism of "Altogether Another World" and presents a sourcebook for Waldman's diverse poetic influences and future development. In the opening stanza, the poem's speaker mulls over priorities:

> I opened this poem with a yawn
> thinking how tired I am of revolution
> the way it's presented on television
> isn't exactly poetry
> You could use some more methedrine
> if you asked me personally
>   (1970, 15) [3]

The yawn at first signifies boredom, not sleepiness or physical fatigue, and either the revolution or, more likely, its televised depiction drives the speaker to alleviate boredom through drugs. Curiously, though, the speaker looks with prematurely aged eyes at a major sixties breakthrough, the televised revolution. She tires of it, escaping into drugs and longing for poetry in art suggestive of Nietzschean romantic pessimism. The stanza testifies to emotional hunger and dissatisfaction with an impoverished reality rather than to joy at life's abundance or intensity.[4] The speaker disdains even O'Hara's personism: "People should be treated personally / there's another yawn." So out of the six words to be repeated throughout the poem in conformity with the sestina's formal demands, three of them— "revolution," "television," and "personally"—have been eliminated by stanza two as possible solutions to the problem raised by a key fourth term, the "yawn." Only the fifth and sixth words, "poetry" and "methedrine," retain agency, not for explaining how the sestina works—in this regard the poem's title misleads—but for overcoming the yawn-as-boredom (cleverly hidden in plain sight by Waldman in the parentheses of the poem's title).

In the third stanza when "it's 4 AM yawn yawn" and yawning now does correspond to physical fatigue, the previously rejected sixties pastimes get a temporary reprieve. The speaker wonders that TV "is like poetry" and, having taken another shot of methedrine, wants to have "one big revolution" "about something that affects you personally." But in the web of desire and disappointment that speed freaks know, the multiple insights of four A.M. always fade two or three days later in the noon heat, unless luck prevails and they crystallize into not many epiphanies but perhaps one, likely bound to be a fetish for a while. At this point the yawn starts to represent more than late-night boredom or even later-night fatigue; it is the methedrine-fueled threshold where dissatisfaction with reality produces utopian desire, one's recognition of the part played in a larger, dialectical struggle with dominant state ideology.[5] "O giant yawn," Waldman writes in the final stanza, and from the inflated trope one can infer that the speaker has now glimpsed as mere, co-optable ideology even all the sixties Eros of the Left. Her particular revolution will not be televised, for in the end the poem sentences its unworthy words. The television goes "silent," the revolution is "violent," and "what's happening to me personally" is "war, strike, starvation." As early as the late sixties, post-Chicago, Waldman sees little future for collective counterideological action.[6]

Still, ideology is not only false consciousness rendered transparent by the liminal experience of the yawn. Ennui in search of interest, the yawn remains giant in its opacity. Of all six repeating words in the sestina, "yawn" alone evades clarity. Often "How the Sestina" can only define it negatively, by what occurs during its absence: "When you're busy and involved you never yawn." In other places, the poem describes it in terms of extremes:

I really like to write poetry
it's more fun than grass, acid, THC, methedrine
If I can't write I start to yawn

In these lines Waldman's poem of the sixties ironically seems drawn more to the Beat call of the fifties. Not revolution but poetry energizes her, with drugs a close second, in the manner of the pro-war Kerouac and Burroughs of the sixties and the less political Ginsberg of the fifties. The joy in this passion for poetry and even in failed articulation of the inexpressible yawn reminds one of Kerouac's fictional Dean Moriarty and his frenzied, faltering rumination on the mystical "IT" of jazz in On the Road, a passage like several others in this novel that depicts the Beat hero fighting off the immanent loss of a moment's passionate intensity by throwing himself into and beyond language.

Still, as Waldman begins to adopt a Beat sensibility, she also demythologizes it, committing herself to its individuality of outsiders-within-a-group but not to its figure of the heroic male hipster/tortured artist. In this respect, *avant la lettre,* she enacts the postmodern impulse to install and subvert simultaneously. She minimizes claims for her own expressive power, unlike the male Beats, but like them tries to maximize her impact on mainstream readers:

> This is a sample of my own revolution
> taking the easy way out of poetry
> I want it to hit you all personally
> like a shot of extra-strong methedrine
> so you'll become your own television
> Become your own yawn!

The phrase "my own revolution" clearly privatizes what the antiwar movement's leaders could only hope would be an ever-greater public rebellion. As Beat progeny, Waldman participates only from afar, contributing but a "sample" of revolution. By changing consciousness alone, one can change political and cultural life runs this argument by the sixties Left and Waldman, a view inherited from Emerson, Whitman, Rimbaud, and Tzara, a logic revisited in Ginsberg's 1966 call for all Americans over fourteen to take LSD in order to spark the revolution. Waldman's speaker urges readers to "become your own television / [b]ecome your own yawn," another version of the sixties call to "do your own thing," a slogan perilously situated on the border between the Beats' dual urges to self-fulfillment and anarchic romanticism. The times, however, demanded Marx's call to change life directly and collectively, not merely change consciousness and individuality (Gitlin, 216). Politically, then, "How the Sestina" reflects the disconnect between a Beat sensibility as manifest in its sixties' offspring, the self-expressive, semi-organized antiwar protest, and the world of realpolitik.

Poetically, through its nature as a repetitious and thus a citational form, the sestina calls to mind Judith Butler's view that "[a] signifier is political to the extent that it implicitly cites the prior instances of itself, drawing the phantasmic promise of these prior signifiers, reworking them into the production and promise of 'the new'" (220). From this perspective "How the Sestina" reads as Waldman's fantasy of social desire devolving to the personal and back again ad infinitum, utopian ambition latent or manifest in all the sestina's seven attempts to use each of the six words. Successive usages accrete definition or desire to the new and draw their past along with them, but this logic breaks down on the yawn. A continuum stretching from desire through neutrality to repulsion contains the other five words. It is plausible to imagine liking, not liking, or being indifferent to revolution, television, poetry, methedrine, and personal contact. As fatigue or boredom, though, and especially when the sestina dictates that additional meanings or incoherent desires be expressed, the yawn tropes into undecidability, requiring something wholly new, not a reworking. Yet this aporia does not break with citationality, collapse the link of public and private, or vitiate a political interpretation. To Waldman the yawn reveals not only false consciousness on the Left but also the nature of ideology itself, the capacity of myriad state and quasi-state institutions to lure political dissenters into defining themselves negatively and individually, by their alienation from sources of power and by the distance between their lifestyles and state-sanctioned norms. A significant accomplishment of Waldman's poem is this discursive performance of political desire and ideology by a poet soon to be better known for oral performance. As Butler states, "performativity describes this relation of being implicated in that which one opposes. . . . a difficult labor of forging a future from resources inevitably impure" (241). In "How the Sestina" the yawn-as-boredom and transient appeal of TV and revolution show the speaker's awareness of tainted materials. The yawn-as-fatigue, violent revolution, and deadly methedrine powerfully suggest the difficulty ideology poses for desire, the phantasmatic identification indicative of state hegemony.

Most of all, though, "How the Sestina" presents another plausible reading of the "giant yawn" and "become your own yawn," not as sublime objects of ideology but as parody. Becoming your own yawn evokes sixties sloganeering with some earnestness but much mockery as well. People or grand events metamorphosing into giant yawns renders the revolution, its practitioners, and its opponents absurd. In several interviews dating back over twenty years, Waldman describes her own sixties poetry as dated or naive, foolishly proceeding on O'Hara's bully nerve or crafting cosmic supermarket works in the manner of Ginsberg.[7] "How the Sestina" is a cosmic supermarket that knows it's a cosmic supermarket, though; that admits it's not a revolution but a sample of one. This sort of wit is knowing and self-conscious, an ambiguous sample designed either to mislead or read blankly, like postmodern parody in which agency is achieved through the seriocomic reworking of codes. Even the title, "How the Sestina (Yawn)

Works," plays personal and political mind games. In addition to mocking itself, the title preempts responses from both the counterculture and the silent, poetry-eschewing majority. "The sestina-parenthesis-yawn" is a nod in agreement with all those who find poetry a yawn, be they on the Left or Right. Then in an about-face the speaker yawns back at the yawners and, with inspired lunacy, turns them into cosmic yawns, finally to conclude with the conciliation of the poem's final line, "I choose all of you for my poem personally."

Nothing is rejected in this vow to poetry and life that anticipates Waldman's shift over the next few years from New York personism and formalism to Beat shamanism and open form. Writing is more fun than drugs because it lets you choose all, which is "the easy way out" of the problem of desire and disidentification: the way in, inward to self-reliance through Buddhism.[8] Ahead lies the development of compassion for all without desire, using language without fetishizing form or content but rather by following rhythms of breath and listening to the mind. Even before employing the open field of Olson and the Beats and formally committing to Buddhism, Waldman's late-sixties sensibility instinctively turns to Dionysian affirmation and unity. Choosing all means privileging nothing, a core belief Waldman later credits to Olson and his ethnopoetics. Her poem "Eyes in All Heads to Be Looked out Of" (1989) takes its title from Olson's *Maximus I,* which advises that there are no ultimate truths, no hierarchies, beyond the given that heads have eyes "to be looked out of" (33). Waldman has written that Olson's "eyes" and eloquent theory

> had been resonating in my ear for a considerable time. It conjured the image of the many-headed Tibetan deities—those with eyes in the center of their foreheads—"wisdom eyes." My idea here was also that the art of seeing (or insight) transcends the notion of hierarchy. Vision produces a sublime democracy. ([1975] 1996, 151)

Consider, though, that throughout civilization a sublime democracy produced by vision has arisen only in poetry, not in reality, which has yet to transcend hierarchy.

Much the same pattern of visionary grasping at transcendence and political grounding in reality holds for the last, fully historicized poem in *Baby Breakdown,* aptly titled "The Revolution." In this poem as in "How the

Sestina," a violent antiwar rally makes the speaker "want to go where I'm not feeling so bad" and "sit . . . watching movies" (1970, 109).[9] Yet in its evocation of Vietnam-era tensions, the poem provides a rich account of a "grand march," comparable to Mailer's *The Armies of the Night* but minus the ego and packed into thirty-three lines. Waldman's "The Revolution" pits one side "bursting with joy" against "the enemy" that "vanishes . . . behind a gun." She veers from moral hierarchy, however, portraying both sides as "suspecting each other's heart to open fire." This even-handedness distinguishes the work as sixties war poetry. A host of critics, including Charles Altieri, Cary Nelson, Robert von Hallberg, A. Poulin Jr., and Paul Breslin, has faulted such poetry for reasons political and poetical: its overreliance on the lyrical "I" and the metaphysics of presence, neglect of the historical and social forces grounding language and underlying the war, demonization of political opponents, and assumptions that language or higher consciousness could stop the war. *Baby Breakdown's* "Revolution," however, is realistic, the politics embedded in the urban landscape and felt life.

In the poem, a "spooky summer" comes alive through images of "buildings polluting the sky," "a barrage of bottles," and political opponents "stalking the main street." This ghostly, death-in-life atmosphere leads to the next-to-last section, which reads like an obituary for utopian desire. After the doom foreshadowed in discrete images, the speaker now paints history in broad strokes:

> and you realize you're still as alive as ever and want to be
> but would like to be somewhere else perhaps Africa
> Start all over again as the race gets darker and darker
> and the world goes on the way I always thought it would
> For the winner is someone we recognize out of our collective past
> which is turning over again in the grave . . .

These lines convey apathy and powerlessness that, post-Vietnam and post-Watergate, have persisted in the United States for three decades. A world proceeding "the way I always thought it would" drones on to a right-wing triumph, perhaps doing real damage less to the present but more to the past and future. The poem highlights how the war belies America's radical origin, "our collective past" of popular resistance to state-sponsored oppression. The Left's demise also has personal consequences, leaving the speaker's future uncertain; only a vague desire "to be somewhere else" survives. The speaker mentions flight but never actually flees. She "would like to be somewhere else perhaps Africa," but this gesture abroad can only be a passing glance, like Kerouac's controversial desire expressed by the character Sal Paradise in *On the Road,* who wants to be anything other than white—a poor black, Mexican, or Japanese. Despite these attempts to reach out to marginalized or non-Western peoples, this Caucasian wish primarily reconstitutes the agency and freedom of both white subjects, Waldman's speaker and Kerouac's character, through the most transitory of links with otherness.

Perhaps in recognition that even noninvolvement reinscribes the state's claim on its subjects, the poem ends in engaged fashion: "It is so important when one dies you replace him / and never waste a minute." Just prior to this closing, the notion of our past turning in its grave suggests a world-weary voice. In contrast, the last lines introduce a thoroughly new speaker talking of immediately replacing the dead. No longer voyeuristic but now fanatic, the voice is a movement insider's advising steely determination to others in a Left circle. The very humanity the Left sought to affirm, as handed down from the Beats, vanishes here into coldhearted, revolutionary rhetoric. Resisting revolution throughout the poem, the speaker succumbs at the end by issuing a call to arms that mimics the Right's ruthlessness and paradoxically shows the triumph of pro-war ideology over utopian desire. As the war continues, the Left is forced to speak the Right's discourse.

Still, does the poem swallow up all desire by marking political revolution with the fetish of the party?[10] Not if one focuses on a telling declaration earlier in "The Revolution." Nonfetishized desire slips away, detaching itself to incubate the multiple selves to come in Waldman's poetry. The state controls bodies, but its power ends there, she suggests by exclaiming "I just want to know / all the angles of death possible under the American sky!" Ideology's hold on identity diminishes in the mind, soon to transform the social violence and colonized identity of the sixties. Here in the middle of the poem, the speaker locates an exit and glimpses a future. Yearning for knowledge, mingling desire with death, Waldman weds her "I . . . want" to Beat writing. Once the discourses of reportage, disengagement, and revolution reach breaking points, only Beat energy for what's "possible under the American sky" can salvage poetry. Similar to di Prima's *Revolutionary Letters,* which refers to the sixties as "another ghost dance," a striking and thoughtful metaphor for the period, Waldman's revolution becomes a chant of the shamaness (di Prima 1975, 212). "To know / all the angles of death" despairs for the revolution but also carries an undercurrent of exuberance, like the Sioux calling on ancestral spirits to halt genocide. Both tribal rituals—of sixties radicals as of Native Americans—seek a deliverance history reconfigures as ecstatic elegy, leaving the poet/shamaness access only to "all the angles of death" and pondering the ends of all desires.

Unfortunately, the seventies dawned inauspiciously for Waldman. Her *No Hassles* (1971) and *Life Notes* (1973) seem mired in sixties personism and political angst or the seventies inwardness that gripped the nation. But by 1975 in *Fast Speaking Woman* (particularly the long title poem), she broke out by way of feminism into fully realized Beat poetry and a more expansive poetic consciousness. A double vision of the sacred and the abyss—as joyous as in Whitman but darker even than in precursors William Carlos Williams and Olson—has always been at the heart of Beat writing, especially that of Kerouac and Ginsberg. In pursuing these Best extremes, the rhapsodic and the bleak, Waldman began writing longer, more ambitious poems and extending her line to the limits of breath in accord with Ginsberg's aesthetics (Foster 1994, 72). This development is unsurprising considering that by the time *Fast Speaking Woman* was published by City Lights (no. 33 in its Pocket Poets series), Waldman had already met Ginsberg, been invited along with him to give readings at Naropa Institute, and been immersed for a decade in the Lower East Side poetry circle which included other first- and second-generation Beat poets (Charters 1983, 531). Waldman has noted that Ginsberg "called me his 'spiritual wife' in front of three thousand people in Czechoslovakia," and *Fast Speaking Woman* illustrates this Ginsbergian turn in her work, particularly in its emphasis on the orality of poetry (Waldman and Schelling, 39). The title poem came alive in public readings owing to Waldman's performance skills, her chanting style and spontaneous breaking into song at some points, improvising new lines to suit the occasion at other times.

In addition to the breath line, "Fast Speaking Woman" also bears other structural similarities to "Howl." Although "Howl" has four sections and "Fast" two, just as Ginsberg's sequence follows the angelic Beats of "my generation" into the demonic worlds of Moloch and the madhouse and concludes magnanimously with universal holiness, "Fast" charts a similar course from wholeness under threat through fragmentation to reintegration. The progression is most evident in refrains (or choruses) that separate long passages using the anaphoric "I" to begin sentences that catalogue and describe many kinds of women. As Waldman indicates, these choruses allow her "to pause and shift rhythm and acknowledge the cleansing impulse of the writing" ([1975] 1996, 38). Two refrains, one about water and flowers and another on the look and feel of heaven, recur in the first section of the poem:

> I'm the automaton woman
> I'm the decadent woman
> I'm the opulent woman
> > water that cleans
> > flowers that clean
> > water that cleans as I go
> ([1975] 1996, 16)

> I'm the hot-rod woman
> I'm the hostile woman
> I'm the equinox woman
> > that's how it looks when you go to heaven
> > they say it's like softness there
> > they say it's balanced there
> > they say it's like land like day like dew
> ([1975] 1996, 23)

A shift in persona, tone, and imagery, however, occurs immediately in the second section. The everywoman of the first part, positioned in heaven, hell, and many spaces in between, now becomes the Hindu goddess Kali. Her terrifying power over death and life signals a corresponding change in the natural elements, disrupting the refrain. Gone are the cleansing images of water and flowers that drip of dewy heaven.

Waldman's Kali is incendiary, no seventies earth mother but a goddess with attitude:

> I'm the Kali woman the killer woman
> woman with salt on her tongue

fire that cleans
fire that catches
fire burns hotter as I go
. . . .
woman combs snakes out of her hair
woman combs demons out of her hair
   ([1975] 1996, 25)

While fire supplants water as the regenerative agent, the speaker's internal-
ization of Kali suggests revealing contrasts between first-generation male
Beats and second-generation Beat feminism. On one hand, "Howl" exterior-
izes its demon in conformist institutional repression that results in Ginsberg's nightmare vision of collective apocalypse and personal crucifixion.
When the poem's speaker utters Christ's final words, in Hebrew, on the
cross, this extreme fate seems at least partially attributable to the fifties Beats'
highly developed sense of victimization and their insularity. On the other
hand, "Fast" admits to carrying the devil within shared by all and catalyzes
this power to oppose male domination, refusing victimization and Beat disdain for the mainstream. More inclusive than "Howl" as it reaches out beyond the Beat circle to quotidian lives, Waldman's poem also envisions
"cannibal woman" devouring men right now rather than Ginsberg's already-
dead male body and those of his generation's best minds ([1975] 1996, 26).
   The same death goddess animates other notable seventies long poems,
demonstrating a gendered polarity again and how Beat women seized a historical moment of patriarchal rupture. For instance, Robert Bly's "The Teeth
Mother Naked at Last" (1973) probes the male psyche responsible for the
Vietnam war and uncovers Kali at the core, a feminine principle the male
poet sees as conducive only to hate, fear, and rage. Alternatively, di Prima's
Loba reincarnates the teeth mother as the she-wolf whose fires and floods
produce "a new / creation myth" of women's desire (1978, 29). Fast-speak-
ing woman and the loba remind readers that Kali's powers include healing
and growth. Inverting the way male Beat despair of the fifties foretells the
lost revolution of the sixties, Waldman's seventies Beat feminism anticipates
women's enhanced opportunities and roles in the eighties and nineties.
   With an ecstatic howl of desire bursting into fulfillment, "Fast Speaking
Woman" closes with the voice of *vagina dentata* fused to the Beat shamaness,
an identity troubling to feminists since the movement's inception:

all the world fits in my mouth
I'm the multiple-universes woman

my hair sparks desire
my mouth breathes holy fire
    ([1975] 1996, 34 emphasis in original)

Certainly, much has been made of the goddess's literary reappearance as a
lapse into essentialism at the very moment when women first gained subjectivity. But the speaker devotes long passages to the experiences and emotions of lowercase "w" women whose goals, like any movement's aims, can
profit by the symbolism and charisma a Kali lends. Helen McNeil points out
that although the essentialist archetype of Beat women poets can be construed as "a lesser position, it was at least their own. Then it could grow"
(195). Poetry such as "Fast Speaking Woman" steals the language from
patriarchy to illustrate feminine self-expansiveness in the view of Alicia
Ostriker, who considers the speaker of Waldman's poem an "urban
tribeswoman" (1986, 204). The tribe is international as well, though, as
shown by the use of Rimbaud's "I is another" as the epigraph to "Fast." The
interchangeable nature of identity that this French allusion highlights and
the out-of-body experiences of the Mazatec shamaness Maria Sabina,
whose Mexican, peyote-inspired chants Waldman adapts for "Fast Speaking Woman," situate the poem in varied cultures, complicating essentialism
with discriminating, Olsonian world-cultural constructionism. Ishmael
Reed has praised "Fast Speaking Woman" for this "interest in a variety of
cultures and art forms," the difference Beat writers male and female have
always craved (264). To be Beat is to be a "timeless seeker" in Waldman's
view, one to whom the risks of cultural imperialism or essentialism pale in
comparison to the alternative of not reaching out to what is other ([1975]
1996, 38). Her anthropological interest since the seventies is inseparable
from the Beat ethos of self and society as ongoing projects of resistance to
ego, coupled with an openness to all human connections that consistently
marks Beat feminism.

   After widening her poetic field in the seventies, Waldman undertook
even more extensive cultural and literary explorations in the eighties and
nineties. Unlike "Fast Speaking Woman," *Iovis: All Is Full of Jove* (1993,
1997) is another sort of long poem, one that employs a distinctly anti-Beat

discourse reminiscent of modernism: classical mythopoetics. This may strike some as an odd turn for Waldman, since the use of myth by male modernists has been critiqued by both the Beats and feminist literary criticism. As Charles Altieri and Michael Davidson have noted, the fifties and sixties work of Olson and Ginsberg comprised a poetic that reacted against the symbolism, historical and mythological Eurocentrism, and sense of linguistic limits in modernism. And as Rachel Blau DuPlessis has argued,

> In the writings of male modernists, femaleness is as fixed and eternal a category as ever before in Euro-literature. . . . The constant mythologizing of Woman is an erasure of women. We-speaking women in historical time are faces masked with a static, unhistorical idea of Woman. (42–43)

But even the neoromanticism of Olson and Ginsberg muted women's concerns, and Waldman's *Iovis* avoids replicating masculinist mythology. Rather, the poem presents a variation upon and continuation of Beat feminism by treating (male) civilization and literature as subjects in process, on trial, traditions to be challenged and remade.[11] Accordingly, Waldman draws on the classical texts of Virgil, who wrote *Iovis omnia plena,* "all is full of Jove," in seeking to revise ancient forms and ideals.

Through its questioning of the literary tradition in a woman speaker's voice, *Iovis* joins an alternative to a once-male preserve, a change emerging with Muriel Rukeyser and H.D. during the thirties and World War II and continuing with women poets as diverse as Gwendolyn Brooks, Adrienne Rich, di Prima, Sonia Sanchez, and Susan Howe. For *Iovis,* Waldman realizes a new model is needed:

> I honor and dance on the corpse of the poetry gone before me & especially here in a debt & challenge of epic masters Williams, Pound, Zukofsky & Olson. But with the narrative of H.D.'s *Helen in Egypt* in mind, and her play with 'argument.' I want to don armor of words as they do and fight with liberated tongue & punctured heart. But unlike the men's, my history & myths are personal ones. (1993, 2–3)

Waldman's decision to "honor and dance on the corpse" of patriarchal modernism reflects the influence on *Iovis* of Williams, Pound, Zukofsky, and

Olson, as well as the Beats. These poets at times forego linear narrative in favor of less fixed structure and alter normal syntax and semantics, destabilizing the self and notions of social order. In particular, the writers *Iovis* cites employ collage and cut-up, techniques Burroughs used both lavishly and provocatively, borrowing and incorporating outside sources of poetry and prose to transform what literature is and how it is read. While the early twentieth century's dadaism and Russian formalism initiate this experimentalism, H.D.'s related "play with 'argument'" provides Waldman's deep structure and methodology. Like *Helen in Egypt*, *Iovis* retells myth from a woman's point of view, arguing with the past by including the heretofore excluded. Both poems embrace postmodernism's strategy of incorporating valuable parts of the past while casting a cold eye on it in totality. Waldman's "my history & myths are personal" echoes H.D.'s reclamation project and continues the overturning of male modernist insistence on poetic myth's impersonality.[12]

As the poem incubates, Waldman hears "the sound of a bigger vatic voice inside any myth, classic archetype, any ritual sacrifice" (1993, 242). The implication that everyday speech suffers in comparison to "a bigger vatic voice" endows myth with authority and prophetic power. Throughout history, poets generally have appropriated myth's authority to legitimize or perpetuate the male dominance *Iovis* desires to revise. Somewhat akin to Ginsberg in the sixties after he tried to abandon the vatic voice of his Blake visions and took up Buddhism, Waldman grasps the illusory nature of the visionary mode, its truths not divinely revealed by gods to prophets but constructed, made by fallible men and women alike. Consistent with this postmodernization of Beat writing, *Iovis* disputes Virgil on linguistic grounds. To the ancient Roman the world was the creation and property of a male god, the woman poet points out with barely suppressed chagrin by emphasizing that *Iovis* grammatically "is the possessive case, *owned by Jove*" (1993, 2, emphasis in original). In Waldman's imagined return to the ground zero of the world's creation, to the heroic world of myth championed (or "owned") by ancient and modern male writers alike, what does she discover? Not an aging patriarch but an infant dancing, *Iovis* asserts metaphorically. This image—strange or offbeat to some readers, perhaps charming to others, and familiar to computer users or *Ally McBeal* viewers—symbolizes a reappropriation of the male line in twentieth-century American long poems of myth and history. The poet relates that "she dances the word into being," creating poetry not so much from language, observation, or imagination as from embodied kinetics that draw with childlike delight on these systems and faculties, the poetry of dance (1997, 242).

Waldman focuses on the music of her body, similarly heterogeneous, to generate a poetics alternately grounded and without ground:

> I get up & dance the poem when it sweeps into litany. I gambol with the shaman & the deer. It is a *body poetics*. I am in the context of those before me who worshipped a goddess whose eyes were mirrors. One eye reflected the 'inside,' the other the gorgeous & dark phenomenal world. Take your pick. Both, both. She, the muse, puts on an invisible protection cord around my neck to protect me from ego. She exceeds my aspiration to disappear. (1993, 2, emphasis in original)

The poet chooses inside and outside—self and world, psyche and other—since both allow for the desired loss of personality and immersion in the rhythmic body. Paradoxically, the "aspiration to disappear" correlates to ego since the pleasures of connecting with others and the world can turn the poet into a self-absorbed prophet. Waldman knows herself and the Beat desire to enact "body poetics" well enough to realize that she needs the muse for more than inspiration. Noted for theatrical chanting and singing, the poet continually risks seduction by her own powerful presence or through fascination with oral performance voices. Accordingly, the "goddess whose eyes were mirrors" of the noumenal and phenomenal performs a crucial service by reminding the poet not to get too caught up in psychical excitement, to make time to reflect on the self and engage the world intellectually rather than experiencing them only in the moment.

Iovis brings an impressive array of technical devices to bear in developing a body poetics that departs from the mid-century Beat emphasis on presence, converging instead with the theoretical underpinnings of language poetry. It is difficult to convey the scope of the poem's rich and strange visual textures; they incorporate practically every twentieth-century shift in poetry's layout since Gertrude Stein, the dadaists and surrealists, and e.e. cummings. To Waldman body is still understood as human corporeality, but she increasingly stresses the materiality of language, especially the ways signification is challenged or semantic indeter-

minacy proffered by the use of typewriter symbols and the density or spar-
sity of words in lines and on pages. Unique format and design features appear throughout *Iovis* (and its two volumes combined total forty-eight
chapters, over 600 pages). Literally writing all over already-oversized pages
or leaving large white spaces, Waldman makes recurrent use of indenta-
tions at various lengths, centered lines, text flushed right, diversified spacing between lines, and nonlinguistic symbols. Simply put, throughout the
poem the line consistently looks fresh and new, as if the definition of poetry has been expanded and its usual look deterritorialized. The closing
section of *Iovis II,* for instance, surrounds single-spaced lines with language
poetry's "equals" sign at the beginning and end of each line: "=breath
finally gives life to stars= / =ours as it were, a break, a foible, long night
museum-clad=" (1997, 287). The dash, period, dot (or bullet), ellipsis (of
varying lengths), and mathematical symbols for "is greater than" and "is less
than" all function similarly in brief or extended passages, as does the use of
bold type, italics, extremely oversized type, and exclusively uppercase or
lowercase letters. Waldman's plethora of wordless signs and alternative
typescripts turns *Iovis* into a semiotic text, highlighting its marking by
rhythmic gestures, its body hieroglyphically inscribed.

Waldman sets no particular pattern but commits to the visually heterogeneous, even nonlinguistic page. She creates a variety of simple, complex,
inanimate, and animate objects, shapes, and life-forms. For example, in addition to pages that include drawings of animals or arrange lines of poetry
to picture the zodiac, winglike clusters, and Saxon towers, a stretch of several pages in *Iovis I* consists of squares and rectangles, anywhere from three
to seven per page. A few brief, logically unconnected words or phrases are
written inside (or sometimes outside) each square or rectangle. *Iovis II* essentially repeats the process but surrounds the words or phrases with
circles instead. Commenting on the writer's boxing or circling of brain-
stormed thoughts for inclusion in the draft, Waldman indicates that her
geometric shapes enclose language "assured now of a place on the *page*"
(1993, 177; emphasis mine). These pages render content secondary to
form-as-design, since the meanings of the words within the shapes are elu-
sive, suggesting that personal history and myth necessarily involve some
obscurity for readers. This deliberate difficulty, however, contrasts with
the simplicity and purity of the squares and circles, which form creation's

semiotic code in *Iovis*. They become symbols of the poem as open text, inviting readers into its process and encouraging them to remain open to the unfamiliar.

Waldman is fully aware of those passages in *Iovis* bordering on incoherence—both in the boxes and circles and elsewhere in the poem—or based on unusual (often Buddhist and Hindu) sources. This awareness is calculated, for her works over the years, her essay/interview "My Life a List" (1979), and separate interviews over the next fifteen years all show gradual relaxation of an earlier decision not to include Buddhist or other jargon-ridden abstractions in her poetry (Waldman 1979, 318; Bartlett 1987, 267; Foster 1994, 74). *Iovis*'s body poetics and private languages move toward Burroughs-style Beat experimentalism, linked back to and reminiscent of the European dadaism and surrealism that certain American modernists adapted for their collage poetry. For example and by way of contrast, few would dispute that Ginsberg, not only Waldman's mentor early on but also cofounder with her of the Jack Kerouac School of Disembodied Poetics (at Naropa Institute), deserves inclusion in the ranks of major avant-garde poets. As Marjorie Perloff has pointed out, though, even Ginsberg's jazz improvisations and explicit references to sexuality function conventionally, a far cry from body poetics:

> Ginsberg's is a mode of continuity: however surrealist, jarring, hilarious, horrendous his conjunction of images may be, he regards the poem as a living *whole* with, somewhat surprisingly, a beginning, middle, and end. . . . Ginsberg, we may conclude, is never the poet of collage, of fragment, of layering and splicing. As such, his poetry now looks, for all its references to "cock" and "balls," reassuringly traditional. (221)[13]

Unlike Ginsberg, Waldman's use of the page, the cut-up, and the a-linear narrative that defies closure subverts the conventions of poetry, not just sexual mores. *Iovis* pushes openness and obscurity to the limit, as demonstrated by its use of Derridean double-column writing and of strikeovers, straight lines drawn through words and at times whole lines of poetry so that they appear under erasure. Like Derrida, of course, the poet paradoxically both includes and excludes these lines, for they are not really crossed out but only appear so, remaining legible under the strikeover as though the censoring poet decided to exclude and then reconsidered, finally showing both the editing impulse and the refusal of its censorship. While these permutations hint of repression, the double columns touch on schizophrenia, cutting the page in half and splitting the line into dual voices sounding simultaneously, disrupting left-to-right reading. Here Waldman's body poetics expands on H.D.'s "play with 'argument'" and Burroughs's outrider style by arguing through subversive play with form, reveling in the polymorphous perversity of the page-as-body.

While *Iovis* practices the politics of form, it also revises traditional Greek creation myth. In Hesiod's account, the lovemaking of the primordial parents, Ouranos and Gaia, originates the world by establishing the male in heaven's dominant position and relegating the woman to lesser agency as earth. In Waldman's reimagining, Gaia is completely powerless during sexual intercourse, consistent with her later subservience to heaven. Shifting narrative point of view to the woman's perspective, the poet suggests that patriarchy is preordained in Hesiod's tale:

> I am helpless
> Ex Stasis
> I'm Gaia
> Father Sky look down on me
> Stars are his eyes
> He enters me
> All is full of him
>   (1993, 7)

Waldman refers to Ouranos as Father Sky even before consummation, insinuating that Hesiod assumed prior to developing the myth that the ruler of eternity had to be a man. The Ouranos of *Iovis* confirms this determination: "stars are his eyes" before intercourse as well, pointing to the male poet's assumption that heaven is by nature masculine. Notice how the woman poet subtly upbraids the way men "look down" on a woman, the Olympian male arrogance that borders on obscenity according to another example later in *Iovis*. In myth, Jove effectively peoples earth through his promiscuity, his lust for mortal women and goddesses and consequent love making. These conquests are no mere philandering but the very core of myth to the likes of

Virgil, heroic manifestations of divine Eros. *Iovis,* on the other hand, envisions the many trysts of Jove and his sons as rape plain and simple:

> All is full of Jove, he fucks everything
> It is the rough way to prove it
> The male gods descend & steal power
> How does it happen
>   (1993, 19)

Here the speaker echoes the use of obscene words by earlier male Beats but also challenges the sexual license patriarchy grants to men. Waldman's transgressive language and question speak to misogyny so strongly that the context of the last three lines induces the thought that the initial line omits a word: not "he fucks everything" but "he fucks everything up." This ambiguous play on "fucking" as making love and "fucking up" as ruining things intersects at Jove, whose "rough way" with women and compulsion to "prove it" ("it" referring to male power) destroy what should be the mutual joy of Eros.

Throughout *Iovis* Waldman counterpoints this pursuit of dominance with her own readings of creation myths for their power to suggest positive self- and world-transformation. As a practicing Buddhist, like many Beats, Waldman prefers the Madhyamika creation myth

> which refutes the idea of solid existence and embraces the view of codependent or co-arising origination. Things do not come from themselves nor do they come from things other than themselves, nor do they arise from both these factors, nor do they come from neither of these factors. Where do they come from? We live in a *Samsaro-dadhi,* or oceanlike world. The strands of our existence come together karmically. (1993, 298)

To a Western sensibility this explanation probably seems to be more of a noncreation myth, so vague is it about how planetary or human matter arises. The nothingness or nonbeing of "solid existence" is precisely the point in Buddhism, which "refutes" the corporeal presence of things to recognize a "codependent," "oceanlike" origin of life that values acceptance of indeterminacy and mystery over causality and certainty. Waldman's

"Things do not come from themselves" encapsulates the negative spirituality of the East that paradoxically grounds compassion and worldliness, qualities critical to *Iovis*. The *neti neti* ("not this, not that") way, seeing the creation as due neither to this nor that, neither both nor neither, involves a philosophy of "canceling identification with object and with subject" according to Joseph Campbell. He adds that this discovery by the Buddha under the Bodhi tree "led to an ironic return to life without commitment to anything at all, but with compassion equally for all. For all things are void" (285).

Iovis's chapter on Buddhism restates this assertion, claiming "there is no / thing in itself" (1993, 307). This denial of essence makes analysis problematic, but Buddhism's rejection of matter does not erode Waldman's commitment to body poetics. The refutation of "thingness" exalts the principle of karma—the energy generated by human actions, somewhat akin to psychic energy and often referred to as the atmosphere something radiates or vibrations someone gives off; in the process, Buddhism in fact plays a symbiotic role in the poet's articulation of the body's forces and music. One of the chief implications of continental critical theory and the language poetry that sprang from it is that the rhythms, echoes, and linguistic and inscripted play Waldman uses form the way language is learned, was created in the past, and will change in the future. The poet links her desire for this productive reversion and future transformation to Buddhist meditation, stating that religious practice moves her to posit *"an oppositional poetics,"* a discourse of the never-experienced and the unutterable on "the edge of this writing, outside the book" (298, 308). [14]

The Buddhist creation myth in *Iovis* exemplifies what Waldman and the Beats long have seen as a pressing need: to bring into poetry and society what the West often has ignored or marginalized. If the strange brew of bad and good karma in the sixties made the poet slow to recognize that disidentification with the state only reproduced its hegemony over a movement lacking adequate collectivization, then history also meant for Beat writing to be revived when Waldman discovered it. Her desire to decipher the yawn and know America's angles of death reflected a nationwide search for a new basis of community. Breathing Kali's holy fire of feminism in the seventies, her poetry turned from revolution to creation, a vision retaining the utopian impulse of Beat body poetics and Olson's ethnopoetics but at once more inclusive and politically effective. In the avant-garde foreground during the antinuclear eighties and poetry-slamming nineties,

Waldman has built toward the critique of patriarchy in *Iovis*, in which Beat desire recodes the cultural past and the conventional page and line.

Notes

1. The New York school of O'Hara and others "held a particular attraction for younger poets. Their work—subtle, witty, urban, visual—included the playfulness of the Surrealists without the ideology," Waldman indicates (1991, 4). She has recalled meeting O'Hara before he died in 1966 and how "[h]e was so matter-of-fact about my wanting to be a poet. Welcome to the club, he said" (Waldman and Schelling, 35). Waldman's interest in oral performance poetry intensified after Olson punctuated the 1965 Berkeley readings with an inspired, rambling reading. In 1968, she became director of New York's St. Mark's Poetry Project, a leading site for avant-garde poetry readings, particularly by the younger branch of the New York school that featured another of Waldman's early mentors, Ted Berrigan. In the seventies, she was poet-in-residence on musical legend Bob Dylan's Rolling Thunder tour, and in the last decade as spoken work has become increasingly popular, she has twice won the Taos (New Mexico) Poetry Circus slam.

2. In other words, as revolution becomes the sublime object of desire, sex, drugs, and rock lose transcendence and become a sublime object of ideology (to borrow Slavoj Zizek's terms). In this section my reading of Waldman is indebted to Zizek 1989 and especially to Zizek 1996a.

3. All of the following quotes from "How the Sestina (Yawn) Works" are from page 15 in Waldman 1970.

4. In a distinction similar to his theory of the Apollonian and Dionysian, Nietzsche sees romantic music, art, and literature as rooted in hunger and poverty, desirous of destruction, whereas the classical in the arts springs from fulfilled natures. He then complicates this distinction by acknowledging that the will to change and destroy arises in both sorts of people, as does the passive desire to eternalize the same. See *The Will to Power*, 419–453.

5. See Jameson, particularly the first and final chapters.

6. "How the Sestina (Yawn) Works" is reprinted in *Baby Breakdown* and in *Helping the Dreamer* (1989); the poem initially appeared in Waldman's first published volume, *O My Life!* (1969).

7. For Waldman's frank assessment of her least successful early poems, see Waldman 1979 and see Foster. In the 1994 interview with Foster, Waldman indicates that as early as her matriculation at Bennington in the mid-sixties, she contacted Ginsberg to arrange a visit to her school. *Giant Night* (1970) provides further evidence of the Ginsberg connection, as the poems "Here It Is No Here It Is" and "New Day" express admiration for Ginsberg's *Planet News* and "Wales Visitation" respectively.

8. In Helen McNeil's view, the Buddhism of Waldman and two other major

Beat women poets, Diane di Prima and Joanne Kyger, functions as a defense mechanism against the irresponsibility and chauvinism of the male Beats. In her thoughtful "The Archaeology of Gender in the Beat Movement," McNeil values the poetry of all three despite what she sees as the sacrifice of gendered identity to religion (195).

9. In the ensuing section, all citations of "The Revolution" are from page 109 in Waldman 1970.

10. The terminology here ("fetish of the party") and the argument in the above paragraph are indebted to Zizek 1996b.

11. In the following section, the argument and some of the terminology are indebted to Kristeva 1980 and 1984.

12. See T.S. Eliot 1964 and 1975."Tradition and the Individual Talent" in his *Selected Essays* (New York: Harcourt, 1964) and "Ulysses, Order, and Myth" in *Selected Prose of T.S. Eliot,* ed. Frank Kermode (New York: Harcourt, 1975). Prior to *Iovis,* Joanne Kyger's *The Tapestry and the Web* (1965) most closely anticipates Waldman's strand of Beat feminism as it continues H.D.'s rewriting of classical myth. Michael Davidson notes that in adapting the tale of Ulysses's wife Penelope, "Kyger's use of persona blurs the distinction between mythical personage and herself . . . [T]he use of myth allows her a degree of chattiness" (189). Waldman's similar blend of the breezily personal and the mythical is no accident; she has acknowledged Kyger as an influence, crediting her skilled characterization (Charters 1983, 531).

13. For a perceptive defense of Ginsberg against eighties critics who have charged the Beat poet with formlessness and naive, left-wing politics, see Perloff. To her, "Howl" is a valuable and poetically accomplished "cultural and historical artifact: it tells us who and how we were in mid-century America; more specifically, it encodes counterculture values and anxieties that are specifically homosexual, Jewish, and lower middle-class" (3). As the Perloff comments quoted above in this essay indicate, though, she also argues that in addition to its social protest and cultural and historical values, "Howl" and much of Ginsberg's poetry use standard formal devices to a greater degree than previously suspected. Interestingly, his poetry is too undisciplined for several eighties critics and too conventional for him to be considered postmodern by Perloff.

14. Buddhism has proven conducive, in Waldman's view, to the poet's assumption of the Adamic role of namer and, in an ethereal sense, creator of the world. She has spoken of writing as a form of Buddhist meditation in which "[y]ou watch how your mind is working. You see how the world is not all that solid, and 'you' who are not all that solid either, is usually thinking it up" (qtd. in Bartlett, 268).

Many Drummers, a Single Dance?

Tim Hunt

Good criticism forces us to consider new possibilities, to reread and re-think. The essays in this collection do that. They map out roads and destinations for the literary landscape known as Beat that have always been there but that we have mostly overlooked in our zeal for the core of male writers—Allen Ginsberg, Jack Kerouac, William S. Burroughs in particular—who were inscribed as *the* Beats (rather than *of* the Beat) when the popular press first discovered Beat dissent and artistic experiment. These studies of women Beat writers come at a pivotal moment. We are finally starting to integrate Beat culture into our accounts of American literature in the 1950s and 1960s, and reconsideration of the Beats must also engage the work of women who wrote Beat and account for their critical neglect (by their male Beat peers, the press, and the academy). If we want to be serious students of the Beats, we no longer have the option of reading and writing as if the writers discussed in these essays were not part of the equation—especially if our aim is a productive understanding of Beat work and culture and not just individual, isolated texts.

Those writing on the Beats have generally wanted to distance the terms

Beat and *Beatnik* from each other as much as possible, reserving "Beat" for the writers' own positive representations of their work and their literary community, while gathering the dismissals of their lives and work in the popular and academic presses under the heading "Beatnik." There's some sense in this. Beatnik began as a derogatory coinage, and when the critical priority was to establish that at least some Beat texts were literary and belonged in the canon, casting *Beat* as an honorific term and *Beatnik* as the label for uninformed, mean-spirited attacks was a useful rhetorical move. Yet the careers of such writers as Diane di Prima, Joyce Johnson, and Hettie Jones suggest that the relationship between these labels needs to be rethought. Their work, and their lives as figured in their writings, demonstrate that being Beat was never about crafting well-wrought literary urns for New Critical analysis. It was an attempt to resist the pressures to commit to the fantasy of suburban bliss and to anesthetize one's self to the nightmare of cold war stalemate. It was an attempt to name and dissect these pressures, and it was an attempt to recover, demonstrate, and (thereby) validate other, more individual modes of consciousness. It was both literary experiment and oppositional (often violational) lifestyle(s). For better and worse, the efforts to advance the Beat project and the attempts to contain it not only involved the production of literary texts and critical wars over their merit and meaning but also played out in panels and forums, commentaries in the popular press, television series, movies, even advertising campaigns. In this broader (and perhaps more haphazard) negotiation of terms and positions, of texts and behaviors, the distinction between the insider's term (*Beat*) and outsider's term (*Beatnik*) could and did blur to the point that even the attacks on Beatniks could help draw people to the possibility of Beat and in part mediate their understanding of it. Even if di Prima in *Memoirs of a Beatnik* plays on and against this slippage or doubleness, Beatnik as a category or domain or set of positions must be an element in our reading of it, if we are to appreciate the way she was engaging the cultural moment and how the terms of the cultural moment also helped shape how and why the book was read.

Similarly, in their memoirs *Minor Characters* and *How I Became Hettie Jones*, Johnson and Jones remind us that media representations of bohemia, Beat, and Beatnik helped shape these writers' initial revolt against 1950s gender codes and middle-class norms and were a factor in their decisions, and presumably the decisions of others, to explore the possibilities of Beat and Beatnik. Their accounts of what it meant to write and how the writing got done also remind us that writers seldom create in the heroic isolation we might fantasize for them. They are part of networks of people who help pay the bills, wash the dishes, type the manuscripts, handle the correspondence, and build the literary communities that help validate the writing and help it find readers. And these accounts remind us that even in the Beat world, for all its rejection of middle-class values and norms, for all its emphasis on the transcendent individual, the roles for women were ones that supported the writing of men and cast women as peripheral figures. As such, the remembering and reconstructing and imaginative probing in works such as *How I Became Hettie Jones* are context for understanding how writing got done in this period and thereby help us understand the broader cultural negotiation of Beat that was not only the process of producing literary texts but also the process of creating literary communities and trying to leverage cultural change through those texts and communities. This remembering also dramatizes the need to recover what we can of the work of women such as Elise Cowen who paid the cost of being rendered insignificant within the world of Beat, since such work reveals most acutely how the Beat ethos was only partly a transcendence of, or rejection of, the norms of postwar culture and society. In Jones, Cowen, and others we see entanglement and escape, both in their own writings and in their relationships with the male writers whose work they loved and encouraged. In them, that is, we see both a rejection of and a partial reinstatement of the codes of their culture, and this is part of the power of their work and why it has as well the power to force revisionary readings of the established Beat canon. We can still appreciate how works like *On the Road* and "Howl" (partly through their own power, partly through the public images of Kerouac and Ginsberg, and partly through the controversies in the media) helped catalyze cultural and social change, but the context of *Minor Characters,* the shards of Cowen's surviving poems, the transformative witness of Hettie Jones demand that we move beyond the impulse to cast the major male Beat writers as figures who transcended their cultural moment (however much they sought to escape aspects of it) and beyond the impulse to treat such works as *On the Road* as freestanding literary monuments. If we fail to do this, not only will we fail to recover writers such as Cowen but we will also continue to miss how the male writers and the works we have begun to validate functioned as part of a larger, more significant project.

Women Beat writers also remind us that literary production is never neat, even if we make histories of it that are. In part, the value of the question of who qualifies as Beat is the impossibility of a satisfactory answer. Joanne Kyger's ties to Gary Snyder and Ginsberg, her travels to Japan and India, mark her as Beat, yet her approach to writing, which owes little to Beat practice, developed as it did almost in spite of her involvement with the Beats. Her work reminds us that the Beats were part of a larger set of literary and cultural experiments in this period that included the poets of the San Francisco Renaissance and the New York and Black Mountain schools. That Kyger moved across these boundaries complicates and disrupts the category of Beat by reminding us that these labels were less the names of discrete schools or systems than tags for groups of people drawn together by both personal and aesthetic tendencies, that the practices of the writers in these overlapping communities were evolving and shifting throughout the period, and that writers could move from one group to another or even be functioning in several communities at once—as the career of Anne Waldman illustrates. Waldman, though a Beat writer, was also influenced by Frank O'Hara, a poet of the New York school, and by Charles Olson, the patriarch/theorist of the Black Mountain school, whose "Projective Verse" is a key document in postwar experimental poetics. While "Projective Verse" parallels the approaches of Ginsberg and Kerouac in its emphasis on the voice as a unit of measure, its emphasis on the written work, the text, as a made object on the page, is finally counter to the poetics Ginsberg and Kerouac were developing and owes more to the experiments of Pound than the example of Whitman (or even William Carlos Williams). That Waldman, in her career, has negotiated O'Hara's "Personism," Olson's "Projective Verse," and Beat spontaneity and orality points to the rich, eclectic mix of postwar literary experiment. And it underscores the danger of treating any of these experimental positions too much in isolation from the matrix of competing and overlapping projects and groups. One can easily multiply the list of interesting and important writers from the 1950s and 1960s who in various ways bear on or link to the Beat without necessarily being perceived or treated as Beat in the literary histories: Ed Dorn, Diane Wakoski, Denise Levertov, Paul Metcalf, Sharon Doubiago come to mind, as does Robert Creeley, whose friendship with Kerouac and interest in his work perhaps marks him as Beat, even as his time at Black Mountain College and links with Olson mark him as Black

Mountain. Such multiple and overlapping lines of affinity and the multiple points of collaboration (especially in the small presses and magazines where people identified with different groups published side by side) remind us that various antagonisms and schisms—as well as the alliances—were at times personal as much as aesthetic or ideological. Here, again, *How I Became Hettie Jones* reflects how Beat was part of a larger constellation of cultural production. And recognizing this, we are in a better position not only to distinguish how the various strands of Beat interweave with other strands of experiment but also to discern the significance of projects like the journal *Big Table* and events like the 1965 Berkeley Poetry Conference, related developments in the other arts (the career of the painter Larry Rivers, for example), and even developments in the mass media (the recordings of Ken Nordine, the humor of Lenny Bruce, the radio work of Jean Shepard). Serious study of the Beats needs to be, also, serious study of the period's complementary and competing artistic and cultural experiments, just as serious study of these other projects needs to be serious study of the Beats.

But perhaps most importantly, scholarship on women Beats reveals the extent to which the Beat writers—in spite of their rejection of the square world of the middle class and its sexual norms—in large part reenacted the era's gender codes with their limited range of roles and expression for women. In part, this reflects how deeply embedded these codes are and their resistance to change. It also reflects the gendered character of the tradition from which the Beats drew much of their inspiration and which they used to help authorize their emphasis on nonconformity, individualism, and transcendental vision. Historically, Emerson is perhaps the central figure in this tradition, both for what he developed in his own texts and because of how his work catalyzed other significant American writers—Whitman's vatic Kosmos, Melville's attempts to sound the depths of the transcendental self in *Moby-Dick,* and Thoreau's sky fishing at Walden Pond. We now take for granted the canonical status of Whitman, Melville, Thoreau, and the figures F.O. Matthiessen celebrated in *American Renaissance: Art and Expression in the Age of Emerson and Whitman* (1941), and we tend to assume that these writers—and the tradition of the "Imperial Self" and the "American Adam"—have always been recognized as foundational. But Melville and Thoreau were almost forgotten figures from the Civil War to the mid-1920s, and Whitman (at least academically) was disreputable and marginal. This literature was first entering the canon and classroom, largely through the critical mediation of such figures as Matthiessen, as the Beats were coming of age, and initially, at least, it functioned not as an authorized site for the literary but as oppositional—an alternative to the sense of tradition that offered Henry James as the epitome of fiction and assumed that the only worthwhile tradition for a poet was the British canon as defined by T. S. Eliot. Joyce Johnson's use of the figure of Melville in *Come and Join the Dance* shows how quickly the canon could absorb a disruptive figure and weave his work into an authorized, conservative master narrative, but in the 1940s Kerouac's allegiance to Melville and Thoreau and Ginsberg's allegiance to Whitman were acts of literary revolt. One problem was that this then-countertradition was itself already gendered—or too easily subsumed to a masculinist position—to challenge the gendered assumptions about writing that women writers of the 1950s confronted. Di Prima, Elise Cowen, and Janine Pommy Vega could join Ginsberg, Gregory Corso, and Snyder in rejecting the hegemony of Eliot (or perhaps more accurately the hegemonic Eliot the academy had constructed) and seeking moments beyond the confining social order, but this act of literary revolt was one that only partly challenged categories of gender in which literary writing was male. That paradigmatic moment of transcendence for American literature—Emerson's experience in *Nature* of becoming a "transparent eyeball"—helps suggest why this was so. It is worth remembering that the process that leads to his moment of vision (which he implies but doesn't actually detail) erases all human connections and obligations, including those of family. This formulation of vision isn't explicitly male; it is available to anyone able to reject social conventions and, for a time at least, put aside human connections. Yet it is a small step from this to a sense that commitments to others—especially sexual, domestic, and parental ones—preclude or compromise visionary experience. From there it is a smaller step to a sense that those who seek vision should avoid or evade such commitments and that men can more plausibly or acceptably do this. Ironically, then, the nineteenth-century American writers that the early Beats saw as precursors and who offered a way to think of literature as a way to move beyond the quotidian and contingent also helped reinscribe or reinforce the gender bias of 1950s containment culture. Melville and Whitman and Thoreau represented a ground for resisting the lures and pressures to conform but their societies of one (or one and a select male comrade or two) seemed to license visionary independence only for those women who avoided or renounced domestic entanglements. The nineteenth-century precursors of the Beats pointed toward radical cultural possibilities for women, even as their texts worked against the more radical thinking about gender that the women sought as they lived out the Beat experience and fashioned their practices as writers. This context underscores the radicalism of di Prima's commitment to the visionary in her life and work while also choosing to have and raise children without entangling relationships with their fathers. It also suggests that part of the terms—and cost — for Brenda Frazer to be able to write *Troia* was having given up her daughter and the absence (in jail) of Ray Bremser, to whom she was addressing the pieces that make up the book. Similarly, Pommy Vega's husband functions as her muse in "Poems for Fernando" perhaps in part because he is dead and, like Bremser, an absence. In this context, the way Joyce Johnson's heroine in *Come and Join the Dance* rejects Melville becomes a figure for her own turning away from the allure of the American romantic tradition to become, in part through her "cool" and more detached style, a writer who deftly and insightfully portrays the Beat more than she enacts it.

Less obviously, but I think importantly, the new Beat scholarship on women writers points to the general dissatisfaction of both men and women who wrote Beat with the rules and logic of the printed page as established by such modern masters as James, Eliot, Fitzgerald, and Hemingway, codified by the New Critics, and enforced by the postwar academy. To the Beats this approach to the page—which dictated that each work be a self-contained, crafted literary object rich with irony, indirection, and complexity and where the masterful deployment of literary conventions was the primary sign of authenticity—was simply too constraining, too indirect, and too impersonal. The directness of sincerity and confession, the immediacies of anger or joy or pain or hilarity all violated the stylistic norms that had grown up around the printed page in the modern period and had become the conditions for writing being considered literary. The Beat desire for the immediacy of passionate speaking and the willingness to risk the jumps and digressions of people actually telling stories (or performing stories as if for an actual other at an actual moment) threatened to reveal the page for what it actually is—not a transparent medium but a screen or barrier, a rupture that confronts the writer (if we focus on the assumptions that sustain this constructed space) with the reader's absence and, similarly, confronts the reader with the writer's absence.

The story of Kerouac drafting *On the Road* in three weeks in the spring of 1951 by feeding a roll of paper directly into his typewriter and typing continuously for long stretches has become a figure for the Beat aesthetic— the risk of (or commitment to) speed, spontaneity, and improvisation yielding discovery and vision. But for Kerouac this experiment was also, I think, an attempt to break through the alienated and alienating conventions of the page in order to find an approach that would recast the page (and writing) from being a space where one composed representations of speech to being instead a medium where one could enact a kind of speaking as if the reader where an actual presence, an actual (and potentially collaborative) listener. Other than perhaps Joyce Johnson, whose stylistic debt to Henry James seems to have enabled her to make peace with the conventions of print and page, many women who wrote Beat, such as Kyger, Waldman, and Pommy Vega, were, like Kerouac, experimenting with ways to break the confines of the page and the rhetorics it seemed to enforce (based on the constraints and authority of a single, fixed point of view). These attempts to make the written page a performative space for writer and reader (or at least to recast the page as the residue of the writer's performative process), to explore, as does Hettie Jones, speaking as well as writing, to play with the gap between the way language functions for the ear and for the eye, may be another reason why women who wrote Beat at times chose to work outside the category of the novel, with its weight of print-based conventions, and instead engaged their lives and readers through the less-determined genres of the memoir and personal narrative. Had Frazer tried to fictionalize, to novelize, her experiences in Mexico she would have had to use her understanding of the needs and expectations of the impersonal reader to shape the book, but instead her decision to write as if talking to someone who shared these experiences allowed her to probe her associations with the material, to bring these reflections and lyric flights to the fore, and to push the linear narrative of the events into the background. In *Troia* Frazer's voice enacts her experience of reflecting on her story. That her voice is fundamentally private even as it reaches us through the public medium of the published page underscores how much her work is written against the grain of the formality of the modern literary page, how much its various risks function as a denial and subversion of that page. And while di Prima's rhetorical and structural games in *Memoirs of a Beatnik*—her seeming insincerity at times, her willingness to confess, then erase the confession, then tease us to know the truth between the stories she flaunts and her flaunting of her ability to deny and assert—might seem the antithesis of Frazer's sincerity, like Frazer she is refusing to write a novel in the traditional sense, indeed is writing against the novel in the traditional sense and using the license of the pornographic memoir (as well as its conventions) to create exchanges with the reader. Frazer's and di Prima's different subversions of the novel and its page become clearer in the context of Kerouac's experiments (and those of Burroughs and Ginsberg as well), but equally Frazer's and di Prima's experiments underscore how much Kerouac's project was, finally, based on a decision to break with the formality, distance, and logic of the page to explore modes of writing emphasizing, instead, risk, sincerity, and associational freedom and that would allow (force?) the reader into the more active position of sincere listener and even collaborator. In this sense, it is not that Kerouac wrote novels and that Frazer and di Prima wrote memoirs. It is that Kerouac, di Prima, and Frazer wrote in ways that subverted what the novel had been and toward new modes of creative discourse.

We are just beginning to map and still trying to understand the Beat phenomenon. We must now consider the whole range of Beat voices and Beat experience, not just the work and lives of the small set of men whose work initially caught the attention of the public, if we are to understand the implications of the cultural and social transformations that the 1940s incubated and that the 1950s and 1960s realized. Most simply, of course, we must read the women who wrote Beat or (as is perhaps more the case with Kyger) wrote their way out of Beat and to do so with an appreciation of the assumptions that shaped their various practices and the cultural, social, and economic realities that at times constrained, at times helped enable, their work. Such readings will also challenge us to rethink in broader ways what it meant to write Beat and be Beat. At this moment when it has become acceptable, even within the academy, to begin to consider seriously that such figures as Kerouac, Burroughs, and Ginsberg were important writers, the danger is that the real radicalism of their projects will be assimilated and to some extent reduced to a variation of the literary that they attempted to resist and subvert through their work. Reading the now almost canonical Beats (the male writers) in the context of the women who wrote Beat can help us understand the actual disruptiveness of the Beat experiment that the best of male Beats represent in their best work. But, equally, reading the work of di Prima, Waldman, Cowen, Johnson, Jones,

Pommy Vega, Helen Adam, Kyger, and Frazer as well as other women associated with Beat in the context of their male contemporaries, peers, sometimes collaborators, sometimes competitors can help us more fully appreciate the literary achievement of Beat women and their contribution to the larger project of breaking with the writing of the past to create a possibility for a literature of the future.

Selected Bibliography

Helen Adam

1924. *Charms and Dreams from the Elfin Pedlar's Pack.* London: Hodder and Stoughton.

1924. *The Elfin Pedlar and Tales Told by Pixy Pool.* New York and London: G. P. Putnam's Sons.

1958. *The Queen o' Crow Castle.* Drawings by Jess Collins. N.p.: White Rabbit Press.

1963. *At the Window.* San Francisco: Gene's Print Shop.

1964. *Ballads.* Illustrated by Jess Collins. New York: Acadia Press.

1964. *San Francisco's Burning: A Ballad Opera.* San Francisco: Oannes Press. Reprint 1985. New York: Hanging Loose Press.

1972. *Counting Out Rhyme.* New York: Interim Books.

1974. *Selected Poems and Ballads.* New York: Helikon Press.

1977. *Turn Again to Me and Other Poems.* New York: Kulchur Foundation.

1978. *The Last Secret.* Binghamton, N.Y.: Bellevue Press.

1979. *Ghosts and Grinning Shadows: Two Witch Stories.* Brooklyn, N.Y.: Hanging Loose Press.

1979. *Last Words of Her Lover.* Vancouver, B.C.: Slug Press.

1980. *Gone Sailing.* West Branch, Iowa: Toothpaste Press.

1983. *Summer 1981.* West Branch, Iowa: Toothpaste Press.

1984. *Stone Cold Gothic.* Edited by Lita Hornick. New York: Kulchur Foundation.

1985. *The Bells of Dis: Poems.* West Branch, Iowa: Coffee House Press.

Diane di Prima

1958. *This Kind of Bird Flies Backwards.* New York: Aardvark Press. Reprint 1963. New York: Paper Book Gallery.

1961. *Dinners and Nightmares.* Reprint 1974. New York: Corinth Books. Expanded ed. 1998. San Francisco: Last Gasp Press.

1965. *The New Handbook of Heaven.* San Francisco: Auerhahn Press.

1965. *Seven Love Poems from the Middle Latin.* San Francisco: Poets Press.

1966. *Haiku.* Topanga, Calif.: Love Press.

1968. *Hotel Albert: Poems.* New York: Poets Press.

1969. *Memoirs of a Beatnik.* New York: Olympia Press. Reprint 1988. New York: Last Gasp Press. Reprint 1998. New York: Penguin Books.

1969. *L.A. Odyssey.* San Francisco: Poets Press.

1971. *Kerhonkson Journal.* Berkeley, Calif.: Oyez.

1971. *Revolutionary Letters.* 3rd. ed. 1974. San Francisco: City Lights Books.

1972. *The Calculus of Variation.* San Francisco: Eidolon Editions.

1973. (Editor). *The Floating Bear: A Newsletter.* La Jolla, Calif.: Laurence McGilvery.

1974. *Freddie Poems.* Point Reyes, Calif.: Eidolon Editions.

1975. *Selected Poems, 1956–1975.* Plainfield, Vt.: North Atlantic Books.

1978. *Loba,* Parts 1–8. Berkeley: Wingbow Press.

1990. *Pieces of a Song: Selected Poems.* San Francisco: City Lights Books.

1991. *Seminary Poems.* Point Reyes Station, Calif.: Floating Island Publications.

1998. *Loba,* Parts 1–16, Books 1 and 2. New York: Penguin Books.

2001. *Recollections of My Life as a Woman: The New York Years.* New York: Viking Press.

Brenda Frazer (Bonnie Bremser)

1969. *Troia: Mexican Memoirs.* New York: Croton Press. Republished 1971 as *For Love of Ray.* London: Tandem Press.

Joyce Johnson

1962. (As Joyce Glassman). *Come and Join the Dance.* New York: Atheneum.

1978. *Bad Connections.* New York: G. P. Putnam's Sons.

1983. *Minor Characters: A Memoir of a Young Woman of the 1950s in the Beat Orbit of Jack Kerouac.* Boston: Houghton Mifflin. Reprint 1990. New York: Washington Square Press. Expanded ed. 1999. New York: Penguin Books.

1989. *In the Night Café.* New York: Dutton.

1990. *What Lisa Knew: The Truths and Lies of the Steinberg Case.* New York: Kensington Press.

1993. "The Children's Wing." In *Turning Toward Home: Reflections on the Family from Harper's Magazine.* New York: Franklin Square Press, 193–202.

1996. "Greenwich Village." In *The Seasons of Women: An Anthology.* Edited by Gloria Norris. New York: W. W. Norton, 127–133.

1999. "Beat Queens: Women in Flux." In *The Rolling Stone Book of the Beats: The Beat Generation and American Culture*. Edited by Holly George-Warren. New York: Hyperion, 40–51.

1999. "Beat Women: A Transitional Generation." *Beat Culture: The 1950s and Beyond*. Edited by Cornelius Van Minnen, Jaap van der Bent, and Melvan Elteren. Amsterdam: VU University Press, 211–221.

2000. (With Jack Kerouac). *Door Wide Open: A Beat Love Affair in Letters, 1957–1958*. New York: Viking Press.

Hettie Jones

1971. (Compiler). *The Trees Stand Shining: Poetry of the North American Indians*. New York: Dial Press. Reprint 1974. New York: Viking Press. Reprint 1976: New York: Dell.

1976. *Big Star Fallin' Mama: Five Women in Black Music*. Reprint 1995. New York: Viking Press.

1980. *I Hate to Talk About Your Mother: A Novel*. New York: Delacorte Press.

1990. *How I Became Hettie Jones*. New York: Dutton.

1996. "Going to Jail." In *In Defense of Mumia*. Edited by S. E. Anderson and Tony Medina. New York: Writers and Readers.

1997. "It Was 1960." In *Generations: A Century of Women Speak About Their Lives*. Edited by Myriam Miedzian and Alisa Malinovich. New York: Atlantic Monthly Press.

1998. *Drive: Poems*. Brooklyn, N.Y.: Hanging Loose Press.

1999. "Babes in Boyland." In *The Rolling Stone Book of the Beats: The Beat Generation and American Culture*. Edited by Holly George-Warren. New York: Hyperion.

Joanne Kyger

1964. (With Phyllis Bailey). *The Persimmons Are Falling*. San Francisco: San Francisco Arts Festival.

1965. *The Tapestry and the Web*. San Francisco: Four Seasons Foundation.

1970. *Places to Go*. Santa Rosa, Calif.: Black Sparrow Press.

1971. *Desecheo Notebook*. Berkeley: Arif Press.

1971. *Trip Out and Fall Back*. Berkeley: Arif Press.

1975. *All This Every Day*. Bolinas, Calif.: Big Sky Press.

1979. *The Wonderful Focus of You*. Calais, Vt.: Z Press.

1981. *The Japan and India Journals, 1960–1964*. Bolinas, Calif.: Tombouctou Books. Republished 2000. *Strange Big Moon: The Japan and India Journals 1960–1964*.

1981. *Mexico Blonde*. Bolinas, Calif.: Evergreen Press.

1981. *Up My Coast*. Point Reyes Station, Calif.: Floating Island Publications.
1983. *Going On: Selected Poems, 1958–1980*. New York: Dutton.
1984. *Revolution in Poetic Language*. Translated by Margaret Waller. New York: Columbia University Press.
1986. (With Robert Grenier). *Phantom Anthems*. Oakland, Calif.: O Books in collaboration with Trike Press.
1989. *Phenomenological*. New York: Institute of Further Studies.
1991. *Just Space: Poems, 1979–1989*. Santa Rosa, Calif.: Black Sparrow Press.
1993. *Going Out: Selected Poems 1958–1980*. New York: Dutton.
1996. *Some Sketches from the Life of Helena Petrovna Blavatsky*. Boulder, Colo.: Rodent Press & Erudite Fangs.
1999. *Patzcuaro*. Bolinas, Calif.: Blue Millenium Press.
2000. *Some Life*. Sausalito, Calif.: Post-Apollo Press.

Janine Pommy Vega

1968. *Poems to Fernando*. San Francisco: City Lights Books.
1977. *Song for César*. Brattleboro, Vt.: Longhouse Press.
1978. *Here at the Door*. Brooklyn, N.Y.: Zonepress.
1979. *Journal of a Hermit &* . Cherry Valley, N.Y.: Cherry Valley Editions.
1980. *The Bard Owl*. New York: Kulchur Foundation.
1984. *Apex of the Earth's Way*. Buffalo, N.Y.: White Pine Press.
1988. (Editor). *Candles Burn in Memory Town: Poems from Both Sides of the Wall*. New York: Segue Books.
1988. *Skywriting*. San Francisco: City Lights Books.
1992. *Threading the Maze*. Old Bridge, N.J.: Cloud Mountain.
1993. *Red Bracelets*. Chester, N.Y.: Heaven Bone Press.
1994. (Editor). *These Are Successful Hands: An Anthology of Poetry from the Women of Huntington House*. New York: Segue Books.
1997. *Tracking the Serpent: Journeys to Four Continents*. San Francisco: City Lights Books.
1999. (Editor). *Voices Under the Harvest Moon: An Anthology of Writing from Eastern Correctional Facility*. New York: Segue Books.
2000. *Mad Dogs of Trieste: New and Selected Poems*. Santa Rosa, Calif.: Black Sparrow Press.

Anne Waldman

1968. *Giant Night*. New York: Angel Hair Books.
1969. *O My Life!* New York: Angel Hair Books.
1969. (Editor). *The World Anthology: Poems from the St. Mark's Poetry Project*. Indianapolis and New York: Bobbs-Merrill.

1970. *Baby Breakdown.* Indianapolis and New York: Bobbs-Merrill.
1971. *No Hassles: An Unhinged Book in Parts.* New York: Kulchur Foundation.
1973. *Life Notes.* Indianapolis and New York: Bobbs-Merrill.
1975. *Fast Speaking Woman: Chants & Essays.* Rev. ed. 1996. San Francisco: City Lights Books.
1976. *Journals and Dreams: Poems.* New York: Stonehill Books.
1980. *Countries: Poems.* West Branch, Iowa: Toothpaste Press.
1983. *First Baby Poems.* New York: Hyacinth Girls Editions.
1984. *Makeup on Empty Space: Poems.* West Branch, Iowa: Toothpaste Press.
1985. *Skin Meat Bones: Poems.* Minneapolis: Coffee House Press.
1987. *The Romance Thing: Travel Sketches.* Flint, Mich.: Bamberger Books.
1988. *Blue Mosque.* New York: United Artists Books.
1989. *Helping the Dreamer: New and Selected Poems, 1966–1988.* Minneapolis: Coffee House Press.
1989. *Tell Me About It: Poems for Painters.* Stout, Ohio: Bloody Twin Press.
1990. *Not a Male Pseudonym.* New York: Tender Buttons Press.
1991. (Editor). *Out of This World: An Anthology of the St. Mark's Poetry Project, 1966–1991.* New York: Crown Books.
1992. *Fait Accompli.* Boulder, Colo.: last generation press.
1993. *Troubairitz.* New York: Fifth Planet Press.
1993. *Iovis: All Is Full of Jove.* Vol. 1. Minneapolis: Coffee House Press.
1994. (Editor, with Andrew Schelling). *Disembodied Poetics: Annals of the Jack Kerouac School.* Albuquerque: University of New Mexico Press.
1994. *Kill or Cure.* New York: Penguin Books.
1996. (Editor). *The Beat Book: Poems and Fiction of the Beat Generation.* Boulder, Colo.: Shambhala Press.
1997. *Iovis: All Is Full of Jove.* Vol. 2. Minneapolis: Coffee House Press.
2000. *Marriage: A Sentence.* New York: Penguin Books.
2001. *Vow to Poetry.* Minneapolis: Coffee House Press.

Works Cited
and Consulted

Adam, Helen. 1924. *The Elfin Pedlar and Tales Told by Pixie Pool.* New York and London: G. P. Putnam's Sons.

———. 1964. *San Francisco's Burning: A Ballad Opera.* San Francisco: Oannes Press. Reprint 1985. New York: Hanging Loose Press.

———. 1974. *Selected Poems and Ballads.* New York: Helikon Press.

———. 1977. *Turn Again to Me and Other Poems.* New York: Kulchur Foundation.

———. 1984. *Stone Cold Gothic.* Edited by Lita Hornick. New York: Kulchur Foundation.

———. The Helen Adam Collection. The Poetry/Rare Books Collection. Buffalo: The State University of New York at Buffalo.

Adam, Helen, and Robert Duncan. 1997. "Selected Correspondence, 1955–1956." *apex of the M* 6 (fall): 136–165.

Allen, Donald M., ed. 1960. *The New American Poetry, 1945–1960.* New York: Grove Press.

Allen, Donald M., and Benjamin Friedlander, eds. 1997. *Collected Prose.* Berkeley: University of California Press.

Allen, Donald M., and Warren Tallman, eds. 1973. *The Poetics of the New American Poetry.* New York: Grove Press.

Alter, Robert. 1985. *The Art of Biblical Poetry.* New York: Basic Books.

Altieri, Charles. 1979. *Enlarging the Temple: New Directions in American Poetry During the 1960s.* Lewisberg, Penn.: Bucknell University Press.

Anderson, Susan. 2000. "A Hut of Words Primitive to Our Nature: Ballad Influences in the San Francisco Renaissance." Masters thesis, Naropa University, Boulder, Colo.

Auerbach, Nina.1982. *Woman and the Demon: The Life of a Victorian Myth.* Cambridge, Mass.: Harvard University Press.

Austin, J. L. 1979."Performative Utterances." In *Philosophical Papers.* Oxford, U.K.: Oxford University Press.

Baraka, Imamu Amiri. 1984. *The Autobiography of LeRoi Jones.* 2nd rev. ed. 1997.

Chicago: Lawrence Hill Books.

———. 1995. "Am/Trak." In *Transbluesency: Selected Poems, 1961–1995*. Edited by Paul Vangelisti. New York: Marsilio.

Bartlett, Lee, ed. 1981. *The Beats: Essays in Criticism*. Jefferson, N.C. : McFarland.

———, ed. 1987. *Talking Poetry: Conversations in the Workshop with Contemporary Poets*. Albuquerque: University of New Mexico Press.

Barthes, Roland. 1986. "The Death of the Author." In *The Rustle of Language*. Translated by Richard Howard. Berkeley: University of California Press.

Battersby, Christine. 1989. *Gender and Genius*. London: The Women's Press.

Belgrad, Daniel. 1998. *The Culture of Spontaneity: Improvisation and the Arts in Postwar America*. Chicago: University of Chicago Press.

Benstock, Sheri. 1986. *Women of the Left Bank: Paris, 1900–1940*. Austin: University of Texas Press.

Bhaghostus, Djbot. 1993. *Run*. Los Angeles: Sun and Moon Press.

Bly, Robert. 1973. *Sleepers Joining Hands*. New York: Harper & Row.

Braude, Ann. 1991. *Radical Spirits: Spiritualism and Women's Rights in Nineteenth–Century America*. Boston: Beacon Press.

Breines, Wini. 1992. *Young, White, and Miserable: Growing Up Female in the Fifties*. Boston: Beacon Press.

Bremser, Bonnie. 1969. *Troia: Mexican Memoirs*. New York: Croton Press.

Breslin, Paul. 1987. *The Psycho-Political Muse: American Poetry since the Fifties*. Chicago: University of Chicago Press.

Buchan, David. 1972. *The Ballad and the Folk*. London: Routledge & Kegan Paul.

Burroughs, William S. 1953. *Junky*. New York: Ace Books. Reprint 1977. New York: Penguin Books.

———. 1959. *Naked Lunch*. New York: Grove Press. Reprint 1992. New York: Grove Weidenfeld.

Burroughs, William S., and Allen Ginsberg. 1962. *The Yage Letters*. Reprint 1973. San Francisco: City Lights Books.

Butler, Judith. 1993. *Bodies That Matter: On the Discursive Limits of "Sex."* New York: Routledge.

Butterick, George. 1983. "Diane di Prima." In *The Beats: Literary Bohemians in Postwar America*. Edited by Ann Charters. Dictionary of Literary Biography, vol. 16. Detroit: Gale Research.

Campbell, Joseph. 1962. *Oriental Mythology*. Vol. 2 of *The Masks of God*. New York: Penguin Books.

Cándida Smith, Richard. 1995. *Utopia and Dissent: Art, Poetry, and Politics in California*. Berkeley: University of California Press.

Cassady, Carolyn. 1990. *Off the Road: My Life with Cassady, Kerouac, and Ginsberg*. New York: Penguin Books.

Chadwick, Whitney. 1985. *Women Artists and the Surrealist Movement*. New York: Thames and Hudson.

Charters, Ann. 1983. "Anne Waldman." In *The Beats: Literary Bohemians in Postwar America*. Edited by Ann Charters. Dictionary of Literary Biography, vol. 16.

Detroit: Gale Research.

———, ed. 1992. *The Beat Reader.* New York: Viking.

Child, Sir Francis. 1965. *The English and Scottish Popular Ballads.* New York: Dover Publications.

Conway, Jill Ker. 1998. *When Memory Speaks: Exploring the Art of Autobiography.* New York: Random House.

Cook, Bruce. 1971. *The Beat Generation.* New York: Scribner. Reprint 1994. New York: Morrow.

Cowen, Elise. Undated. "Dream," "Enough," "Interview," "Jehovah," "Someone I could kiss," and "Teacher—your body my Kabbalah." Unpublished manuscript.

Cully, Margo, ed. 1992. *American Women's Autobiography: Fea(s)ts of Memory.* Madison: University of Wisconsin Press.

Damon, Maria. 1996. "Victors of Catastrophe: Beat Occlusions." In *Beat Culture and the New America: 1950–1965.* Edited by Lisa Phillips. New York: Whitney Museum of Art, 141–149.

Davidson, Michael. 1989. *The San Francisco Renaissance: Poetics and Community at Mid-Century.* New York: Cambridge University Press.

Michael Davidson, Lyn Hejinian, Ron Silliman, and Barrett Watten. 1992. *Leningrad: American Writers in the Soviet Union.* San Francisco: Mercury House.

De Man, Paul. 1979. "Autobiography as De-facement." *Modern Language Notes,* 94: 919–930.

D'Emilio, John. 1983. *Sexual Politics, Sexual Communities: The Making of a Homosexual Minority in the United States, 1940–1970.* Chicago: University of Chicago Press.

Dery, Mark. 1999. *The Pyrotechnic Insanitarium: American Culture on the Brink.* New York: Grove Press.

di Prima, Diane. 1958. *This Kind of Bird Flies Backwards.* New York: Aardvark Press. Reprint 1963. New York: Paper Book Gallery.

———. 1961. *Dinners and Nightmares.* Reprint 1974. New York: Corinth Books. Expanded ed. 1998. San Francisco: Last Gasp Press.

———. 1969. *Memoirs of a Beatnik.* New York: Olympia Press. Reprint 1988. New York: Last Gasp Press. Reprint 1998. New York: Penguin Books.

———. 1971. *Revolutionary Letters.* 3rd ed. 1974. San Francisco: City Lights Books.

———. 1975. *Selected Poems 1956–1975.* Plainfield, Vt.: North Atlantic Books.

———. 1978a. "Light / and Keats." In *Talking Poetics from Naropa Institute.* Edited by Anne Waldman and Marilyn Webb. Boulder, Colo.: Shambhala Press.

———. 1978b. *Loba,* Parts 1–8. Berkeley: Wingbow Press.

———. 1990. *Pieces of a Song: Selected Poems.* San Francisco: City Lights Books.

———. 1991. *Seminary Poems.* Point Reyes Station, Calif.: Floating Island Publications.

———. 1995. "Recollections of My Life as a Woman / Diane di Prima." New York: Thin Air Video. Video recording.

———. 2001. *Recollections of My Life as a Woman: The New York Years.* New York:

Viking Press.

Doolittle, Hilda (H.D.). 1914. "Oread." *Egoist* 1 (2 February): 54–55.

———. 1961. *Helen in Egypt*. New York: New Directions.

Douglas, Ann. 1999. "Strange Lives, Chosen Lives: The Beat Art of Joyce Johnson." In *Minor Characters: A Beat Memoir*. New York: Penguin Books, xiii–xxix.

Dragomoshchenko, Arkadii. "The Eroticism of Forgetting." *Poetics Journal* 10 (1998): 79–87.

Douglas, Susan J. 1994. *Where the Girls Are: Growing Up Female with the Mass Media*. New York: Random House.

Duncan, Robert. 1960. *The Opening of the Field*. New York: Grove.

———. 1962. "What Happened: Prelude." *Open Space Magazine* (San Francisco), February.

———. 1964. *Roots and Branches*. New York: New Directions.

———. 1985. *Fictive Certainties*. New York: New Directions.

———. 1997. *Selected Poems*. Edited by Robert J. Bertholf. New York: New Directions.

———. Undated. *Homage to Coleridge*. Unpublished manuscript. The Robert Duncan Archive at the Poetry/Rare Books Collection. Buffalo: The State University of New York.

DuPlessis, Rachel Blau. 1990. *The Pink Guitar: Writing as Feminist Practice*. New York: Routledge.

Edelman, Lee. 1993. "Tearooms and Sympathy, or, The Epistemology of the Water Closet." In *The Lesbian and Gay Studies Reader*. Edited by Henry Abelove, Michele Aina Barale, and David M. Halperin. New York: Routledge.

Ehrenreich, Barbara. 1983. *The Hearts of Men*. New York: Anchor Books.

Eliot, T.S. 1964. "Tradition and the Individual Talent." In *Selected Essays*. New York: Harcourt.

———. 1975. "Ulysses, Order, and Myth." In *Selected Prose of T.S. Eliot*. Edited by Frank Kermode. New York: Harcourt.

Ellingham, Lewis. 1982a. "Interview #1 with Robert Duncan." Unpublished transcript. Poetry/Rare Books Collection. Buffalo: The State University of New York.

———. 1982b. "Tape Interview of Ebbe Borregaard and Joanne Kyger by Lewis Ellingham on May 28 at Bolinas, California." Unpublished manuscript. Poetry/Rare Books Collection. Buffalo: The State University of New York.

Ellingham, Lewis, and Kevin Killian. 1998. *Poet, Be Like God: Jack Spicer and the San Francisco Renaissance*. Hanover, N.H. and London: Wesleyan University Press.

Escoffier, Jeffrey. 1998. *American Homo: Community and Perversity*. Berkeley: University of California Press.

Faas, Ekbert, ed. 1978. "Allen Ginsberg." In *Towards a New American Poetics: Essays and Interviews*. Santa Barbara, Calif.: Black Sparrow Press.

Faderman, Lillian. 1991. *Odd Girls and Twilight Lovers: A History of Lesbian Life in Twentieth-Century America*. New York: Penguin Books.

Foster, Edward Halsey. 1992. *Understanding the Beats*. Columbia: University of

Southern Carolina Press.

———. 1994. "An Interview with Anne Waldman." *Talisman* 13 (fall): 62–78.

Foucault, Michel. 1984. "What Is an Author?" In *The Foucault Reader*. Edited by Paul Rabinow. New York: Pantheon.

Fraser, Kathleen. 2000. *Translating the Unspeakable*. Hanover, N.H. and London: Wesleyan University Press.

Frazer, Brenda (Bonnie Bremser). 1969. *Troia: Mexican Memoirs*. New York: Croyton Press.

———. 2000. E-mail correspondence to Nancy Grace, June 26.

French, Warren. 1991. *The San Francisco Renaissance*. New York: Twayne.

Friedan, Betty. 1963. *The Feminine Mystique*. New York: Norton.

Friedman, Amy L. 1996. "'I saw my new name': Women Writers of the Beat Generation." In *The Beat Generation Writers*. Edited by A. Robert Lee. London: Pluto Press.

Friedman, Susan Stanford. 1998. *Mappings: Feminism and the Cultural Geographies of Encounter*. Princeton, N. J.: Princeton University Press.

Genet, Jean. 1964. *The Thief's Journal*. Translated by Bernard Frechtman. New York: Grove Press.

George-Warren, Holly, ed. 1999. *The Rolling Stone Book of the Beats: The Beat Generation and American Culture*. New York: Hyperion.

Gilman, Charlotte Perkins. [1894] 1973. *The Yellow Wallpaper*. Old Westbury, N.Y.: The Feminist Press.

Ginsberg, Allen. 1956. "Howl." In *"Howl" and Other Poems*. San Francisco: City Lights Books.

———. 1961. "Kaddish." In *"Kaddish" and Other Poems*. San Francisco: City Lights Books.

———. 1973. "How Kaddish Happened." In *Poetics of the New American Poetry*. Edited by Donald M. Allen and Warren Tallman. New York: Grove Press.

———. 1976a. *Introduction to Helen Adam at the Naropa Institute*.

———. 1976b. "Spontaneous Poetics, Lecture #2 with Guest Helen Adam." In *The Complete Naropa Lectures of Allen Ginsberg*. Edited by Randy Roark. Unpublished manuscript. 11 June.

———. 1980. "Improvised Poetics." Interview with Michael Aldrich, Edward Kissam, and Nancy Blecker. In *Composed on the Tongue: Literary Conversations, 1967–1977*. San Francisco: Grey Fox.

———. 1984. *Collected Poems 1947–1980*. New York: Harper & Row.

Gitlin, Todd. 1987. *The Sixties: Years of Hope, Days of Rage*. New York: Bantam Books.

Glassman, Joyce. 1962. *Come and Join the Dance*. New York: Atheneum.

Gold, Herbert. 1993. *Bohemia*. New York: Simon and Schuster.

Golding, Alan. 1998. "*The New American Poetry* Revisited, Again." *Contemporary Literature* 39: 180–211.

Grace, Nancy. 1995. *The Feminized Male Character in Twentieth-Century Literature*. Lewiston, N.Y.: The Edwin Mellen Press.

————. 1999a. "Interview with Brenda Frazer." Unpublished. 13 September. Wooster, Ohio.

————. 1999b. "Women of the Beat Generation: Conversations with Joyce Johnson and Hettie Jones." *Artful Dodge*, no. 36/37: 106–133.

Graves, Robert. 1955. *The Greek Myths*. Vol. 2. New York: Penguin Books.

Gruen, John. 1966. *The New Bohemia*. New York: Shorecrest. Reprint 1990. New York: a cappella books.

Guest, Barbara. 1962. *Poems*. New York: Doubleday.

Haggard, H. Ryder. 1886. *She: A History of Adventure*. New York: The Review of Reviews.

Halberstam, David. 1993. *The Fifties*. New York: Villard.

Hampl, Patricia. 1996. "Memory and Imagination." In *The Anatomy of Memory*. Edited by James McConkey. New York: Oxford University Press.

Harris, William J., ed. 1999. *The LeRoi Jones/Amiri Baraka Reader*. 2nd ed. New York: Thunder's Mouth Press.

Hemingway, Ernest. 1940. *For Whom the Bell Tolls*. New York: Scribner's.

Holmes, John Clellon. 1952. *Go*. Rev. ed. 1980. New York: New American Library.

————. 1988. "The Beat Poets: A Primer 1975." In *Passionate Opinions: The Cultural Essays*. Fayetteville: University of Arkansas Press.

Homer. 1969. *The Odyssey*. Translated by Richmond Lattimore. New York: Harper & Row.

Hoover, Paul. 1994. "Introduction." In *Postmodern American Poetry*. Edited by Paul Hoover. New York: Norton.

Hutcheon, Linda. 1988. *A Poetics of Postmodernism: History, Theory, Fiction*. New York: Routledge.

James, Henry. 1948. *The Art of Fiction and Other Essays*. New York: Oxford University Press.

Jameson, Fredric. 1981. *The Political Unconscious: Narrative as a Socially Symbolic Act*. Ithaca, N.Y.: Cornell University Press.

Jelinek, Estelle C. 1986. *The Tradition of Women's Autobiography from Antiquity to the Present*. Boston: Twayne Publishers.

Johnson, Joyce. 1983. *Minor Characters: A Memoir of a Young Woman of the 1950s in the Beat Orbit of Jack Kerouac*. Boston: Houghton Mifflin. Reprint 1990. New York: Washington Square Press. Expanded ed. 1999. New York: Penguin Books.

————. 1989. *In the Night Café*. New York: Dutton.

Johnson, Joyce, and Jack Kerouac. 2000. *Door Wide Open: A Beat Love Affair in Letters, 1957–1958*. New York: Viking Press.

Johnson, Ronna C. 2000. "'You're putting me on': Jack Kerouac and the Postmodern Emergence." *College Literature* Special Issue 27, no. 1 (winter), Teaching Beat Literature: 22–38.

Jones, Hettie. 1990. *How I Became Hettie Jones*. New York: Dutton.

————. 1997. "Spotlight on Hettie Jones." *PEN Newsletter* 95 (September–October).

————. 1998. *Drive: Poems*. New York: Hanging Loose Press.

Jones, LeRoi. 1960. "How You Sound??" In *The New American Poetry*. Edited by Donald M. Allen. New York: Grove Press.

———. 1961. *Preface to a Twenty Volume Suicide Note*. New York: Totem Press.

———. 1963. *Blues People*. New York: Morrow.

———. 1964. *Dutchman and The Slave*. New York: Morrow.

———. 1973. "Hunting Is Not Those Heads on the Wall." In *The Poetics of the New American Poetry*. Edited by Donald M. Allen and Warren Tallman. New York: Grove Press.

Julian of Norwich, Dame. 1977. *Revelations of Divine Love*. Translated by M. L. del Mastro. Garden City, N.Y.: Image Books.

Kandel, Lenore. 1966. *The Love Book*. San Francisco: Stolen Paper Review Books.

Katz, Marilyn A. 1991. *Penelope's Renown: Meaning and Indeterminacy in the Odyssey*. Princeton: Princeton University Press.

Kempe, Margery. 1985. *Book of Margery Kempe*. Translated by B. A. Windeatt. Harmondsworth, U.K.: Penguin Books.

Kerouac, Jack. 1957. *On the Road*. New York: Viking. Reprint 1991. New York: Penguin Books.

———. 1958. *The Subterraneans*. Reprint 1981. New York: Grove Press.

———. 1959. "The Origins of the Beat Generation." *Playboy* (June): 31–32, 42, 79. Reprint 1979. In *On the Road: Text and Criticism*. Edited by Scott Donaldson. New York: Viking Press.

———. 1960. *Tristessa*. New York: McGraw-Hill.

———. 1978. *Desolation Angels*. New York: Capricorn Books.

Kerouac, Joan Haverty. 2000. *Nobody's Wife: The Smart Aleck and the King of the Beats*. Berkeley, Calif.: Creative Arts Books.

Killian, Kevin. 2000. "Jack Spicer's Secret." Paper presented at The Opening of the Field: A Conference on North American Poetry in the 1960s, 28 June–2 July, The University of Maine, Orono.

Kirschenbaum, Blossom S. 1987. "Diane di Prima: Extending La Famiglia." *MELUS* 14, 3–4 (fall/winter): 53–67.

Knight, Brenda. 1996. *Women of the Beat Generation: The Writers, Artists and Muses at the Heart of a Revolution*. Berkeley: Conari Press.

Krim, Seymour. 1960. *The Beats*. New York: Fawcett.

Kristeva, Julia. 1980. *Desire in Language: A Semiotic Approach to Art and Literature*. Edited by Leon S. Roudiez. Translated by Thomas Gora, Alice Jardine, and Leon S. Roudiez. New York: Columbia University Press.

———. 1981. "Oscillation between Power and Denial." Interview, translated by Marilyn A. August. In *New French Feminisms*. Edited by Elaine Marks and Isabelle de Courtivron. New York: Schocken Books.

Kyger, Joanne. 1965. *The Tapestry and the Web*. San Francisco: Four Seasons Foundation.

———. 1974. "A Conversation with Joanne Kyger." Interview by Lawrence Nahem. *Occident* 8, new series: 142–157.

―――. 1977. "Three Versions of the Poetic Line." Interview by Robert Bertholf with Joel Oppenheimer and Ed Dorn. *Credences* 4: 55–66.

―――. 1979. *The Wonderful Focus of You.* Calais, Vt.: Z Press.

―――. 1981. *The Japan and India Journals: 1960–1964.* Bolinas, Calif.: Tombouctou Books. Republished 2000. *Strange Big Moon: The Japan and India Journals 1960–1964.* Berkeley, Calif.: North Atlantic Books.

―――. 1983. "Congratulatory Poetics." Interview by Diana Middleton-McQuaid and John Thorpe. *Convivio*:109–120.

―――. 1984. *Revolution in Poetic Language.* Translated by Margaret Waller. New York: Columbia University Press.

―――. 1989. *Phenomenological.* Canton, N.Y.: Institute for Further Studies.

―――. 1992. *Joanne Kyger.* Vol. 16 of Contemporary Authors Autobiography Series. Edited by Joyce Nakamura. Detroit, Mich.: Gale Research.

―――. 1996. *Some Sketches from the Life of Helena Petrovna Blavatsky.* Boulder, Colo.: Rodent Press & Erudite Fangs.

―――. 1999. *Patzcuaro.* Bolinas, Calif.: Blue Millennium Press.

―――. Undated. "Thoughts on being a woman poet starting in the '50s." Unpublished manuscript. Bolinas, Calif..

Lee, A. Robert. 1996. *The Beat Generation Writers.* London: Pluto Press.

LeJeune, Phillip. 1989. "The Autobiographical Pact." In *On Autobiography.* Edited by Paul John Eakin. Translated by Katherine Leary. Minneapolis: University of Minnesota Press.

Loewinsohn, Ron. 1959. *Watermelons.* New York: Totem Press.

Mackey, Nathaniel. 1993. *Djbot Bhaghostus's Run.* Los Angeles: Sun and Moon Press.

―――. 1997. *Bedouin Hornbook.* Los Angeles: Sun and Moon Press.

Mann, Ron, director and producer. 1982. *Poetry in Motion.* Distributed by Home Vision Cinema/Public Media Inc. 2000 (Chicago).

Marcus, Greil. 1997. *Invisible Republic: Bob Dylan's Basement Tapes.* New York: Henry Holt.

McNally, Dennis. 1979. *Desolate Angel: Jack Kerouac, the Beat Generation, and America.* New York: Random House.

McNeil, Helen. 1996. "The Archeology of Gender in the Beat Movement." In *The Beat Generation Writers.* Edited by A. Robert Lee. London: Pluto Press.

Metalious, Grace. 1956. *Peyton Place.* New York: Messner.

Meyerowitz, Joanne, ed. 1994. *Not June Cleaver: Women and Gender in Postwar America, 1945–1960.* Philadelphia: Temple University Press.

Miles, Barry. 1989. *Ginsberg: A Biography.* New York: HarperCollins.

Miller, Nancy K. 1988. *Subject to Change: Reading Feminist Writing.* New York: Columbia University Press.

―――. 2000. "But Enough About Me, What Do You Think of My Memoir?" *The Yale Journal of Criticism* 13, no. 2: 421–436.

Moffeit, Tony. 1989. "Interview with Diane di Prima." Unpublished. Boulder, Colo.

Mokey, Susan. 1998. *Desires of Their Own: Twentieth-Century Women Novelists and Images of the Erotic.* Ann Arbor, Mich.: University Microfilm.

Mulvey, Laura. 1989. *Visual and Other Pleasures.* Bloomington: Indiana University Press.

Nagy, Gregory. 1996. *Homeric Questions.* Austin: University of Texas Press.

Natsoulas/Novelozo Gallery Press. 1990. *Lyrical Vision: The 6 Gallery 1954–1957.* Davis, Calif.: Natsoulas/Novelozo Gallery Press.

Nelson, Cary. 1981. *Our Last First Poets: Vision and History in Contemporary American Poetry.* Urbana: University of Illinois Press.

———. 1989. *Repression and Recovery: Modern American Poetry and the Politics of Cultural Memory, 1910–1945.* Madison: The University of Wisconsin Press.

Nielsen, Aldon. 1994. "LeRoi Jones as Intertext." In *Writing Between the Lines: Race and Intertextuality.* Athens: University of Georgia Press.

———.1997. *Black Chant: Languages of African-American Postmodernism.* Cambridge, U.K.: Cambridge University Press.

Nietzsche, Friedrich. 1967. *The Will to Power.* Edited by Walter Kaufmann. Translated by Walter Kaufmann and R. J. Hollingdale. New York: Random House.

Notley, Alice. 1992. "Homer's Art." In *The Scarlet Cabinet.* New York: Scarlet Editions.

———. 1994. "Epic and Women Poets." In *Disembodied Poetics.* Edited by Anne Waldman and Andrew Schelling. Albuquerque: University of New Mexico Press.

———. 1996. *The Descent of Alette.* New York: Penguin Books.

O'Hara, Frank. 1974. "Personal Poem." In *The Selected Poems of Frank O'Hara.* New York: Random House.

Olson, Charles. 1983. *The Maximus Poems.* Edited by George Butterick. Berkeley: University of California Press.

———. 1997. "Projective Verse." Reprinted in *Collected Prose.* Edited by Donald M. Allen and Benjamin Friedlander. Berkeley: University of California Press.

Oppen, George. 1966. *Discrete Series.* Cleveland, Ohio: Asphodel Book Shop.

Ostriker, Alicia Suskin. 1982. "Blake, Ginsberg, Madness, and the Prophet as Shaman." In *William Blake and the Moderns.* Edited by Robert J. Bertholf and Anna S. Levitt. Albany: State University of New York Press.

———. 1987. *Stealing the Language: The Emergence of Women's Poetry in America.* London: The Women's Press.

———. 1997. "'Howl' Revisited: The Poet as Jew." *American Poetry Review* 26 (July/August): 28–31.

Peabody, Richard, ed. 1997. *A Different Beat: Writings by Women of the Beat Generation.* London: High Risk Books.

Perloff, Marjorie. 1990. *Poetic License: Essays on Modernist and Postmodernist Lyric.* Evanston, Ill.: Northwestern University Press.

Persky, Stan. 1964. "Proposition." *Open Space* no. 0.

Plimpton, George, ed. 1999. *Beat Writers at Work.* New York: Modern Library.

Pommy Vega, Janine. 1968. *Poems to Fernando.* San Francisco: City Lights Books.

———. 1979. *Journal of a Hermit &.* Cherry Valley, N.Y.: Cherry Valley Editions.

———. 1997. *Tracking the Serpent: Journeys to Four Continents.* San Francisco: City Lights Books.

Pommy Vega, Janine, and Hettie Jones. 1999. *Words Over Walls: Starting a Writing Workshop in a Prison.* New York: PEN.

Portugés, Paul. 1978. *The Visionary Poetics of Allen Ginsberg.* Santa Barbara, Calif.: Ross-Erikson.

———. 1980. "Allen Ginsberg's Paul Cézanne and the *Pater Omnipotens Aeterna Deus.*" *Contemporary Literature* 21 (summer): 435–449.

Poulin, A. Jr. 1991. "Contemporary American Poetry: The Radical Tradition." In *Contemporary American Poetry.* 5th ed. Edited by A. Poulin Jr. Dallas: Houghton Mifflin.

Prevallet, Kristin. 1997. "An Extraordinary Enchantment: Helen Adam, Robert Duncan, and the San Francisco Renaissance." *The Edinburgh Review* (fall).

Reed, Ishmael. 1993. *Airing Dirty Laundry.* Reading, Mass.: Addison-Wesley.

Rexroth, Kenneth. 1975. *Golden Gate: Interviews with Five San Francisco Poets.* Edited by David Meltzer. San Francisco: Wingbow Press.

Rich, Adrienne. 1976. *Of Woman Born: Motherhood as Experience and Institution.* New York: Norton.

Rosetti, Christina. 1979. *The Complete Poems of Christina Rossetti.* Edited by R. W. Crump. Baton Rouge: Louisiana State University Press.

Russo, Linda. 2000."On Seeing Poetic Production: The Case of Hettie Jones." Paper delivered at The Opening of the Field: A Conference on North American Poetry in the 1960s. 28 June–July 2, The University of Maine, Orono.

Savran, David. 1990. *Taking It Like a Man: White Masculinity, Masochism, and Contemporary American Culture.* Princeton, N. J.: Princeton University Press.

Schumacher, Michael. 1992. *Dharma Lion: A Critical Biography of Allen Ginsberg.* New York: St. Martin's Press.

Shulevitz, Judith. 2000. "Schmatte Hari." *The New Yorker* (April 24 & May 1): 206–211.

Shulman, Alix Kates. 1978. *Burning Questions.* New York: Knopf. Reprint 1990. New York: Thunder's Mouth Press.

Shelley, Mary. 1965. *Frankenstein.* New York: Dell.

Skerl, Jennie, ed. 1997. *A Tawdry Place of Salvation: The Art of Jane Bowles.* Carbondale: Southern Illinois Press.

———, ed. 2000. *College Literature* special issue 27, no. 1 (winter). Teaching Beat Literature.

Skir, Leo. 1996. "Elise Cowen: A Brief Memoir of the Fifties." In *Women of the Beat Generation: The Writers, Artists and Muses at the Heart of a Revolution.* Edited by Brenda Knight. Berkeley, Calif.: Conari Press.

Smith, Harry. 1997. *A Booklet of Essays, Appreciations, and Annotations Pertaining* to *The Anthology of American Folk Music*. *The Anthology of American Folk Music*. 3 vols. Washington, D.C.: Smithsonian Folkways Recordings.

Smith, Sidonie. 1987. *A Poetics of Women's Autobiography: Marginality and the Fictions of Self-Representation*. Bloomington: Indiana University Press.

Snyder, Gary. 1960. *Myths and Texts*. New York: Totem Press.

———. 1977. "North Beach." In *The Old Ways*. San Francisco: City Lights Books.

Solomon, Barbara Probst. 1960. *The Beat of Life*. New York: Lippincott.

Spicer, Jack. 1975. "After Lorca." In *The Collected Books of Jack Spicer*. Los Angeles: Black Sparrow Press.

———. 1998. *The House that Jack Built: The Collected Lectures of Jack Spicer*. Edited by Peter Gizzi. Hanover, N.H. and London: Wesleyan University Press.

Stewart, Susan.1991. *Crimes of Writing: Problems in the Containment of Representation*. New York: Oxford University Press.

Stoker, Bram. 1911. *The Lair of the White Worm*. London: W. Foulsham.

Stull, James N. 1993. *Literary Selves: Autobiography and Contemporary American Nonfiction*. Westport, Conn.: Greenwood Press.

Sukenick, Ronald. 1987. *Down and In: Life in the Underground*. New York: Morrow.

Teresa of Avila. 1972. *Interior Castle*. Translated by E. Allison Peers. Garden City, N.Y.: Image Books.

Tytell, John. 1976. *Naked Angels*. New York: Grove Press.

von Hallberg, Robert. 1985. *American Poetry and Culture, 1945–1980*. Cambridge, Mass.: Harvard University Press.

Wakefield, Dan. 1992. *New York in the Fifties*. Boston: Houghton.

Waldman, Anne. 1969. *O My Life!* New York: Angel Hair Books.

———. 1970. *Baby Breakdown*. New York: Bobbs-Merrill.

———. 1975. *Fast Speaking Woman: Chants & Essays*. Rev. ed. 1996. San Francisco: City Lights Books.

———. 1979. "My Life a List." In *Talking Poetics from Naropa Institute*. Edited by Anne Waldman and Marilyn Webb. Vol. 2 of *Annals of the Jack Kerouac School of Disembodied Poetics*. Boulder, Colo.: Shambhala Press.

———. 1984. "An Interview with Diane di Prima." In *The Beat Road*. Edited by Arthur and Kit Knight. California, Pa.: A. Knight.

———. 1989. *Helping the Dreamer: New and Selected Poems, 1966–1988*. Minneapolis, Minn.: Coffee House Press.

———, ed. 1991. *Out of this World: An Anthology of the St. Mark's Poetry Project, 1966–1991*. New York: Crown Books.

———. 1993. *Iovis: All Is Full of Jove*. Vol. 1. Minneapolis, Minn.: Coffee House Press.

———, ed. 1996. *The Beat Book: Poems and Fiction from the Beat Generation*. Boulder, Colo.: Shambhala Press.

———. 1997. *Iovis: All Is Full of Jove*. Vol. 2. Minneapolis, Minn.: Coffee House Press.

Waldman, Anne, and Andrew Schelling, eds. 1994. *Disembodied Poetics: Annals of the Jack Kerouac School*. Albuquerque: University of New Mexico Press.

Watson, Steven. 1995. *The Birth of the Beat Generation: Visionaries, Rebels, and Hipsters, 1944–1960*. New York: Pantheon Books.

Watten, Barrett. 1996. "Being Hailed in and by the 1950s." Paper presented at the conference American Poetry in the 1950s, 21–24 June, University of Maine, Orono.

———. 1997. "The Bride of the Assembly Line: From Material Text to Cultural Poetics." *Impercipient Lecture Series* 1, no. 8 (October): 69–81.

———. Forthcoming. "What Is Literature?" in *Assembling Alternatives*. Edited by Romana Huk. Hanover, N.H. and London.: Wesleyan University Press.

Weiners, John. 1996. *707 Scott Street*. Los Angeles: Sun and Moon Press.

Weinreich, Regina. 2000. "The Beat Generation Is Now About Everything." *College Literature* special issue 27, no.1 (winter): 263–268.

Wilentz, Elias, ed. 1960. *The Beat Scene*. New York: Corinth Books.

Whalen, Philip. 1960. "Further Notice." *Yugen* no.1.

Woolf, Virginia. 1929. *A Room of One's Own*. New York: Harcourt.

Zizek, Slavoj. 1989. *The Sublime Object of Ideology*. London: Verso.

———. 1996a. "Fantasy as a Political Category: A Lacanian Approach." *Journal for the Psychoanalysis of Culture and Society* 1, no. 2 (fall): 77–85.

———. 1996b. "The Fetish of the Party." In *Lacan, Politics, Aesthetics*. Edited by Willy Apollon and Richard Feldstein. Albany: State University of New York Press.

About the Contributors

Ann Charters has had over thirty years' involvement in reading, collecting, teaching, and writing about Beat literature. She began collecting books written by Beat authors while still a graduate student at Columbia University and after completing her doctorate she worked directly with Jack Kerouac in 1966 to compile a bibliography of his work. After his death, she wrote the first Kerouac biography and edited the posthumous collection *Scattered Poems.* She was the general editor for the two-volume encyclopedia *The Beats: Literary Bohemians in Postwar America,* as well as for *The Portable Beat Reader, The Jack Kerouac Reader,* and two volumes of Kerouac's *Selected Letters.* She published a collection of her photographic portraits in a book called *Beats and Company.* Most recently, she has edited the anthology *Beat Down to Your Soul: What Was the Beat Generation?* She is a professor of American literature at the University of Connecticut in Storrs.

Maria Damon teaches literature at the University of Minnesota, Twin Cities. She is the author of *The Dark End of the Street: Margins in American Vanguard Poetry* and coauthor (with Betsy Franco) of *The Secret Life of Words.* Her critical articles have appeared in *Literature Nation, pleasureTEXTpossession, Eros/ion,* and *Semetrix.* She is a member of the National Writers' Union.

Nancy M. Grace is an associate professor of English and director of the Program in Writing at The College of Wooster in Ohio. She is the author of *The Feminized Male Character in Twentieth-Century Literature* and has published articles and presented papers on Jack Kerouac, Ernest Hemingway, women writers associated with the Beat movement, and feminist pedagogy.

Tim Hunt is a professor of English at Washington State University, where he also teaches in the Program in Electronic Media and Culture. He is the author of *Kerouac's Crooked Road: Development of a Fiction* and the editor of *The Collected Poetry of Robinson Jeffers.* He is also rhythm guitarist in Derridean Debris.

Ronna C. Johnson is a lecturer in English and American studies at Tufts University, where she has also been director of women's studies. She has published essays on John Okada, Harriet E. Wilson, and Jack Kerouac, as well as studies of postwar U.S. writers and critics. She is completing a book-length study on Kerouac and postmodern anticipations, an essay from which was recently published in a special issue of *College Literature.* She is currently writing on Beat poet Lenore Kandel.

Anthony Libby is a professor of English at The Ohio State University, where he also directs the Computers in Composition and Literature Program. He is the author of *Mythologies of Nothing: Mystical Death in American Poetry, 1940–1970; The Secret Turning of the Earth,* which won the Wick Poetry Prize in 1995; and articles on Robert Bly, Frank O'Hara, and other American poets.

Kristin Prevallet is a poet and the author of *Perturbation, My Sister: A Study of Max Ernst's Hundred Headless Woman* and *The Parasite Poems.* She is editing a collection of Helen Adam's poetry and collages to be published by The National Poetry Foundation.

Peter Puchek is an independent scholar and has published articles on Robert Browning, T. S. Eliot, William Faulkner, and Francis Ponge.

Linda Russo is a doctoral candidate in the Poetics Program at The State University of New York at Buffalo. She is the coeditor of *verdure,* a magazine of poetry and poetics and the author of several books of poetry, including *Secret Silent Plan.*

Tony Trigilio is an assistant professor of English at Columbia College Chicago. He is a poet and the author of *"Strange Prophecies Anew": Rereading Apocalypse in Blake, H.D., and Ginsberg.*

Barrett Watten is an associate professor of English at Wayne State University and the author of two forthcoming volumes of criticism, *The Constructivist Moment: From Material Text to Cultural Poetics* and *Horizon Shift:*

Progress and Negativity in American Modernism. His critical articles have appeared in *Genre, Poetics Today, Modernism/Modernity, Qui Parle, The Impercipient Lecture Series, Postmodern Culture, Textual Practice,* and *Cultural Studies.* His most recent creative work is *Bad History.* As editor, he brought out two journals of poetry and poetics, *This* (1971–1982) and *Poetics Journal* (1982–1998), and he has served as associate editor of *Representations,* corresponding editor of *Artweek* (1989–1995), and on the editorial board of *Criticism.*

Index